Ernst Cassirer

SUNY series in
Contemporary Continental Philosophy

Dennis J. Schmidt, editor

Ernst Cassirer

A "Repetition" of Modernity

S. G. Lofts

Foreword by
John Michael Krois

STATE UNIVERSITY OF NEW YORK PRESS

Published by
State University of New York Press, Albany

Printed in the United States of America

For information, address the State University of New York Press, State University Plaza, Albany, NY 12246

Production by Kristin Milavec
Marketing by Patrick Durocher

Library of Congress Cataloging-in-Publication Data

Lofts, Steve G., 1959–
Ernst Cassirer : a "repetition" of modernity / S. G. Lofts : foreword by John Michael Krois.
p. cm. — (SUNY series in contemporary continental philosophy)
Includes bibliographical references and index.
ISBN 0-7914-4495-3 (hardcover : alk. paper). — ISBN 0-7914-4496-1 (pbk. : alk. paper)
1. Cassirer, Ernst, 1874–1945. I. Title. II. Series.
B3216.C34L64 2000
193—dc21 99-39699
CIP

10 9 8 7 6 5 4 3 2 1

Pour
Jacqueline et Jean-Louis Bustin
en tout amitié

Contents

Foreword

A Reading of the Philosophy of Ernst Cassirer

Steve Lofts' interpretation of Cassirer's philosophy as developed in this book, derives from his reading of Cassirer's philosophy of symbolic forms in the context of contemporary continental philosophy, and in particular as a form of structuralism *avant la lettre.* Without resorting to an ahistorical textual interpretation, or subsuming Cassirer's philosophy under the rubric of a philosophical school (e.g., neo-Kantianism) Lofts has read and reread Cassirer (and this means a lot of reading), thinking while he reads, and treating Cassirer as a thinker in his own right. In his work he guides the reader through the labyrinth of Cassirer's oeuvre. We discover in the course of our odyssey a very different Cassirer than the one we are accustomed too. We discover a Cassirer who was acutely aware of the historical and cultural changes we glibly call postmodernity, who's philosophical enterprise was to reaffirm and transform the project of modernity in such a way as to overcome its traditional shortcomings. Many of the topics that have become the acknowledged focal point of both the continental and analytic directions of philosophy prove to be central to Cassirer's philosophy of symbolic forms. It is to the author's credit to have shown, without doing violence to Cassirer's work or losing sight of what renders it unique, that this thoroughly modern thinker still has something to contribute to the contemporary philosophical debate.

In the past, the breadth Cassirer's conception of culture has often led to a superficial, piecemeal reception of his thought. As a result the systematic unity of his philosophy of culture and symbolic forms has been largely overlooked. In Lofts' study, particular topics are treated in relation to one another through an underlying systematic unity of culture; the chapters on art and religion are outstanding examples of this. Lofts' reading moves from one element or stage in the symbolic process of cultural meaning to another, bringing to the foreground the internal systematic unity of this process. The philosophical implications of Cassirer's acclaimed investigations into the Renaissance and the Enlightenment and the historical orientation of his thought have yet to be sufficiently understood. The emphasis that is placed throughout this work upon the historicity of being demonstrates once and for all that Cassirer was a philosopher of historicity and not a historian of philosophy. In one of the best analyses yet of Cassirer's metaphysics of the symbolic form, we discover in the conclusion of this work that Cassirer was a thoroughly speculative and even dialectical thinker.

By taking Cassirer's works in their own terms, Lofts has shown that the philosophy of symbolic forms embodied a new kind of thinking whose importance we are only now becoming able to recognize in light of subsequent developments in philosophy and cultural studies.

JOHN MICHAEL KROIS

Acknowledgments

Every work has its history, and this one is no exception. It is a pleasure to acknowledge and thank a few of the many people who have played, in one way or another, an important role in this history. This work was first written as my doctoral dissertation at the Université catholique de Louvain. Of the many people around me at that the time to whom I owe so much, special recognition must go to Professor G. Gérard and Professor Ph. W. Rosemann. Each in his own way provided me with more help than I could have ever hoped for. Many of the ideas were then rewritten in French and published as a short essay in the series *Accent* under the title: *La vie de l'esprit: Essai sur l'unité systématique de la culture et de la philosophie des formes symboliques*. (I would like to thank Les Éditions Peeters for their kind permission to reprint material from this French essay.) Evidently, rendering one's ideas into another language required rethinking them in this language. This difficult task of re-thinking my English reading of a German philosopher into French was aided by the comments and support of, among others, Professor M. Dupuis. His insights, both philosophical and personal, have always proven sage and will not be quickly forgotten. The second part of the introduction, "The Strategy of Reading," was presented as a paper in a seminar on editorial methodology held at the Université catholique de Louvain, and later published in *Éditer, traduire, interpréter: Essais de méthodologie philosophique*. I would like to thank the participants of this seminar for their questions, objections, and discussion that brought to my attention a number of weaknesses in the first draft but also a number of unseen strengths. (I would also like to thank the editors of the Philosophes médiévaux for their permission to publish the English version of this text.) The work that is being presented here is a slightly revised version of the original doctoral dissertation. It has profited from its history and from my discussions with students and colleagues at both the Université catholique de Louvain and Katholieke Universiteit Leuven. In particular I would like to thank Professor Fabien Capeillères, Geert van Eekert, Olivier Feron, Professor Enno Rudolph, Professor E. Orth, and Professor Massimo Ferrari for sharing with me their knowledge of Cassirer and for their comments and objections to my interpretation. This work has also greatly profited from John Michael Krois' comments on the original doctoral dissertation. His profound knowledge of Cassirer and generosity have not ceased to be a source of inspiration. I am very grateful for both. The handwriting used in the cover design is Cassirer's and comes from the manuscript for the *Metaphysics of the Symbolic* (*ECN*, I, p. 3). The quote appears on p. 201 of the present work. Printed with permission of Yale University Press. Finally, the writing of this work has also had a personal history. My dearest thanks goes out to my mother, my wife Agnieszka, and all my friends for their understanding, patience, and support over the years.

Abbreviations and References

For the most frequently cited texts by Cassirer, the following abbreviations have been employed:

Aufbau	"Die Sprache und der Aufbau der Gegenstandswelt"
Davos	"Davoser Disputation zwischen Ernst Cassirer und Martin Heidegger"
ECN, I	*Ernst Cassirer: Nachgelassene Manuskripte und Texte, vol. 1*
"Erkenntnistheorie"	*"Erkenntnistheorie nebst den Grenzfragen der Logik und Denkpsychologie"*
ETR	*Einstein's Theory of Relativity*
Essay	*An Essay on Man*
IC	*The Individual and the Cosmos in Renaissance Philosophy*
ID	*Determinism and Indeterminism in Modern Physics*
Logic	*The Logic of the Cultural Sciences* (Page references are to the German Edition)
LM	*Language and Myth*
MS	*The Myth of the State*

PK	*The Problem of Knowledge: Philosophy, Science, and History since Hegel*
PSF	*The Philosophy of Symbolic Forms:* Vol. I, *Language;* Vol. II, *Mythic Thought;* Vol. III, *The Phenomenology of Knowledge;* Vol. IV, *The Metaphysics of the Symbolic.*
SF	*Substance and Function*
SMC	*Symbols, Myth and Culture: Essays and Lectures of Ernst Cassirer*
"The Problem of the Symbol"	*"The Problem of the Symbol and Its Place in the System of Philosophy"*
" 'Spirit' and 'Life' "	" 'Spirit' and 'Life' in Contemporary Philosophy"
"Structuralism"	*"Structuralism in Modern Linguistics"*

For full details see the bibliography. The first page number given refers to the English translation and, where appropriate, the second to the German original. For those works for which there is no English translation, the reference refers to the original and the translation is my own. Many of the English translation of Cassirer's works are unfortunately not accurate. Where necessary I have amended the translation. Due to the quantity of modifications made, I have not indicated amended passages. Though less scholarly, this has shorten the work by more than ten full pages! Where the translation has required restructuring I have given a new translation and indicated that the translation is my own. Where I believe that the modification or the translation was important to my argument I have added the German.

Introduction

The Strategy of Reading . . .

is . . . what orders and governs this complex of interwoven repetitions.

—J.-L. Nancy and Ph. Lacoue-Labarthe, *The Title of the Letter: A Reading of Lacan*

A Reading of Cassirer

A thoroughly central figure in the neo-Kantain movement and the pre-World War II philosophical scene, Ernst Cassirer was quickly displaced to the margins of philosophy after his death in 1945. Today the name of Cassirer is seldom, if ever, mentioned in lectures on, or introductions to the history of philosophy, and the critical work on his philosophy of symbolic forms remains insignificant by comparison to that devoted to contemporaries such as Heidegger and Husserl. This picture of marginality, however, is perhaps not the whole truth. For though seemingly forgotten by the students of contemporary philosophy, the presence of Cassirer can nevertheless be established, as it were, in the "margins" and "between the lines" of a number of the key figures in contemporary thought. To note but a few of the more significant examples: Cassirer is one of the rare authors to be quoted by Heidegger in *Being and Time.* What is more, Heidegger devoted an equally rare critical study to the second volume of the *Philosophy of Symbolic Forms* and engaged Cassirer in a debate on the interpretation of Kant at Davos in 1929.[1] Finally, as we shall see in our investigation into the structure of myth, Heidegger's concept of "poetic dwelling" and "the fourfold" owe much to his reading of Cassirer. When one looks closely at Merleau-Ponty's *Phenomenology of Perception,* not to mention his other works, the importance of his reading of the third volume of the *Philosophy of Symbolic Forms* is more than evident.[2] Likewise, it can be shown that such figures as Foucault,[3] Bataille,[4] Lévi-Strauss,[5] and Blumenberg[6] have all read and derived inspiration from Cassirer. Cassirer's influence can also be found beyond the domain of philosophy. The art historian Erwin Panofsky, for example, has written a work entitled: *Perspective as a Symbolic Form*. The French psychoanalyst Jacques Lacan, too, must have read Cassirer, as in his own review *Scilicet* there appears a long critical study on the three volumes of the *Philosophy of Symbolic Forms* entitled "La raison avant Freud."[7]

It would be difficult to determine the precise nature or degree of influence that Cassirer has exerted on any one of these thinkers or upon the philosophical tradition after him. Certainly a reading of these authors in light of Cassirer's work would prove most fruitful and illuminating. However, a more interesting adventure might be to reread Cassirer's work in light of the work of those who have read him. Such is essentially the approach adopted by this study. However, the reader will not find here a comparative study that lists the convergences and divergences between Cassirer and any particular thinker. Rather, the primary task of this work is to provide a systematic and philosophical introduction to Cassirer's "critique of culture." It treats Cassirer as a thinker in his own right, and limits itself to interpreting Cassirer's work. The pages that follow thus undertake a close textual reading of Cassirer's philosophy of symbolic forms that seeks to develop his philosophy of culture. However, this reading is undertaken from the perspective of contemporary philosophy. The reader familiar with the work of George Bataille, Jacques Derrida, Foucault, Hiedegger, Lacan, or Merleau-Ponty will perhaps recognize something of their presence in my interpretation of Cassirer.

On a more general level, my reading of Cassirer is situated in the growing awareness that postmodern thought has arrived at an impasse. For having effectively done away with the modern paradigm of man as that being who, through his faculty of understanding, is able to transcend and thus know reality, and through this knowledge is able to transform himself and reality, postmodern discourse seems to be lost in its own labyrinth of equally meaningful, and thus equally meaningless signs. It seems unable to question its own tacit assumptions, to critique its own perspective, to transcend itself and thus overcome its present condition. And how could it be otherwise, for such a positive and constructive "project" as self-critique, and such lofty ideals as "progress" and "change" belong to the very project of modernity that it rejects—thus, the postmodern "project" is, and can be nothing more than an "antiproject." Unable to take up anything more than a negative position, unable to suggest a new direction, to put forward a positive ideal of change—without at the same time deconstructing and subverting it in the process—postmodern theory has become entrapped in its own imaginary discourse and absorbed by the present age of multinational consumer capitalism.[8] Having denounced its historical roots, and unable to envision future possibilities, the postmodern condition is one of status quo stagnation—it finds itself, ironically, caught up in the vicious and imaginary circle of the "eternal return" of the same that it sought to subvert and escape. As Félix Guattari has already expressed it in his 1987 article "The Postmodern Dead End":

> A certain idea of progress and modernity has gone bankrupt, and in its fall it has dragged along all confidence in the notion of emancipation through social action. At the same time social relations have entered an ice age: hierarchy and segregation have solidified, poverty and unemployment tend now to be accepted as inevitable evils.[9]

There is today a general return to the thought and work of the tradition. This return is not, however, a naive and dogmatic avowal of outdated philosophical views, but rather an authentic "repetition" of the tradition, as Heidegger would say, that seeks to actualize certain inherent possibilities of the past. This reading of Cassirer belongs to this general and growing movement that we might call the " 'repetition' of modernity." It sets out to show how, while recognizing the shortcomings of the modern project of reason, Cassirer's philosophical project was to transform modernity from within; and this not through its rejection, but rather by its faithful embracing.

This work is also a reflection of its time. Since the end of the Second World War, there has been a growing and radical new awareness of the plurality of cultures. It has become increasingly evident that no one culture can provide us with the ideal token or form of humanity, but rather that there are a myriad of expressions of humanity, each of which possesses its own dignity and intrinsic value. On the other hand, there has also been a growing movement toward an all-encompassing homogenous global culture, toward what has been called the "global village." Our times are thus marked by a double movement toward what we might paradoxically call a "multicultural culture": a culture that has as its identity the unity of a plurality of different and autonomous cultures, an identity that is at once inclusive and exclusive of difference. The effort to forge this new multicultural culture can be seen on every level of society—economic, political, social, and intellectual. It is in this context that we must understand the growing interest in the philosophy of Ernst Cassirer today. For as a pioneer in the science of spirit (*Geisteswissenschaft*), Cassirer's philosophy of symbolic forms has as its original and principal aim to establish the methodological foundations for the sciences of culture. Toward this end, Cassirer undertook to transform the "critique of reason" of Kant into a "critique of culture" that would establish the structure and function of the different universal forms of human understanding that constitute the cultural world of meaning and the life of the human spirit. Beyond the myriad of its different historical expressions, Cassirer thus sought to determine the universal form of humanity by determining the universal form of culture. Perhaps no thinker since Hegel has attempted to provide such a general and global theory of the human spirit. Cassirer, however, never renders the systematic unity of the system of symbolic forms explicit. Readers often find themselves lost in the wealth of historical and anthropological material presented by Cassirer. Where Cassirer's summary of other authors ends and Cassirer begins is not always clear. Our reading of the philosophy of symbolic forms attempts to render explicit the systematic unity implicit in Cassirer's account of culture.

The Strategy of Reading . . .

Introduction or Interpretation?

Our reading of Cassirer is admittedly an interpretative one. What, however, is the proper methodology of interpretation? There is perhaps no other way to understand the nature of interpretation than to enter into the process of interpretation itself. Let us thus approach the question of interpretation by way of an interpretation of what Cassirer himself has written on the subject in chapter 10 of *An Essay on Man*, entitled quite simply "History," and in this way establish the methodological principles of our approach to Cassirer.

Now, in order to do justice to a thinker, according to Cassirer following Kant, it is necessary to "understand him better than he understood himself."[10] In my interpretation of Cassirer I have therefore attempted to understand Cassirer better than Cassirer understood himself. I have tried to make explicit that which remains implicit in his work, and from time to time this has required that I go further than he himself has gone, or might have gone. This approach may seem presumptuous to some who would argue that the goal of the historian should be to recount that which a thinker "actually" said, rather than what might have been said. But in fact this approach is the only one open to the historian—at least according to Cassirer. For, as Cassirer writes:

> the facts of the philosophical past, the doctrines and systems of the great thinkers are meaningless without an interpretation (*Essay*, p. 179 f.). The texts say nothing until they are made to speak through the labors of the historian. They are not only incomplete but in many, if not in most cases obscure or contradictory. To lighten this darkness and remove these contradictions a special art of interpretation is needed, an historical "hermeneutics." (*PK*, p. 323/326)

Let us reread and interpret a little these few phrases.

[T]he facts of the philosophical past, the doctrines and systems of the great thinkers are meaningless without an interpretation." "The texts say nothing until they are made to speak through the labors of the historian."

The Object of History

What is the object of historical investigation? The answer would seem rather evident: historical research seeks to know the past. However, "the past is gone forever." It has always already vanished into the nothingness of oblivion. As such, the past no longer exists, and insofar as it "exists," it is always something lost and distant. Thus, the only way that we can as historians approach the past is through our "memory" of it—and through this act of "remembrance" provide the past with "a new ideal existence" (*Essay*, p. 174). Historical thought is a process of "recollection," by which the past is "reconstructed" in and for the present. However, if the past is no longer present, from what does the historian begin this process of "recollection"? Here too the answer would seem rather evident: the historian reconstructs the past from the "material traces" that have been left by the past for the present. But these physical "traces" are not seen by the historian as mere physical objects, but rather as symbols that represent the "materialization of the spirit of a former age" (*Essay*, p. 177). "Not things or events but documents or monuments are the first and immediate object of our historical knowledge" (*Essay*, p. 175). The material letter of the text is in itself nothing more than a physical object possessing a place in time and space, and subject to the laws of nature. As a physical thing the material text is not a part of the past, but rather something found only in the present. The material figure of the letter, however, only becomes a "letter" in the moment of its being read, in the moment that it is taken as a meaningful sign, as a "historical fact." It is only through the "complicated process" of historical recollection that this "mere thing" is "charged with meaning" and transformed into a symbol that provides us with an insight into the past. "The historian must learn to read and interpret his documents and monuments not only as dead remnants of the past but as living messages from it, messages addressing us in a language of their own. The symbolic content of these messages is, however, not immediately observable. It is the work of the linguist, the philologist, and the historian to make them speak and to make us understand their language" (*Essay*, p. 177). The meaning of the historical object is therefore dependent upon the act of recollection: "historical objects have true being only so long as they are remembered—and the act of remembrance must be unbroken and continuous" (*Essay*, p. 185).

[T]he facts of the philosophical past, the doctrines and systems of the great thinkers are meaningless without an interpretation." "The texts say nothing until they are made to speak through the labors of the historian. ***They are not only incomplete but in many, if not in most cases obscure or contradictory.***"

An Empirical Reconstruction

Although historical documents are never to be understood simply in terms of their mere physical existence, their material dimension must never be forgotten by the historian: for the spirit of the letter only exists in its embodiment in the materiality of the letter. For this reason, the reconstruction of the past always begins by way of an "empirical reconstruction." In this respect, Cassirer is himself a champion of scrupulous historical objectivity.

> He [the historian] has to collect all the documents in the case in order to submit them to the highest court of law, to the history of the world. If he fails in this task, if by party favoritism or hatred he suppresses or falsifies a single piece of testimony, then he neglects his supreme duty. (*Essay*, p. 189; cf. also *PK*, p. 318 f.)

However, the historical material of the past has not always weathered the passage of time. The historian often has only fragments from which to work. These fragments must be collected and organized before they can be understood. In the case of philosophy, the process of establishing the complete editions of the writings of the tradition proves to be the first difficult step in the long process of historical recollection. Cassirer himself began his philosophical career by establishing the critical editions of Leibniz and Kant. Today, the work being done by John Michael Krois and the editors of Cassirer's *Nachlass* is essential to our future understanding of Cassirer's philosophy as much remains to be discovered in his unpublished papers.

The Law of the Text

Historical knowledge is of course not reducible to a knowledge of the chronological order of events. Rather history "wants to teach us to understand the life of the past," not just cataloge it (*Logic*, p. 92). "Behind these fixed and static shapes, these petrified works of human culture, history detects the original dynamic impulses" (*Essay*, p. 185). The historian seeks to uncover the "creative energies" that animate these historical facts. Insofar as we are concerned here with philosophical history, it is a question of determining the spirit of the material letter of the text. However, as we well know, the concept that an author is attempting to express is not always perfectly clear even to the author himself. For this reason the concept often remains in an "implicit state" in his work. As Kant points out, in reading an author we find that he has often "not sufficiently determined his concept, he has sometimes spoken, or even thought, in opposition to his own intention" (*Essay*, p. 180).

The concept that governs a thinker's thought must be made "explicit in order to be comprehended in its true meaning, and this transition from an implicit to an explicit state is the work of the future" (*Essay*, p. 180); and this "work of the future" is the work of the historian. The material reconstruction of the text, therefore, cannot itself render the "essence" of a philosophy. Rather, what the historian seeks is the "unknown law" that animates these different fragments.[11]

The Structure of the Work: φ(*x*)

For Cassirer every philosophical system or text, as an expression of spiritual existence, represents "a coherent whole in which all parts are interdependent upon each other" ("Structuralism," p. 110). As an "organic whole" it is governed by a "law" that determines the structure of its internal unity. The law determines the "belonging together" (*συνάγειν εἰς ἕν*) of all the particulars fragments of this meaningful manifold (*PSF*, III, p. 383/447). The law of the whole is always immanent in each member of the series that it constitutes as "the rule of progression" that assigns each its "place" and internally orders them into an organic totality. The law of the series is thus never expressed in any one of its members, nor is it expressed by the sum of all of its members: for it represents the whole of the series as the law that determines the internal limit of every possible member of that series—even those that do not, properly speaking, exist. All meaning, insofar as it represents a "one in the many," possesses this structure and polarity between the universal law of the series (φ), on the one hand, and the multiplicity of particulars ($x_1, x_2, x_3, \ldots$), which obey the law, on the other. In each fragment of the past, as the "materialization of the spirit of a former age" (*Essay*, p. 177), there is hidden the law of the whole to which it belongs. Immanent in every part, every chapter, every key word of an author's work there is found the whole. Thus the historian must search in each of the material fragments the law of the whole. A close word-for-word reading of any philosophical text will bring out the whole of the philosophy to which this text belongs.

[T]he facts of the philosophical past, the doctrines and systems of the great thinkers are meaningless without an interpretation." "The texts say nothing until they are made to speak through the labors of the historian. They

are not only incomplete but in many, if not in most cases obscure or contradictory. ***To lighten this darkness and remove these contradictions a special art of interpretation is needed, an historical 'hermeneutics'*** "

The Strategy of Reading . . .

To reconstruct the past through recollection, through a process of reading and interpretation that seeks to reveal the law that structures the whole, such is the noble and arduous task of the historian. But what is the proper methodology of interpretation? Interpretation involves, evidently, a thorough reading of the text. A methodology of interpretation is therefore a strategy of reading. In reading a text, we generally begin at the beginning and follow the text to its conclusion. Upon arriving at the end it is inevitable that we must return to the beginning, for only once we have read the text and have an idea of where the text intends to lead us are we in a position to follow it more faithfully and thoughtfully. However, in the course of our rereading, paying as we will closer attention to the letter of the text, to its turn of phrases, to the tensions that verge on contradictions, and so forth, we will no doubt discover a number of elements and connections that had escaped our attention—and perhaps we will even discover that the text takes us somewhere else than we had first imagined. In fact, it is possible that we will discover in the text something unknown even to its author: for the author of the text, in writing the text, is the last person in a position to read it. The reader brings something to the text that the writer can never bring: namely, another perspective. To read a text is to reinscribe it into the context of the particular perspective of the reader. All reading, therefore, is inherently a process of rewriting. As our understanding of the text is perpetually transformed with each new reading, which is in fact a rewriting, we are continually being forced to return to the beginning. "As soon as we have reached a new center and a new line of vision in our own thoughts we must revise our judgements," and this "process of interpretation never comes to a complete standstill" (*Essay*, p. 180). The result of this process is graphically reflected, as Cassirer goes on to say, "in our portrait of Socrates. We have the Socrates of Xenophon and Plato, we have a Stoic, a skeptic, a mystic, a rationalistic, and a romantic Socrates. They are entirely dissimilar. Nevertheless they are not untrue; each of them gives us a new aspect, a characteristic perspective of the historical Socrates and his intellectual and moral physiognomy" (*Essay*, p. 180). Each reading of Socrates reveals yet another possible expression of the hidden law that constitutes the thought of Socrates. The example of Socrates is rather poetic, as Socrates did not of course himself write, and thus we know of Socrates only through the writings of others, that is to say, through the interpretations of others. Socrates represents, if you will, the philosophical past par excellence. A past forever lost, that exists quite literally only in the memory of philosophical historical recollection. It is a past that can only be approached indirectly through the traces found in the interpretation of the historical fact.

> To define historical fact as "concordance with the facts"—*adaequatio rei et intellectus*—is . . . no satisfactory solution of the problem. It begs the question instead of solving it. That history has to begin with facts and that, in a sense, these facts are not only the beginning but the end, the alpha and omega, of our historical knowledge, is undeniable. But what is an historical fact? All factual truth implies theoretical truth. (*Essay*, p. 174)

The doctrines and systems of the great thinkers of our philosophical past present themselves to us as historical facts. The meaning of these facts will be determined by the perspective in which we read them—by the "unknown law" that animates our own thought. In other words, the "facts" of history are nothing outside our horizon of understanding, and their meaning changes when they are understood from a different perspective. However, does the historian not seek the law that originally governed these historical facts? In reading a text by Plato, Heidegger, or Cassirer are we not interested in determining the law of the author in question? The question that naturally arises, then, is from what hermeneutical horizon can we properly read a text from the past? The question itself is perhaps ill-formed: for it treats the past, or the theory of an author, as if it were a *Ding an sich*, existing independently of the theoretical framework in which it is interpreted, which of course it is not. That is why, just as there are numerous Socrates' there are numerous Aristotles, Aquinas', Descartes', Leibniz', Hegels, Heideggers, Foucaults, Cassirers . . . There is not a single thinker in our tradition for whom divergent readings cannot be found. And for the most prominent of them it is precisely the plurality of readings that has made them prominent figures in our tradition. To be limited to *one* reading is the death of a text: the more multifarious its readings the richer its life.

Is then the interpretative framework completely arbitrary? And if not, from what perspective can we judge the correct one? Certainly it is not arbitrary. And equally certainly, the criterion is not the correspondence of our model with the "original." To answer this question it is necessary to enter into the temporal structure of the dynamic of interpretation, for the type of reading we are dealing with here is not just a hermeneutics, but "historical 'hermeneutics.' "

The Temporal Structure of Interpretation

> There is . . . a prophecy of the past, a revelation of its hidden life. History cannot predict the events to come; it can only interpret the past. But human life is an organism in which all elements imply and explain each other. Consequently a new understanding of the past gives us at the same time a new prospect of the future, which in turn becomes an impulse to intellectual and social life. For this double view of the world in prospect and in retrospect the historian must select his point of departure. He cannot find it except in his own time. He cannot go beyond the conditions of his present experience. Historical knowledge is the answer to definite questions, an answer which must be given by the past; but the questions themselves are put and dictated by the present—by our present intellectual interests and our present moral and social needs. (*Essay*, p. 178)

This passage requires some interpretation and explanation. For Cassirer there is a constant tension between the tradition and a movement toward the future, which resolves itself in the present. As our understanding of the past changes, so does our vision of the future. Subsequently, the transformation of our vision of the possibilities open to us in the future results in a reevaluation of our present. The present is, therefore, always a product of the presence of the past as actuality and of the presence of the future as possibility. *"Le présent est chargé du passé, et gros de l'avenir"* (Leibniz, cited in *Essay*, p. 50). In the final analysis the presence of the present is nothing more than the future possibility of the past, or in other words, the present is always already a product of an interpretation of the past in the light of the future possibilities that the past itself has opened up for the present. One writes and reads in the present: one writes, however, in light of a future possibility—namely, the possibility of being read; and one reads so as to return to a voice of the past that speaks of, and to, a future possibility—but as the future is always yet to come, the possibilities opened up to the present by the past can never fully be exhausted. Writing, then, opens up the future possibility of reading; whereas reading represents the present possibility of writing.

Let us make this more concrete. When we initially approach the text of any philosopher, we can do so only because this text is already invested with a certain degree of meaning—only insofar as it is already invested with meaning can it stand present as something approachable, as a historical fact. As such, this text is already defined by its place in the tradition in which it is situated—be it a central mainstream or a marginal place. In order to understand its meaning, we must, to a certain degree, appropriate and make our own the interpretative structure provided by the same tradition to which it belongs—as a reader we are not, after all, some transtraditional entity existing beyond and independent of a tradition. Rather to the contrary, we are, insofar as we are a reader, only in the moment that we enter into, take up, and further the tradition of a reading. Thus, already implicit in the taking up of a text is the process of investing it with its meaning.

The meaning of any text depends upon the interpretative elements that are used to read it—elements that, it is important to note, cannot but be taken from the same pool of meaning structures that make up the tradition to which the text belongs. In this way, we see that while the possible meanings of a text are in principle infinite, there always being the possibility of a future rereading, the present possibilities are limited by the selection of interpretative frameworks presently available, the meaning structures that are, as it were, "present-at-hand." The meaning of the text is, therefore, at once fixed and open. Its past interpretation provides us with the horizon of its present meaning, as the work of an important philosopher or of a marginal philosopher, as the work of the teacher of Aquinas or of the student of Albert the Great, as the work of a devoted Christian or that of a heretic. . . . Its meaning is, however, open insofar as the meaning of the text depends upon the framework in which it is read—this interpretative framework again coming from the tradition. In reading a work in an untraditional framework, or better, from another perspective than is customary, we may be able to bring out a new meaning, to show a new relation to other elements in the same system of meaning, thus changing its position in the whole, thus changing its meaning and subsequently changing the meaning of the whole. The interpretation of a text is not like a coin that can be passed from hand to hand without itself being changed—an example often used by Cassirer and others to characterize language. Rather, meaning is possible only in living dialogue, in a dynamic process of exchange, of reading which is a rewriting, rewriting in the sense that one rethinks the idea in order to understand it, but also in the sense that one appropriates the idea for oneself.[12] The final meaning of a text, like the final meaning of a conversation, comes only with the last word, with the last reading. Until that point, there always exists the possibility of another turn in the conversation, of a new reading.

So the meaning of a text is always open to a new interpretation, that is to say, its signification is always in the process of being uncovered and determined. That is why the present can never completely "exhaust" the possibility of the past, or better the infinite future possibility of the past. The possibility of any meaning represents an actualization of a future possibility which lies in the past. The continuous process of interpretation and reinterpretation of a text represents an actualization of a possible meaning already present in the text—we are, as it were, *forever running into the future chasing our past.*[13]

The Subjectivity of History

Historical recollection is, as we have seen, a question of reconstruction. The historical past is essentially a construction by and for an historian. The great historian "Menard writes:

> . . . truth, whose mother is history, who is the rival of time, depository of deeds, witness of the past, example and lesson to the present, and warning to the future. . . .

History, *mother* of truth; the idea is astounding. Menard, a contemporary of William James, does not define history as a investigation of reality, but as its origin. Historical truth, for him, is not what took place; it is what we think took place."[14] Even more *astounding* is that this would also seem to be the position of Cassirer. Against historians like L. von Ranke, who maintain that the "genuine task of the historian is to describe [the past] 'as it actually was,' " Cassirer maintains that even if the historian could achieve this impossibility, "it is still true that 'what has been' acquires a new meaning when placed in the perspective of history. . . . The task of history does not consist merely in making us *acquainted with* past existence and life, but in teaching us how to *interpret* its meaning" (*Logic*, p. 77). All historical recollection is a reconstruction by and for the historian. "All mere knowledge of the past would remain for us a 'lifeless picture' if no other powers were involved than those of reproductive memory" (*Logic*, p. 77). The historian "infuses into his concepts and words his own inner feelings, and thus gives them a new sound and a new color—the color of a personal life" (*Essay*, p. 187). The profundity of a reading depends upon the profundity of its reader. Is then the truth simply relative to the reader? Is there no historical objectivity in reading? Cassirer is more than aware of the problem:

> The fundamental dilemma of historical thought begins at precisely this point. Undoubtedly it is the richness and variety, the depth and intensity, of his personal experience which is the distinctive mark of the great historian. Otherwise the work would remain lifeless and colorless. But how can we hope in this way to attain the ultimate objective of historical knowledge, how can we find out the truth of things and events? Is not a personal truth a contradiction in terms? (*Essay*, p. 187)

Without his personal experience, without the passion that animates his thought and work, the historian would lack the perspective and means to engage in the recollection of the past. "If I put out the light of my own personal experience I cannot see and I cannot judge of the experience of others. Without a rich personal experience in the field of art no one can write a history of art; no one but a systematic thinker can give us a history of philosophy" (*Essay*, p. 187). Cassirer's philosophy is a history of philosophy only in appearance. In reality it is a thoroughly systematic philosophy of history.

The Problem of Relativity

Could it not, however, be objected that this view leads to a position which maintains that all interpretations are equally viable? That there are, in fact, no misinterpretations? Or possibly, nothing but misinterpretations? If all meaning is nothing but an interpretation, and all interpretations are equally valid, would not the "meaning of meaning" be destroyed? All meaning is relative to its interpretative context, however this relativity of meaning does not necessarily entail its destruction, nor the destruction of the "truth." How then are we to overcome this antithesis between the demand for historical objectivity and the subjectivity of historical recollection? The problem is overcome by the particular structure of historical recollection: history is part science and part art.

History as a Form of Science

For Cassirer history and science only represent two different expressions of one and the same force of spirit that is found in all theoretical scientific thought. "In his quest of the truth the historian is bound to the same formal rules as the scientist. . . . he obeys the same general laws of thought as a physicist or biologist. So far as these fundamental theoretical activities of the human mind are concerned we can make no discrimination between the different fields of knowledge. . . . Historical and scientific thought are distinguishable not by their logical form but by their objectives and subject matter" (*Essay*, p. 176). As forms of theoretical knowledge they possess "an inner unity and a logical homogeneity" that overcomes the "heterogeneous" nature of the objects that they study[15] (*Essay*, p. 176).

The "Poetic Spirit" of the Historian

There is, of course, an essential difference between science and history; namely, the goal in scientific knowledge is to extinguish all expressive or "anthropological elements" in its interpretation of nature, history, however, cannot negate the "anthropomorphic" dimension without destroying itself.

> Like language or art, history is fundamentally anthropomorphic. To efface its human aspects would be to destroy its specific character and nature. But the anthropomorphism of historical thought is no limitation of or impediment to its objective truth. History is not knowledge of external facts or events; it is a form of self-knowledge. In order to know myself I cannot endeavor to go beyond myself, to leap, as it were, over my own shadow. I must choose the opposite approach. In history man constantly returns to himself; he attempts to recollect and actualize the whole of his past experience. But the historical self is not a mere individual self. It is anthropomorphic but it is not egocentric. Stated in the form of a paradox, we may say that history strives after an "objective anthropomorphism." (*Essay*, p. 191)

But how are we to achieve this "objective anthropomorphism"? In part the desired objectivity is achieved through the fact that the activity of the historian is governed by the logic and structure of science. But science only gives us knowledge of "the exterior world" (cf. *Essay*, p. 143), the world that can be seen and touched. History, however, does not desire to know the external manifestations of spirit, but rather the original dynamic impulses that animate these external manifestations—not the material sign but the spiritual signification, not the act but the impulse to act, not the word but the passion: such are the proper objects of historical recollection. "History is a history of passion; but if history itself attempts to be passionate it ceases to be history. . . . The historian must lose his interest in things and events in order to see them in their true shape" (*Essay*, p. 191 f.). To accomplish this task the historian has need of another mode of expression than that of science. As Goethe expresses it, the historian must possess an "imagination for the truth of reality (*eine Phantasie für die Wahrheit des Realen*)," a "poetic spirit" (*Essay*, p. 204). For like the artist, the historian must provide us with a representation of the history of passion without himself getting caught up in the passion of history. "The aesthetic experience—the experience of contemplation—is a different state of mind from the coolness of our theoretical and the sobriety of our moral judgement. It is filled with the liveliest energies of passion, but passion itself is here transformed both in its nature and in its meaning. Wordsworth defies poetry as 'emotion recollected in tranquillity' " (*Essay*, p. 147). There is of course an essential difference between art and history, for the drama that is recollected in art has no basis in the reality of the past: "The emotions aroused by the poet do not belong to a remote past. They are 'here'—alive and immediate" (*Essay*, p. 147). In fact, the artist provides us with an insight into the pure forms of human existence, without ever referring to any particular existence as such. Even where art aims at realism, the reality that it creates remains a work of fiction. Any resemblance between the dramatic reality of art and any particular reality found in the world is quite simply a *méconnaissance*. It is rather the historian who provides us with the pure form of the actual drama of the world as it has been lived.

> [History] does not go beyond the empirical reality of things and events but moulds this reality into a new shape, giving it the ideality of recollection. Life in the light of history remains a great realistic drama, with all its tensions and conflicts, its greatness and misery, its hopes and illusions, its display of energies and passions. This drama, however, is not only felt; it is intuited. Seeing this spectacle in the mirror of history while we are still living in our empirical world of emotions and passions, we become aware of an inner sense of clarity and calmness—of the lucidity and serenity of pure contemplation. "The spirit," wrote Jakob Burckhart in his *Reflections on World History*, "must transmute into a possession the remembrance of its passage through the ages of the world." (*Essay*, p. 205 f.)

The Paradox of History

There is thus a certain paradox involved in the process of historical recollection by which the past is reconstructed through its interpretation for and by the present. For although we set out to uncover something that is fundamentally other, in the final analysis what we discover via the mirror of history is ourselves. And what of the past, what of that which was actually thought, actually said?

> *Warum kann der lebendige Geist dem Geist nicht erscheinen?*
> *Spricht die Seele, so spricht, ach! schon die Seele nicht mehr!*
> Why can the living spirit not appear to the spirit?
> When the soul speaks, alas, it is no longer the soul that speaks!

. . . but the historian.

A Prelude to Reading

Toward an Interpretation of the Unity of Cassirer's Philosophy

Our reading and interpretation of Cassirer cannot begin *ex nihilo,* but rather must, following what we have said above, define its problem in terms of the already existing readings of Cassirer. The traditional approach to Cassirer, despite its value, is characterized by one major shortcoming: it does not explain the unity of Cassirer's philosophy. Echoing the sentiments of a number of commentators, Ralph Lindgren points out that an "adequate understanding of the meaning of any one of Cassirer's doctrines awaits a grasp of the unity of his thought."[16] Throughout the literature on Cassirer, the "unity" or hidden law of the philosophy of symbolic forms remains elusive. Part of the reason for this almost certainly stems from the fact that the vast majority of the critical literature on Cassirer has been written by authors whose interest in Cassirer has been only passing and secondary. Thus, while these works provide valuable insights into any one of a number of specific aspects of Cassirer's thought, they do not, either individually or collectively, provide an adequate interpretation of its whole. Even the full-length studies on Cassirer do not manage to capture the internal unity of Cassirer's conception of man and culture. Rather, here too we find a tendency to isolate elements without explaining their relation to each other or to their structural unity. To cite but a few examples from the literature, Carl Hamburg in his study *Symbol and Reality* focuses exclusively on the "core-idea" of the philosophy of symbolic forms, namely Cassirer's concept of the symbolic, and that from the narrow perspective of the epistemological problem that it poses for semantic and pragmatic philosophy. The two volumes by Seymour Itzkoff, *Ernst Cassirer: Scientific Knowledge and the Concept of Man* and *Ernst Cassirer: Philosopher of Culture,* focus upon Cassirer's theory of science as a continuation of the neo-Kantian project. Not only does Itzkoff not demonstrate the unity of Cassirer's thought, but in fact he does not even seem to believe that such a unity exists. David Lipton's study *Ernst Cassirer: The Dilemma of a Liberal Intellectual in Germany, 1914–1933* is a sociological study and says little directly relevant to Cassirer's theoretical ideas. The most recent publication in English, *Cassirer: Symbolic Forms and History,* by John Michael Krois is perhaps the most comprehensive study on Cassirer to date. While the project of Krois' study is to demonstrate the "basic philosophical orientation"[17] of Cassirer's thought, in the final analysis his reading too remains eclectic.[18] Two other works that warrant mention are Thomas Knoppe's *Die theoretische Philosophie Ernst Cassirers. Zu den Grundlagen transzendentaler Wissenschafts- und Kulturtheorie* and Massimo Ferrari's *Il giovane Cassirer e la scuola di Marburgo*. Those interested in the relation between the thought of Cohen and Natorp and that of Cassirer would greatly profit from either of these two works.[19] However, here too we find that the structure or unity of Cassirer's philosophy of symbolic forms is marginalized by an effort to establish the philosophical sources and genesis of his thought. The problem of the unity of the philosophy of symbolic forms thus remains a central problem in the literature on Cassirer. As a recent commentator has written:

> The symbol is the central point of the philosophy of symbolic forms, the only point allowing us to grasp, apart from its essence, its systematic unity. However, even during Cassirer's own lifetime, this element was considered to be one of the most difficult, and indeed obscure. This has given rise to the following interpretative error: either the systematicity of Cassirer's thought is denied—and thus becomes nothing more than a brilliant history—, or one of the symbolic forms is taken as the paradigm of the symbolic function as such, and the totality of the philosophical enterprise is explained starting from this symbolic form.[20]

My interpretation, therefore, emphasizes the unity of the Cassirerian project of the philosophy of symbolic forms, along with the unity of his view of the human world of culture. Such, as we shall see, is the nature of Cassirer's philosophical perspective: the whole always comes, logically speaking, before the parts. The parts do not exist prior to the whole, and cannot be understood outside their place and function in the whole. For Cassirer, "human life is an organism in which all elements imply and explain each other" (*Essay*, p. 178). At each step, I attempt to move from defining each element in its own terms, to determining its function in the whole structure of Cassirer's conception of the human world.

The problem of the unity of Cassirer's work is reflected in the obvious embarrassment in which Cassirer scholarship finds itself when it attempts to define a satisfactory frame of reference for its interpretation of the Cassirerian project. In his review of the collection of articles on Cassirer published in the "Living Philosophers" series edited by Paul Schilpp, Iredell Jenkins writes: "What comes as a definite and cumulative shock is the uncertainty that these authors evidence concerning their interpretations and criticisms: their seeming inability to be satisfied as to what Cassirer's position actually is."[21] What is lacking, Jenkins continues, is a general "frame of reference" in which to situate Cassirer and problems concerning Cassirer's thought. The classical interpretation at work in each of the articles in this collection, and much of the literature concerning Cassirer, for that matter, regards Cassirer as the last, and perhaps most eminent, representative of the Marburg school of neo-Kantianism. As to the importance of Kant and neo-Kantianism for the thought of Cassirer there can be little or no doubt. In *Determinism and Indeterminism in Modern Physics*, Cassirer himself affirms that his philosophical position remains thoroughly in keeping with the spirit of neo-Kantianism, and specifically the neo-Kantianism of the Marburg school: "Thus, my bond with the founders of the Marburg school is not loosened, and my debt of thanks with regard to them is not diminished, if it follows from the following investigations that . . . I have arrived at substantially different results" (*ID*, p. 132). This adherence to the transcendental method of critical philosophy aside, one is not then justified to reduce Cassirer's thought to a simple reworking of ideas already developed by other neo-Kantians, such as Cohen and Natorp. Much, though not all, of the literature on Cassirer spends the majority of its time examining the ideas of Cohen and Natorp rather than those of Cassirer.

If Cassirer's debt to Kant, Cohen and especially Natorp cannot be denied, neither can his other intellectual debts. Those familiar with Hegel cannot help but recognize the often Hegelian overtones of Cassirer's language. Some interpreters such as Donald Verene, for example, have even gone so far as to argue "that the philosophy of symbolic forms is derived from Kant only in a broad and secondary sense and that its actual foundations are in Hegel."[22]

In the final analysis, of course, Cassirer's thought is neither neo-Kantian nor neo-Hegelian, but rather a synthesis of a number of diverse intellectual sources—the Heraclitean notion of *Λόγος* and *κόσμος*; Kant's conception of transcendental philosophy and of the schematism; Natorp's psychology; Goethe's sense of "organic form" or "morphology" and his concept of the *Urphänomen*; Schelling's and Hegel's notions of the self-reflective and self-developing character of the concept; Leibniz's and Hertz's theory of the sign; Humboldt's theory of language; the movement from substance-based physics to field theory; Husserl's concept of intentionality . . . to mention but a few. All these sources must be taken into account in any comprehensive philosophical presentation of Cassirer's own perspective. Research into the intellectual roots of Cassirer's thought is by no means without merit, but it can never be taken in exchange for an interpretation of what I have called the hidden law or strategy of his thought. Without doubt, the presence of Heraclitus, Kant, Hegel, Leibniz, Goethe, . . . can be felt in Cassirer's thought; however, our task cannot rest with an analysis of the individual elements. Rather, we must seek the hidden law or strategy that brings these elements together into an organic unity. "A system always presupposes, if not an identical nature, at least an identical structure. As a matter of fact this structural identity—an identity of form, not of matter—has always been emphasized by the great historians" (*Essay*, p. 172). This "identity of form," or "that which brings the elements of the series a, b, c, . . . together, is not itself a new element, that was factually blended with them, but . . . is the rule of progression, which remains the same, no matter in which member it is represented. The function f (a,b), f (b,c) . . . which determines the sort of dependence between the successive members is obviously not to be pointed out as itself a member of the series which exists and develops according to it" (*SF*, p. 17/21 f.). As we saw in our reflections on the paradoxical structure and dynamics of interpretation and reinterpretation, our understanding of this "rule of progression," or the hidden law, cannot be derived from the past, from the "elements of the series." Rather, what is required is a perspective, a "line of vision" to organize the series—and this rule of progression can only come from the future possibilities of the past, future possibilities that are successively brought out in the present. In the pages that follow, the philosophy of symbolic forms is presented as a *type* of "structuralism" *avant la lettre* resulting from a fusion and critical transformation of Kant's transcendental critical philosophy, on the one hand, and Hegel's phenomenology of spirit, on the other. In a sense this approach is not without its predecessors. In the introduction to his book *Cassirer: Symbolic Forms and History*, Krois for one maintains that Cassirer's work prefigures "semiotics, structuralism, and hermeneutics."[23] Unfortunately, Krois never takes up this claim in a more detailed fashion.[24] Of course, "this whole cannot be presented all at once but must be unfolded progressively by thought in its own autonomous movement and rhythm" (*PSF*, I, p. xiv/vi). Thus, "in what follows what counts is not to listen to a series of propositional phrases, but to follow the movement of the showing."[25]

One

The "Crisis" in the Project of Rationality

A "Crisis" in Rationality

Toward the turn of the century, there remained little doubt in the minds of many that not all was well in the project of rationality, that our faith in rationality, upon which occidental culture had been founded for some two millennia, was itself unfounded. This crisis in the self-knowledge of reason first manifested itself in the realization that the sciences paradigmatic of modern rationality, such as mathematics and physics, were unable to account for the principles upon which they were constructed, and thus were themselves incapable of providing the foundations for human knowledge—which, since Descartes and Galileo, had been assumed to be the case. This failure of modern rationality brought about a more general crisis in Western rationality itself, of which modern rationality was but a particular, though important and paradigmatic expression. Some, most notably Edmund Husserl, took up the formidable challenge of salvaging reason and the project of Western rationality, calling for a reinscription of rationality and the "re-establishment" of the Greek ideal of knowledge, and spoke of the vital importance of philosophy as a "rigorous science" to the identity and survival of European culture. Others, most notably Martin Heidegger, took up the no less formidable challenge of unveiling and exposing the illusory nature of reason, calling rather for a decentering of rationality and the "repetition" of the Greek ideal of knowledge, and spoke of the vital importance of the end of philosophy for the beginning of the "thinking" of difference and the survival of *Dasein*. The project of the philosophy of symbolic forms shares many of the basic concerns from which the critique of reason and modernity begins.[1] Cassirer's response to the crisis in rationality and the project of modernity was not, however, one of rejection, but rather one of reaffirmation. Like

Husserl, Cassirer speaks of the ethical imperative of re-establishing the Greek "ideal" of reason and knowledge, and of the importance of philosophy for human culture. However, unlike Husserl Cassirer's project of re-establishment begins by way of recognizing the need for a much wider and more comprehensive conception of objectivity and reason. Wide enough, in fact, to include domains of being and meaning that cannot but be seen as being essentially irrational in nature—at least irrational in terms of our traditional conception of scientific reason. To suggest that anything resembling irrationality has a place in the interior of rationality itself was, for Cassirer as it was for Husserl, a meaningless and unthinkable notion.[2] Cassirer was thus forced in the end to abandon the term reason itself: for as we shall see "reason is a very inadequate term with which to comprehend the forms of man's cultural life in all their richness and variety" (*Essay*, p. 26).

Without doubt Cassirer remains a thoroughly modern philosopher. However, his philosophy of symbolic forms provides us, as it were, with a "repetition" of modernity, an authentic appropriation and transformation of Western rationality from within—and this through a re-establishment, or as Cassirer might say, a "renaissance" of the Greek ideal of logos and knowledge.[3] This repetition of modernity marks a twofold return to the Greek conception of knowledge: in the sense in which Husserl understood it, as the project to establish the "unity" of knowledge of Being, on the one hand, and in the sense in which Heidegger understood it, as the simultaneous disclosure (*ἀλήθεια*) and concealment (*λήθη*) of the truth of logos, on the other.

This chapter sets out to render explicit the implicit problems that underlie Cassirer's whole philosophy. The chapter is divided into three sections. The title of each section refers to one of the three basic expression employed by Cassirer to characterize his philosophical project: namely, a "critique of culture," a "philosophy of representation," and finally a "phenomenology of culture." Each section considers the project of the philosophy of symbolic forms from the perspective of one of the main issues inherent in the now classic critique of modernity: namely, logocentrism, the metaphysics of presence, and finally, the problem of the relation between the immanence of life and the transcendence of spirit.

From a "Critique of Reason" to a "Critique of Culture"

The "Crisis" as a Loss of Unity

The analysis of the "crisis" of modern man presented by Cassirer is in many respects not unlike the one presented by Husserl in *The Crisis of European Sciences and Transcendental Phenomenology*. Like Husserl, Cassirer, too, believes that the most striking symptom of the impasse that Western rationality has reached is to be found in the disunity and, indeed, "anarchy" of the different domains of human knowledge (cf. *Essay*, p. 21 f.), especially the "cleft" existing between the sciences of nature and the sciences of culture (cf. *Logic*, p. 36). And, again akin to Husserl, Cassirer believes that philosophy has failed in its task to provide the intellectual center around which the different branches of knowledge can be organized and thus unified into a system that transcends their individual particularity: "Philosophy was unable to maintain this unity, nor was it able to put a stop to the growing fragmentation. Hegel's system is the last great attempt to embrace the whole of knowledge and to organize it by virtue of one ruling thought. But Hegel was not able to reach this goal" (*Logic*, p. 34 f.).[4] Finally, again akin to Husserl, Cassirer considers that this loss of unity, "this antagonism of ideas is not merely a grave theoretical problem but an imminent threat to the whole extent of our ethical and cultural life" (*Essay*, p. 21 f.).[5]

What is the cause of this disunity? In chapter 1 of *An Essay on Man*, entitled "The Crisis in Man's Knowledge of Himself," Cassirer sets forward an answer to this question by way of a reading of the history of the quest of Western thought for self-knowledge, a history beginning with the Greeks and provisionally ending in nineteenth-century and twentieth-century empiricism. Cassirer concludes his study by stating that each of the modern theories of man proves to be nothing more than a "procrustean bed on which the empirical facts are stretched to fit a preconceived pattern" (*Essay*, p. 21). Each theory proves to be its own paradigm of human existence, independent and isolated from every other competing paradigm. Each theory proclaims to present *the* nature of human existence without being able to account for the others—assuming that it wanted to do so—nor for its own theoretical and metaphysical presuppositions.

> [The problem is that] the modern theory of man [has] lost its intellectual center. . . . Metaphysics, theology, mathematics, and biology successively assumed the guidance for thought on the problem of man and determined the line of investigation. The real crisis of this problem manifested itself when such a central power capable of directing all individual efforts ceased to exist. . . . [A]n established authority to which one might appeal no longer existed. Theologians, scientists, politicians, sociologists, biologists, psychologists, ethnologists, economists all approached the problem from their own viewpoints. To combine or unify all these particular aspects and perspectives was impossible. . . . The personal factor became more and more prevalent, and the temperament of the individual writer tended to play a decisive role. (*Essay*, p. 21)

Logocentrism and the Failure of Philosophy

The responsibility for this loss of a general unitary paradigm of human existence, and thus for the loss of a general framework of theoretical research into man and the world, lies with philosophy itself: for it has been the task of philosophy since its birth in ancient Greece to provide the "highest instance of unity (*Einheitsinstanz*), the definitive verdict" (*PSF*, I, p. 82/14). The failure of philosophy to establish this universal unity stems from its partisanship with one or another sphere of cultural life. The different dogmatic systems of metaphysics "stand in the midst of the battle, and not above it: despite the conceptual universality towards which they strive, they stand only for one side of the conflict, instead of encompassing and mediating the conflict itself in all its breadth and depth." In this way "they cut themselves off from particular aspects of cultural life and the concrete totality of its forms" (*PSF*, I, p. 82/14). What is more, where other forms of spirit are recognized, they are reduced to that form of spirit that is found in scientific thought: namely, to "logic." Philosophy has understood the "*universitas* of spirit, the concrete totality of spirit" only when, and to the extent that it has succeeded in deducing it from "a *logical* principle." "Thus the pure form of logic becomes . . . the prototype and model for all spiritual existence and every form of spirit" (*PSF*, I, p. 83/15). This "panlogicism" finds its highest and purest expression in the system of Hegel in which "all the diverse forms of spirit set forth in the *Phenomenology* seem to culminate in a supreme logical summit. . . . Of all the cultural forms, only that of logic, the concept, cognition, seems to enjoy a true and authentic *autonomy*" (*PSF*, I, p. 83/15). All the other moments in the concrete life of spirit are sublated into the existence of the concept.

The Systematic Unity of the Symbolic Forms of Culture

The philosophy of symbolic forms aims to overcome the crisis of Western rationality by establishing a new intellectual center, the symbolic function, and in so doing provide a new paradigm of human existence and a new unitary framework and direction for scientific knowledge. Cassirer's whole philosophical outlook begins from the recognition of the autonomy of a plurality of dimensions of spirit. The concept of the symbol function, as that "which recurs in each basic cultural form but in no two of them in exactly the same shape" (*PSF*, I, p. 84/16), provides Cassirer with a "standpoint situated *above* all these forms and yet not merely outside them: a standpoint which would make it possible to encompass the whole of them in one view, which would seek to penetrate nothing other than the purely immanent relation of these forms to one another, and not their relation to any external, 'transcendent' being or principle" (*PSF*, I, p. 82/14). In this way, the philosophy of symbolic forms "can maintain the claim of unity and universality, which metaphysics had to abandon in its dogmatic form. Not only can it unite these various ways and directions of our knowledge of the world in itself, but in addition, it is capable of recognizing the legitimacy of every attempt to understand the world, every interpretation of the world that the human spirit is capable of, and of understanding them in their specificity" (*Logic*, p. 20). Our task in the following pages will be to determine the basic structure of the symbolic function and its different manifestations, as well as demonstrate their codetermination within the dynamic unity of culture.

From a "Metaphysics of Presence" to a "Philosophy of Representation"

On another and deeper level the crisis of Western rationality is due to a lack of critical self-distance. Entangled in what Jacques Derrida has termed the "metaphysics of presence" and the "myth of the given," our tradition has allowed itself to be absorbed in an illusory immediacy of the real that can never become "present." The belief in this has rendered our tradition incapable of stepping back and taking a distance to itself and the different forms of human culture as a means of representation. Cassirer's concept of the symbolic allows him to argue that all reality is always already mediated by symbols, that each symbolic form at once reveals and conceals reality. From the perspective of the philosophy of symbolic forms, the "dualistic antithesis is sublated. The illusion of an original division between the intelligible and the sensuous, between 'idea' and 'phenomenon,' vanishes. . . . Through [the different 'image' worlds of each of the symbolic forms] alone we see what we call 'reality,' and in them alone we possesses it" (*PSF*, I, p. 110 f./47 f.). In this context, Cassirer advances a critique of Husserl that it will be interesting to compare to that of Derrida as this will help us to better understand not only the originality of Cassirer's thesis, but also its radical nature.

Derrida's Critique of Husserl's Concept of Sign

Derrida's critique of Husserl's concept of sign is well known, so that it is not necessary to rehearse it in all its detail here. In *La voix et le phénomene* Derrida formulates his critique upon the basis of a deconstruction of the Husserlian distinction between the indicative and the expressive sign. An expressive sign, according to Husserl, is one in which there obtains an intimate unity between the signifier and the signified, in such a way that there does not seem to be any distance between them. An indicative sign, on the other hand, only points to that which it signifies, which thus remains at an irreducible distance from the signifier. Although Husserl admits that all linguistic signs function at once as expressive and as indicative signs, he nevertheless accords a certain primacy to the expressive dimension. For he remains convinced that expression, as the immediate presence of the object to the subject and of the subject to itself, is the ideal of signification. In keeping with the Cartesian approach, the soliloquy, as the immediate present of the subject to itself without the mediation of a foreign "other," is the Husserlian paradigm of signification. It is precisely at this point that Derrida begins his deconstruction of Husserl's position, by insisting upon the inextricable co-constitutionality, if you will, of the indicative and the expressive dimensions of signification—upon the irreducible nature of the "play of 'différance' between the expressive and indicative sign," as R. Bernet has put it.[6] As R. Bernet has shown, Derrida's critique is more subtle than some commentators would have it, representing not a simple move from the Husserlian-type phenomenology of present to a phenomenology of absence. Rather, Derrida's point is that there is no presence without absence, but also no absence without presence. Signification is the presencing of the absence of the real.

Cassirer's Critique of Husserl's Concept of the Sign

Cassirer's critique of Husserl goes very much in the same direction, although it takes a different point of departure. Cassirer agrees with Husserl's analysis of consciousness in terms of intentionality, and the clear distinction it entails between meaning in consciousness and the misleading problem as to the "factual" existence of something existing before or without its "meaning." Husserl, however, falls into the trap of distinguishing within consciousness between two aspects, namely, between an element of sensuous experience (ὕλη), on the one hand, and an element of intentionality, or meaning (μορφή), on the other. When, moreover, Husserl goes on to ask how it is that these two elements can come together to form a meaningful whole, he completely deviates from the very principles of his own thought:

> We attempt to express this systematic relationship by considering the fundamental sensory experience with which we are dealing in this case as received into, determined, and given form by various "symbolic forms." However, this way of speaking should not and may not be understood as though we were dealing here with a case of the separation or temporal succession of "form" and "matter." If we may distinguish these in the manner of Husserl's terminology, between the sensory material and animating acts, between the sensual ὕλη and intentional μορφή, then this abstract separation can never mean that these may be separated in the phenomenon or that in itself formless matter were something given that is gradually taken up into various modes of interpretation and subsequently given shape by them. Whoever in this way converts the Kantian "dualism" of form and matter, which

> is a difference of meaning and transcendental "validity," into a separation of things actually existing next to and apart from each other has thereby already missed the decisive point of view needed for the profound understanding of this difference. ("The Problem of the Symbol," p. 416; also cf. *PSF*, III, p. 196 ff./228 ff.)

As is evident from this quote, in which Cassirer defines his own philosophy of symbolic forms over against the Husserlian approach, Cassirer conceives of his thought as a continuation and strict application of the Kantian distinction between form and matter *as the two co-constitutive and interdependent* elements of experience. There is, for Cassirer as for Derrida, no representation without the "presence" of something represented;[7] yet this "presence" is always already mediated by the sign, so that it can never actually become a "pure presence":

> This dialectic of metaphysical ontology can be avoided only if, from the very start, "content" and "form," "element" and "relation" are conceived not as terms independent of one another, but as concurrent and mutually determining one another. . . . Only in and through this *representation* (*Repräsentation*) does what we call the condition and the *"presence"* (*Präsenz*) of the content become possible. . . . Only because in this way we can ascertain in the actual content of consciousness something that is not, in the given something that is not given—does there exist for us a unity which on the one hand we designate as the subjective unity of consciousness, and on the other as the objective unity of the object. (*PSF*, I, p. 98 f./32 f.)

As we shall see, for Cassirer even the presence of the subject to itself is mediated by the presence and alterity of the sign. Spirit can only know itself in the "mirror" of its objective expression, in the "mirror of its culture" (*Logic*, p. 102). In the "soliloquy" the subject is "spilt" by the symbolic function. Only in this way does the subject become present to itself as a *"persona"* "in the basic etymological meaning of the word, which goes back to the mask and the role of the actor" (*Logic*, p. 54). The mask of the subject, his *persona*, reveals the subject to himself as to the world by hiding the subject.

To express this dialectic between of representation and presence, between form and matter, the sensuous sign and its nonintuitive meaning, Cassirer introduces his famous concept of "symbolic pregnance" (*symbolische Prägnanz*).[8] As we shall see, the different symbolic forms represent different modes of meaning, or better, different modes of the presence of meaning, as each cultural form constitutes a specific mode of "seeing" (*Sicht*). What is not made clear by Cassirer, and which we will endeavor to make clear at the end of the next chapter and throughout our reading of Cassirer, is that each of these different modes of seeing or different modes of representation constitutes a different moment in the dynamic structure of the basic presence of meaning itself, in the basic structure and process of seeing. In every moment of seeing, in every presence of meaning—and thus every presence—all the different dimensions of meaning studied by Cassirer are implicitly present. The presence of meaning comes about only in the interplay between the different modes of representation, in the play between their difference. It is clear that it is a question of a dynamic process and not a static structure. This dynamic process of meaning is none other than the life of objective spirit.

From a "Phenomenology of Spirit" to a "Phenomenology of Culture"

In the preceding two sections we have considered Cassirer's philosophical project from the perspective of his twofold critique of modernity: namely, as a tradition of logocentrism, on the one hand, and as a metaphysics of presence, on the other. As we have already said, Cassirer sees in Hegel's system the clearest expression, and indeed the pinnacle of the logocentric tradition. Nevertheless, his own philosophy of symbolic forms, as a philosophy of spirit, owes much more to Hegel's phenomenology of spirit. In order to better clarify in what way Cassirer's phenomenology of culture differs from Hegel's phenomenology of spirit, it is first useful to consider his critique of Bergson's metaphysics of life, as one of the clearest expression of what Cassirer understood by life-philosophy (*Lebensphilosophie*). Cassirer's strategy consists in showing that the Hegelian emphasis upon *Logos* naturally leads to a deconstruction of spirit from within, to the affirmation of the rights of life by spirit from within the realm of spirit itself. On the other hand, Cassirer raises the discussion concerning Bergson in order to demonstrate, in a complementary and inverse movement, how a "metaphysics of life" that seeks to return to a form of "pure intuition" without symbols, and thus to a pure and immediate presence, must also deconstruct itself from within, insofar as life, in order to realize itself, requires the otherness of spirit.

Bergson's theory of "pure intuition" aims to overcome what Bergson sees as the limitation of symbolic representation: "La métaphysique," Bergson writes, "est la science qui prétend se passer des symboles" (cited in *PSF*, III, p. 36/43). As the work of spirit, language and symbols cannot, according to Bergson, capture the "heterogeneity" of the *élan vital,* which shows itself in the life of the "pure ego." For linguistic metaphors cannot but "reify" life, thus destroying its immediate vitality and objectifying it in the distanciation inherent in spatial representations. In short, symbols, as spiritual forms, "conceal" the truth of life rather than "reveal" it. To these arguments Cassirer replies by means of a rhetorical question: "Must all form as such necessarily signify concealment rather than manifestation and revelation?" (*PSF*, III, p. 39/47). Evidently not—life possesses no immediate presence even to itself and requires spiritual formation in order to gain any "visibility" at all:

> Life cannot *apprehend* itself by *remaining* absolutely within itself. It must give itself form; for it is precisely by this "otherness" ("*Andersheit*") of form that it gains its "visibility" ("*Sichtigkeit*"), if not its reality. To detach the world of life absolutely from form and oppose the two means nothing other than to separate its "reality" from its "visibility." (*PSF*, III, p. 39/47)

In other words, there can be no "inward" movement, no apprehension of the self through introspection, without and prior to the "outward" movement of the incarnation of the life of the self, the pure ego, in the world of spiritual forms (cf. *PSF*, III, p. 40/48).

Hegel's phenomenology of spirit avoids the mistake of the philosophy of life, represented here by Bergson, insofar as Hegel realizes the necessity of life's entering into communion with spirit—and this not just in some accidental and extrinsic fashion, but in order for life to achieve its own "being-for-itself." This positive appreciation of Hegel is most evident in Cassirer's 1931 essay on " 'Spirit' and 'Life.' " Although Hegel's system is "logocentric," this does not mean, according to Cassirer, that there is no place for life in the Hegelian dialectic:

> [I]t would be a complete misunderstanding of his system to bring against it the reproach that by reason of its panlogistic tendency it denies the rights of Life—that it has sacrificed the vital sphere to that of logic. Even a mere glance at the historical development of the Hegelian doctrine is sufficient to invalidate this objection: for it is precisely in the writings of Hegel's early period that . . . a new, systematically most fruitful concept of Life is coined. (" 'Spirit' and 'Life,' " p. 875/260 f.)

Following this "new, systematically most fruitful concept of Life," spirit needs the exteriority of life in order to realize its interior "depth." On the other hand, life needs spirit, for as such it is "speechless" and unable to give itself expression. Life has always already entered the domain of spirit, so that the "battle" between spirit and life does not remain exterior to spirit, but rather takes place within its own realm:

> The real drama takes place not between Spirit and Life, but in the midst of Spirit's own realm, indeed at its very focus. . . . Spirit is only, insofar as it turns against itself in this manner; its own unity is thinkable only in such contrariety. Hence, Spirit is not only . . . the ascetic of *Life*, not only that which can say "No" to all organic reality; it is the principle which *within itself* may negate itself. . . . Nature knows suffering and death, destruction and annihilation; but it knows nothing of that self-disintegration whereby man turns against himself. As the being who alone is *capable* of questioning, man is also the being who is and remains to himself thoroughly problematical, the being eternally *worthy* of questioning. (" 'Spirit' and 'Life,' " p. 876 f./261 f.)

In the overtones, if not in the letter of this passage, one can already see where Hegel and Cassirer will part company. Whereas for Hegel, the "battle" between life and spirit, and the battle within spirit, finds its ideal resolution in that final moment of "absolute knowledge," Cassirer is convinced that there can be no ultimate harmony, but only an open-ended struggle. In spite of all his positive appreciation of the Hegelian dialectic, Cassirer therefore rejects its *dénouement*—the absorption of life into spirit, nature into idea, difference into identity, and opacity into transparency. For in Hegel, "nature retains nothing in her own right; she possesses only an apparent independence. All her being

function a more general and abstract definition. This is way, in the second section, we turn to a consideration of the philosophy of symbolic forms as a type of structuralism *avant la lettre*. This is undertaken by way of a comparison of Gilles Deleuze's seven-point definition of structuralism with Cassirer's philosophy of symbolic forms. Having established the basic structure of the symbolic function, we turn in the final section of this chapter to introduce—in fact, to logically deduce—the different cultural forms that make up the totality of the cultural realm.

From a Theory of the Concept to a Theory of the Symbolic

From Substance to Function

The project of the *Philosophy of Symbolic Forms* was first conceived, as Cassirer himself informs us, "at the time of the investigations summed up in [his] book *Substanzbegriff und Funktionsbegriff* (Berlin, 1910)" (*PSF*, I, p. 69. v). Cassirer's move in *Substance and Function* could be described as a transformation and inversion of the basic assumptions underlying Aristotelian logic. The necessity for this inversion became clear to Cassirer through his acquaintance with recent developments in mathematics and physics. These developments, in turn, suggested to him the fruitfulness of the Hegelian notion of the "concrete universal." The important position that Hegel holds even at the earliest beginnings of Cassirer's philosophical reflections is rarely adverted to in the critical literature.

Chapter 1 of *Substance and Function*

Aristotelian logic, which has dominated the field throughout its history, cannot be understood independently of the metaphysics that underlies it (cf. *SF*, p. 4/4 f.). Now this metaphysics is, as has often been pointed out, a substance-based theory of being. For Aristotle, only substantial being (οὐσία) *is* in the full sense of the word; relations, quantities, qualities, time, space, and so forth, are only accidents that, in order to be, require a substance in which they inhere. The substance-centered logic that naturally follows from this metaphysics is a logic of concepts and of abstraction. The Aristotelian theory of concept-formation presupposes the existence of autonomous substances, which it takes as its *terminus a quo*, and proceeds to isolate within each individual substance the "essential" properties and features that this individual substance has in common with others. In this way, Aristotelians arrive at "abstract" species and genera as sets of essential properties shared by any number of individual substances.

Cassirer calls for an inversion in the perspective of Aristotelian logic. The process of understanding being cannot take its inception in the particular substance; for how are we to know what the "essential" properties and characteristics of a substance are—those properties without which it would not be what it "essentially" is?

> If we group cherries and meat together under the attributes red, juicy and edible, we do not thereby attain a valid logical concept but a meaningless combination of words, quite useless for the comprehension of the particular cases. (*SF*, p. 7/8)

Cassirer's solution involves a decentering of the substance-centered logic. Rather than taking a being as the *terminus a quo* of a judgment, it is necessary to regard it as its *terminus ad quem*: the judgment thus representing the process of the differentiation of a function relation or universal. We need, in other words, to ascertain the general law by which the being is generated, rather than trying to isolate and abstract elements from within that being and put them together into arbitrary sets of attributes. Being thus comes to be seen as unfolding itself in a series of particular and determined beings, each of which represents a concrete expression of the law governing the series as a whole. All that the individual being *is*, is nothing more than the *place* in the series assigned to it by the functional law. And now it becomes clear that what is "essential" to a being are the *relations* in which it finds itself, and not any underlying "substance," as the Aristotelian tradition would have it.

> Hence if we understand representation as the expression of an ideal rule, which connects the present, given particular with the whole, and combines the two in an intellectual synthesis, then we have in representation no mere subsequent determination, but a constitutive condition of all experience. Without this apparent

> representation, there would also be no "presentation," no immediately present content. (*SF*, p. 284/377)

The deficiencies of the theory of abstraction were not overcome by the psychological approach. Instead of placing, like Aristotle, the concept *in* the real and making it, as a substantial form, the moving force of reality itself, thinkers such as Berkeley and Mill conceive of the concept as a product of the mind (cf. *SF*, p. 9 ff./11 ff.). Whereas Aristotle understands the universal in terms of an actual element of reality, the psychological approach views the universal as abstract, existing independently of any actual realization. Neither Aristotle nor Berkeley or Mill can, however, sufficiently account for the process of abstraction or universalizeation itself.

In order to avoid the problems of the traditional theory of abstraction, a conception of the universal is required that, in fusing Aristotle's substantialism with Berkeley's and Mill's psychologism, transforms both. Cassirer thus puts forward a conception of the universal such that it will at once possess the realness of the Aristotelian universal (without, as Aristotle does, taking the universal as being so immanent to being as to be a particular of the series that the universal itself generates), and the ideality of the psychological and subjective schemas posited by Berkeley and Mill (without, as these thinkers do, severing the universal from the concrete reality of the world—without, in other words, regarding the universal as transcending the particular, with the consequence that it becomes unable to explain the reason of its being).

Cassirer discovers the paradigm for this "concrete universal" satisfying these conditions in the mathematical concept of function $y = \varphi(x)$. In the third volume of the *Philosophy of Symbolic Forms*, Cassirer provides a summery of the essential structure of this function concept:

> If we conceive of the concept as defined, not by a listing of what falls under it, but purely intentionally by the indication of a definite *propositional function* (*Satzfunktion*), this propositional function $\varphi(x)$ contains two factors which are obviously dissimilar. The universal *form* of the function as designated by the letter φ stands out sharply against the *values* of the variable x which may enter into this function as a "true" value. The function determines the relation between these values, but it is not itself one of them: the φ of x is not homogeneous with the x series, x_1, x_2, x_3, etc. (*PSF*, III, p. 301/352)

The φ of the propositional function φ(x) represents the "*law*" that determines the totality of "*possible* members" (x) that are said to "belong together" (x_1, x_2, x_3 . . .). The unity between the universal φ and the particular x must not be thought of as an "aggregate" of independent elements (φ + x), but rather as an "organic unity" φ(x), whereby the universal φ is immanent in every particular x: hence the expression, the "one in the many (*Eines im Vielen*)" (*PSF*, III, p. 336/392). This is precisely what the sensationalist and intellectualist approaches fail to recognize. The sensationalists, for their part, "take the φ as though it were it itself an x, or as though it were at most the mere sum of x's, an $x_1 + x_2 + x_3$ and so on (*PSF*, III, p. 327/382). The intellectualist approach only reverses this by treating the variable x as though it were "an absolute, detached and unconditioned being" (*PSF*, III, p. 327/381). But whether we reduce the universal to the particular, or the particular to the universal, one way or another we fall into the trap of a "correspondence" or "copy theory" of truth and knowledge, and thus into a "myth of the given," which Cassirer never tires of discrediting. In separating the two elements and designating one as the measure over against the other, as both the sensationalist and intellectualist approaches do, we fail to recognize that the two are reciprocal moments of one and the same relation of meaning. Although the law φ transcends the series of x's, this transcendence must not be interpreted as a transcendence in being, but rather as a transcendence in meaning: for the φ of the series is always immanent in each member of the series that it constitutes as "the rule of progression" that assigns each its "place" and internally orders the members of the series into an organic whole. The law of the series is thus never embodied in any one of its members, nor is it equal to the sum total of its members: for it represents the whole of the series as the law that determines the internal limit of every possible member of that series.

> That which brings the elements of the series a, b, c, . . . together, is not itself a new element, that was factually blended with them, but . . . is the rule of progression, which remains the same, no matter in which member it is represented. The function f (a, b), f (b, c) . . . which determines the sort of dependence between the successive members is obviously not to be pointed out as itself a member of the series which exists and develops according to it. (*SF*, p. 17/21 f.)

The essential feature of all true conceptual structures, therefore, is to unify and differentiate the manifold of particulars (infinitely finite in themselves) by providing an "ideal *reference point*." All the particulars "order themselves according to this point of reference, and through this unity of direction a unity of 'essence' is stamped upon them—though this essence is not to be taken ontically but logically, as a pure determination of meaning" (*PSF*, III, p. 303/354). What is more, "in regard to the universal factor of meaning which the concept sets up and makes stand out, all the things that fall under it are not only similar but identical: in order to be thought of as special 'instances' of a concept, each one of the particular examples must satisfy the *whole* concept, i.e., the totality of the conditions it embraces" (*PSF*, III, p. 303/353 f.). Finally, "the convergence by which . . . heterogeneity is overcome does not signify that a substantial sameness or accord is disclosed in the elements of the manifold but that, however different they may be from one another, they are taken as factors of a context of meaning, that each in its own place and role constitutes the totality and function of this meaning" (*PSF*, III, p. 304/354 f.).

From Concepts to Symbols and the Symbolic

Cassirer's investigations in *Substance and Function* were limited to the process of concept formation in the mathematical sciences of nature. It was in accounting for the advent of non-Euclidean systems of geometry, that Cassirer was progressively forced to consider the problem in more and more general terms.

> More and more we have been forced to recognize that the area of theoretical meaning that we designate with the names "knowledge" and "truth," no matter how significant and fundamental, represents only *one* layer of meaning. In order to understand it, in order to recognize its structure (*Struktur*), we must compare and contrast this layer with other meaning dimensions. We must, in other words, conceive the problem of knowledge and the problem of truth as particular cases of the more general *problem of meaning*. ("Erkenntnistheorie," p. 81 f.)

And with this we arrive at the project of the philosophy of symbolic forms:

> It is the task of systematic philosophy, which extends far beyond the theory of knowledge, to free the idea of the world from this one-sidedness. It has to grasp the *whole* of the symbolic forms, the application of which produces for us the concept of an ordered reality, and by virtue of which subject and object, ego and world are separated and opposed to each other in definite form, and it must refer each individual in this totality to its fixed place. (*ETR*, p. 447/109 f.)[1]

As we shall see, the structure of the propositional function $\varphi(x)$ developed above will function as the conceptual expression of the universal structure of every symbolic form. Insofar as each symbolic forms represents a particular mode of structuring the world, it is, if you will, the mathematical expression of the structure of structure. That Cassirer continues to speak of the universal function of the symbolic in terms of one of the members of the series it constitutes—namely the mathematical concept of the natural sciences—is unfortunate as it is at times confusing. The reader often wonders in what way, for example, mythical, religious, or aesthetic meaning can be said to be conceptual. Can it not be objected here that in taking the mathematical concept of function as the model for the symbolic as such, Cassirer has broken with one of his own methodological principles and that he has reduced all the different forms of understanding to one form, namely the form of the logical concept? Cassirer himself recognizes this danger:

> Of course it can be argued that such an approach takes the part for the whole: that a truly logical and phenomenological analysis of the concept [i.e. the symbolic function] must attempt to apprehend it in the *totality* of its meaning (*Bedeutungstotalität*), in *all* (*Gesamtheit*) its achievements and phases of achievement, whereas mathematics and exact science [the concept $\varphi(x)$] disclose it to be sure in perfection but by that very token only at the end of its development. (*PSF*, III, p. 296/346)

To our surprise, however, there is no attempt to justify himself against this possible objection! Cassirer simply states that "far from altering [his] previous analysis of the exact concept," his analysis of the "natural world concept" has only "confirmed it from a new angle" (*PSF*, III, p. 297/347).

It is, of course, inherent to Cassirer's philosophical point of view of the "general movement of consciousness" that "this process itself would disintegrate into isolated and unrelated particulars, permitting no synthesis into *one* result, if there were not . . . the general possibility of apprehending the whole in the part and the part in the whole" (*PSF*, I, p. 99 f./34). Thus, that one of the parts should have as its function to represent the whole that animates all the parts, including itself, would seem to follow logically from the very structure of the process by which "spirit proceeds towards its objectivization, i.e., its self-revelation" (*PSF*, I, p. 78/9): for only then would the universal have come to know itself in and through the particular. In the same way that in Heidegger Being is accessible only through beings, and more specifically through that one being most concerned with its own being, namely *Dasein*, the symbolic function of the "concept" is accessible only through the different symbolic forms, and most specifically through that form which is self-conscious of its own symbolic nature, namely the concept of science. "For what distinguishes science from the other stages (*Stufen*) of cultural life is not that it requires no mediation of signs and symbols and confronts the unveiled truth of 'things in themselves,' but that, differently and more profoundly than is possible for the other forms, it knows that the symbols it employs are *symbols* and comprehends them as such" (*PSF*, II, p. 26/34). We will return to the problem of the reflectivity of the symbolic function as the condition of possibility of its own self-presentation implicitly throughout our study and explicitly in the conclusion.

The Symbolic Function as the Dynamic Structural Form of Spirit

The Symbolic as *Strucktur* and *Aufbau*

Before we examine Cassirer's concept of the symbolic form in terms of structuralism, we must ask ourselves what permits us to undertake such an interpretation. To begin with, we find that throughout his work Cassirer consistently employees the term *Struktur* and its Germanic synonym, *Aufbau,* in speaking about the specific nature of the different symbolic forms.[2] What distinguishes one symbolic forms from another—myth from language, language from art, and so forth—is that in each case we are dealing with a different *Strukturform,* "structural form" (cf. *PSF*, II, p. 11; 12 n7/15; 16 n1). The task of the philosophy of symbolic forms is to determine the specific law or "coherent structural principle" (*einheitliches Strukturgesetz*) (*Logic*, p. 13) that defines the *Strukturform* of each of the different domains of culture insofar as it stands over against the others, and insofar as it forms a unitary whole with the others (cf. *PSF*, II, p. 19/25). In its approach "its inquiry is directed not toward a common origin, but toward a common *structure* (*Struktur*)" (*PSF*, II, p. 254/303). It seeks, by "describing the *structure* of language, myth, religion, art, and science" to "give us insight into the fundamental *structure* of each of these human activities, and which at the same time would enable us to understand them as an *organic whole*" (*Essay*, p. 68, my emphasis).

Aufbau is, as I have said, a synonym of *Struktur*, for it frequently occurs in the same context as the latter. One example is to be found in volume I of the *Philosophy of Symbolic Forms*, where in discussing language, Cassirer remarks that "in this sense every new form represents a new 'structure' of the world, in accordance with specific criteria, valid for it alone (*Jede neue Form stellt in diesem Sinne einen neuen 'Aufbau' der Welt dar*. . .)" (*PSF*, I, p. 177/124). However, there is also an important difference in meaning between *Struktur* and *Aufbau*, which is reflected in the English translation of these terms; for *Struktur* is rendered by "structure" whereas *Aufbau* is variously translated as "structure," "building," or "construction." This reflects the fact that *Aufbau* is derived from the verb *aufbauen*, "to build up," "to construct," and thus possesses a more dynamic meaning than *Struktur*. Hence, Cassirer speaks of the *Aufbau der anschaulichen Wirklichkeit* through the symbolic forms, that is, "the building of intuitive reality" (*PSF*, III, p. 142/165). Due to the synonymy of *Struktur* and *Aufbau* in Cassirer's writings, the verb *aufbauen* can also be translated as "to structure." It is interesting to note that the word "structure" comes from the Latin *structura*, which is itself derived from *struere*, which means "to construct." Each spiritual energy "constructs" the world insofar as it gives to this world its internal "structure" and in this way "determines the inner form of being" (*PSF*, I, p. 74/4).

The Presence of Structuralism

Of course, the prima facie presence of such terms as *Struktur* and *Aufbau* in Cassirer's work does not in itself prove any affinity, on his part, with "structuralism." Can such an affinity be shown within the work of Cassirer? It is not without significance that toward the end of his career, when Cassirer started discovering the writings and ideas of the principle structuralist—notably, Jakobson, de Saussure, and Trubetzkoy—positive references and assessments immediately begin to appear in his work.[3] However, still more interesting is what Cassirer says about structuralism in a small paper entitled "Structuralism in Modern Linguistics" presented to the Linguistic Circle of New York only a few days before his sudden death. After discussing the basic methodological principles of the "morphology" of Goethe, Geoffroy de Saint-Hilaire, and in particular Cuvier, Cassirer writes:

> I have quoted this passage [from Cuvier] at some length, for I think, we may use it for making a very interesting mental experiment, we may exchange every biological term of Cuvier for a linguistic term. In this case we should have, before our very eyes, the problem of modern linguistic structuralism. (*Structuralism*, p. 107)

Cassirer thus clearly equates the Goethean project of "morphology" with that of structuralism: "the methodological views and ideals that we find on both sides are very much akin" (ibid., p. 109). In this sense, linguistic structuralism is to be understood as a "morphology" of language. Certainly, Cassirer insists, "language is neither a mechanism nor an organism, neither a dead nor a living thing. It is no thing at all, if by this term we understand a physical object" (ibid., p. 110). However, taking up Humboldt's terminology, we must understand language, and every other symbolic form for that matter, not as an ε"ρον but as an ἐνέργεια. "To put it shortly, we must say that language is 'organic,' but that it is not an 'organism' " (ibid.), and insofar as it is "organic," insofar as the whole comes logically before the parts so that each of the parts takes its meaning from its place in the whole, it can be approached from the point of view of its structure. In this way, Cassirer goes on to maintain that "the program of structuralism developed by Bröndal is, indeed, very near to Humblodt's ideas" (ibid., p. 117).[4]

Now, in the preface to the first volume of the *Philosophy of Symbolic Forms* Cassirer characterizes his project as a " 'morphology' of spirit ('*Formenlehre*' *des Geistes*)" (*PSF*, I, p. 69/v). The term "morphology" here cannot be understood in any other sense than the one given by Goethe.

And insofar as Cassirer himself has equated Goethe's project of "morphology" with that of structuralism, we would seem permitted to say that Cassirer has himself drawn the link between his own philosophy of symbolic forms and structuralism.[5] In the same way that "Humboldt transferred Goethe's idea to a new field of investigation," namely to that of language, Cassirer transfers Goethe's idea to the field of "*Geist*" as a whole. Whereas Goethe had attempted to provide a theory of organic types (*Bildung und Umbildung organischer Naturen*) and "Humboldt spoke of linguistics types," Cassirer will speak of the fundamental types of *Geist*. By *Geist* we are to understand here "all those functions which constitute and build up the world of human culture," and "it is one of the first and principal tasks of a philosophy of human culture to analyze these various functions, to show us their differences and their mutual relations, their opposition and their collaboration" (ibid., p. 114)—and thus their internal lawful unity as an organic system of functions.

In his *An Essay on Man* we find yet another indication that Cassirer seems to have recognized the affinity between structuralism and his own philosophy of symbolic forms. In the chapter on language, Cassirer maintains that the changes linguistics has undergone in this century are similar to those found in physics. Both are now guided by the "new principle which we may call structuralism" (*Essay*, p. 121). Cassirer illustrates this through the analysis of the new paradigm of "field physics" introduced by Faraday and Maxwell, on the one hand, and the structuralist theory of language developed by Ferdinand de Saussure, on the other. However, in drawing this parallel between "field physics" and linguistic structuralism as two expression of the new principle of structuralism, Cassirer is at the same time showing in what way his own philosophy of symbolic forms is also an expression of this new principle, although *avant la lettre*. For in *The Logic of the Cultural Sciences* Cassirer draws a clear and explicit parallel between the field physics of Faraday and Maxwell and his own philosophy of symbolic forms. Field physics is one of the examples Cassirer uses to illustrate the return of the concept of form and wholeness in the sciences of nature; or as he already puts it in the 1940 text, the emergence of the "*concept of structure (strukurbegriff)* as the dominate principle" of science (*Logic*, p. 92 f.). This concept of form is the same as the one that is employed by the sciences of culture, and by the philosophy of symbolic forms.

The Generic Structure of the Symbolic Form, or the Structure of Structure

What has been said in the preceding lines about the relationship between Cassirer and structuralism has, of course, remained somewhat on the surface of the question at hand. That there should be some affinity between structuralism and the philosophy of symbolic forms is in the final analysis not that surprising. For as Gilles Deleuze reminds us: "Structuralism is not separable from a new transcendental philosophy."[6] Nevertheless it could be justly asked if there is any real affinity between the *content* of Cassirer's theory of the symbolic and the ideas of structuralism. "Structuralism" is, of course, a notoriously elusive term, and indeed those labeled as being structuralist have often declined the title, insisting that what they are doing is very different from structuralism, though certainly along the same lines. However, if this category is to have any meaning at all, it is necessary to provide a basic definition of what we mean by a "structuralist." Fortunately, Deleuze has already provided us with just such a definition in his articles *"À quoi reconnaît-on le structuralisme?"* We can use his seven-point definition here to bring out the basic structure of the symbolic form and at the same time demonstrate the basic affinity between the philosophy of symbolic forms and structuralism.

(i) The Symbolic: The Third Realm

> Now the first criterion of structuralism is the discovery and recognition of a third order, of a third realm: that of the symbolic. . . . Here again, everything begins from linguistics: beyond the word in its reality and its acoustic parts, beyond the images and the concepts associated with the words, the structuralist linguist discovers an element of a completely other nature, the structural object.[7]

It is interesting to note that already in her classic study on Lacan, A. Lemaire has recognized the fact that "according to Cassirer, the symbolic function is the mediation which confers sense upon the sensuous. The symbolic order is a third order, which means that it is organized between the subject and the real."[8] Or in the words of Cassirer himself, "we find in man a third link which may be described as the *symbolic system*" (*Essay*, p. 24), an intermediary world, a

Zwischenreich, which stands between spirit and reality (cf. " 'Spirit' and 'Life,' " p. 874/51).

At every turn in Cassirer's analysis of philosophical problems, we find that everything comes down to a fundamental and paradoxical relation of reciprocity holding between two distinct and seemingly independent elements: between, for example, the sensuous presence of the image and its ideal meaning, the I and the other or the world, spirit and life, and so forth. In his reading of the history of philosophy, Cassirer repeatedly demonstrates how the unity between these two elements has continuously been broken, and one of the elements taken as the absolute measure over against the other. Time and again, either the immanent element (the real, the sensuous presence of the image, etc.) or the transcendent element (the idea, the nonintuitive meaning, etc.) has been favored as the basis upon which a philosophical system has been build: the second element has at best been attributed an inferior and accidental function, or at worst been completely dismissed as a nonessential hindrance that should be overcome or eliminated. The concept of the symbolic, however, "does not fit into the traditional metaphysical classifications and dualism but goes beyond them. The symbolic never belongs to the sphere of immanence or to the sphere of transcendence; its value, rather, consists precisely in the fact that it overcomes this opposition which arises from a metaphysical theory of two worlds. It is not the one *or* the other but represents the 'one *in* the other,' and the 'other *in* the one' " (*PSF*, III, p. 383/447). The symbolic is the element that constitutes the relation between the concrete sensuous presence of the content of consciousness and its nonintuitive meaning. In the algorithm $\frac{S}{s}$ the symbolic is the bar that at once differentiates and unites the signified and the signifier, the real and the image, life and spirit, but which is irreducible to neither. It is the universal law φ that functions as the rule of progression, organizing that various elements (x_1, x_2, x_3) into a "symbolic system."

(ii) Being Is Position

> The elements of a structure have neither extrinsic designation nor intrinsic signification. What remains? As Lévi-Strauss reminds us rigorously, they have nothing else but a *meaning*: a meaning which is necessarily and exclusively "position."[9]

Symbols are essentially nothing more than the presence of meaning, and "this meaning does not consists in what they [the different symbols] 'are' in themselves, nor in something that they copy, but in a specific trend of ideal formation—not in an outward object towards which they aim, but in a determinate mode of objectivization" (*PSF*, III, p. 383/447). The symbol thus has "neither extrinsic designation nor intrinsic signification." Rather, its meaning, as we have already seen above, is its position in the series to which it belongs:

> The point as a simple and particular position is possible only "in" space, i.e., logically speaking, under presupposition of a *system* comprising all designations of position; the ideal of the temporal "now" can be defined only in relation to a *sequence* of moments and to the order of succession that we call "time"—and the same is true of the relation between the thing and its properties. All these relations . . . disclose the same fundamental characteristic of consciousness, namely, that the whole is not obtained from its parts, but that every notion of part already encompasses the notion of the whole, not as to content, but as to general structure (*Struktur*) and form. Every particular belongs from the outset to a definite *complex* and in itself expresses the rule of this complex.[10]

The idea that the meaning of a particular element of a structure is its position within the whole applies above all to the each of the symbolic forms as an expression of the symbolic function: for "each particular form takes its meaning solely form the *place* in which it stands, a system in which the content and significance of each form would be characterized by the richness and specific quality of the relations and concatenations in which it stands with other spiritual energies and ultimately with their totality" (*PSF*, I, p. 82/14).

(iii) The Symbolic as Differential Calculus

> In the end, what do these symbolic elements or units of position consist in? . . . [T]he corresponding elements are taken in a differential relationship. *Dy* is completely indeterminate with regard to *y*, *dx* is completely indeterminate with regard to *x*; each has nei-

> ther existence nor value nor signification. And still, the relation $\frac{dy}{dx}$ is completely determined, the two elements determine each other reciprocally in the relation. It is this process of a reciprocal determination within the relation that allows us to define the symbolic nature.[11]

The symbolic involves, as we have just seen, a twofold "reciprocal determination." On the one hand, there is a "reciprocal determination" between the intuitive content of consciousness and the nonintuitive meaning that it represents.

> For no content of consciousness is in itself merely "present," or in itself merely "representative"; rather, every actual experience indissoluably embraces both factors. Every present (*Gegenwärtige*) *functions* in the sense of representing (*Vergegenwärtigung*), just as all representation (*Vergegenwärtigung*) demands a link with something present (*Gegenwärtiges*) in consciousness. (*PSF*, III, p. 199/232)

Furthermore, this relation between the intuitive presence and its meaning proves to be fully dynamic. A "genuine relation of reciprocity manifests its presence: the formation of intuition is the actual vehicle required by representation, and on the other hand the use of intuition as a means of representation unceasingly brings out new 'facets' and factors in intuition and forms it into an increasingly richer and more differentiated whole" (*PSF*, III, p. 141/164). We find ourselves here at the theoretical heart of the philosophy of symbolic forms. This reciprocal relation between the signifier and the signified manifests itself in each symbolic form, though in each one according to a different modality that determines its specific mode of spiritual formation. It is here that Cassirer introduces his concept of "symbolic pregnance":

> It is with a view to expressing this reciprocal determination (*Wechselbestimmung*) that we introduce the concept and the term "symbolic pregnance" (*symbolische Prägnanz*). By "symbolic pregnance" we mean the way in which a lived perception, as a "sensuous" experience, contains at the same time a certain nonintuitive "meaning" which it brings to an immediate and concrete representation. (*PSF*, III, p. 202/235)

At no time must that which is represented by the sensuous presence be taken as something existing independently of that which represents it. What "merely *is* (without representing anything) never exists in the actual consciousness" (*PSF*, III, p. 141/164). For signification only arises in and through a "reciprocal movement" (*PSF*, III, p. 203/259), or a peculiar oscillation between the "signifier" ("*Bedeutendem*") and the "signified" ("*Bedeuteten*") (*PSF*, II, p. 25/33). In other words, the meaning of any symbol or content of consciousness is always defined in terms of its relation to the whole of the transcendental structure and subsequently to every other element within the same structure. For example, every reference to a "here" has meaning only in terms of its relation to a "there," and every reference to a "me" comes about in and through a reference to a "thou," the "present" is juxtaposed to the "not present," which in turn is internally differentiated into a "past" or a "future," and so on. "Accordingly there is no 'something' in consciousness that does not *eo ipso* and without further mediation give rise to 'another' and to a series of others. For what defines each particular content of consciousness is that in it the whole of consciousness is in some form posited and represented. Only in and through this *representation* does what we call the 'presence' of the content become possible" (*PSF*, I, p. 98/33). The meaning of the content of consciousness is its difference to another, and this difference is determined by the symbolic function that constitutes the law of the series in which each element as a particular content of consciousness belongs. To characterize this "reciprocal determination" between different elements of the same transcendental structure Cassirer too invokes a mathematical metaphor taken from differential calculus.

> If we wish to characterize this process by a mathematical metaphor and symbol, despite the fact that it goes beyond the sphere of the mathematical, we might . . . choose the term "integration." The element of consciousness is related to the whole of consciousness not as an extensive part to a sum of parts, but as a differential to its integral. . . . The "integral" of consciousness is constructed not from the sum of its sensuous elements (a, b, c, d, . . .), but from the totality, as it were, of its differentials of relation and form (dr_1, dr_2, dr_3, . . .). The full actuality of consciousness is merely the unfolding of what was present as "potency" and generally possibility in each of its separate factors. (*PSF*, I, p. 104 f./41)

(iv) Differentiation

> Structures are necessarily unconscious, in virtue of the elements, relations and points which constitute them. All structure is an infrastructure, a microstructure. In a certain way [structures] are not actual. What is actual is that in which the structure incarnates itself or, rather, that which it constitutes in incarnating itself. But in itself, it is neither actual nor fictional; neither real nor possible. . . . Of structure one can say: [it is] *real without being actual, ideal without being abstract.*[12]

Each of the various symbolic forms represents a different "organ" by which spirit constitutes a world of signification. "Language, myth, art—each produces from itself its own world of forms which can be understood only as the expression of the spontaneity of spirit. But because this spontaneous activity is not carried out in the form of free reflection, it is hidden from itself" (*PSF*, II, p. 217/259). The structure of the different symbolic forms and, *a fortiori*, of the symbolic as such remains therefore "wholly unconscious" (ibid.), as the different symbolic forms and the symbolic function are co-constitutional. Thus, the symbolic function is never itself actual, and is accessible only in and through its objective concrete manifestation, that is, through the different cultural forms, which, in turn, objectify themselves only in the actual cultural phenomena. "One and the same fundamental *function*, the function of the symbolic as such, unfolds itself in its different cardinal directions and creates within them ever new structures. It is the totality of these structures that identifies and distinguishes the specifically human world" (*Logic*, p. 26 f.). And again, each of the different symbolic forms, as a substructure, is accessible only through its concrete manifestations. "The content of spirit is disclosed only in its manifestations; the ideal form is known only by and in the aggregate of the sensible signs which it [spirit] uses for its expression" (*PSF*, I, p. 86/19). "In this sense the mythical gods [for example] signify nothing other than successive self-revelations of the mythical consciousness" (*PSF*, II, p. 217/259). Hence, Cassirer too could have said that "all structure is infrastructure," that all structure has always already incarnated itself in substructures, without which it would not exist, and finally that the symbolic function is *"real without being actual, ideal without being abstract."* This also explains why Cassirer will repeatedly insist on the fact that spirit can know itself only in and through its reflection in the "mirror of its culture." It also explains why, as we shall see, the ego is for Cassirer essentially a mask that provides us with our identity as a personal subject.

The presence of meaning is in reality always the coming into being of meaning. The symbolic is a dynamic process moving from an implicit, and thus virtual, state to an explicit, and thus fully actualized, state. As we have seen every presence of meaning is comprised of two factors: a nonintuitive meaning that incarnates itself in a sensuous lived presence.

> The duality of these factors [the sensuous presence of the sign and the spiritual-psychical meaning of which it is an "incarnation"] is, to be sure, *embedded* (*angelegt*) in every phenomenon of consciousness, however primitive; but this potency is not from the very beginning unfolded into actuality. . . . It always appears as something living, divided within itself, as a ἕν διαφερόμενον ἑαυτῷ. But although the difference exists, it is not yet *posited* as such; this occurs only when consciousness passes from the immediacy of life to the form of the spirit and of spontaneous spiritual creation. It is only in *this* transition that all those tensions which are implicit in the sheer facticity of consciousness unfold: what previously was a concrete unity despite all its inner antitheses now beings to separate (*auseinandertreten*) and to "interpret" ("*auslegen*") itself in a special analysis. (*PSF*, III, p. 93/109 f.)[13]

(v) Seriality

> [T]he symbolic elements which we have previously defined, taken in their differential relations, necessarily organize in a series. But as such, they are related to another series, constituted by other symbolic elements and by other relations, . . . all structure is serial, multi-serial, and would not function without this condition.[14]

In Cassirer's language, no symbolic forms can exist independently of the others, and in fact each constitutes a necessary moment in the coming to be of meaning. "If these forms as a whole do constitute a systematic unity, the fate of any one of them is closely bound up with that of the others . . . any destruction of a single member of the system endangers the whole if this whole is regarded not as a mere aggregate but as an organic, spiritual unity" (*PSF*, II, p. xvi/viii). We shall see throughout our study that each of the symbolic forms possesses a unique and immediate relation to the others. "This is why language and myth [as well as language and art, myth and religion, art and religion, language and science, etc.] maintain a perpetual reciprocal contact—their contents support and necessitate each other" (*PSF*, II, p. 40/53). Each is found in the interior of the other: "the one *in* the other" as Cassirer has said above.

(vi) The Empty Place

> It appears that structure envelops a completely paradoxical object or element. . . . In fact, it is with respect to it that the variety of terms and the variation of differential relations are in each case determined. The two series of a structure are always divergent (in virtue of the laws of differentiation). But this single object is the point of convergence of the divergent series as such. It is "eminently" symbolic, but precisely because it is immanent in the two series at the same time. How to call it, if not Object – *x*, Object of riddle or big Mobile?[15]

In every symbolic forms there is found this "Object = x" around which all the elements are grouped.

> [In each case] what holds the series together is not their [the members of the series] similarity or the frequency with which they are given in empirical succession or coexistence, but the common *function* of indication which they fulfill: the fact that with all their sensuous heterogeneity, they relate to a common *reference point* (namely the X of the identical "object" ("*Gegenstand*")). (*PSF*, III, p. 139 f./162)

In each series there is a zero point that functions as an ideal point of reference. All the particulars "order themselves according to this point of reference, and through this unity of direction a unity of 'essence' is stamped upon them—though this essence is not to be taken ontically but logically, as a pure determination of meaning" (*PSF*, III, p. 303/354). Although the symbolic function itself can never be a member of the series, there nevertheless must be one member who represents its presence within the series. For each member derives its meaning from its relation to and difference from another member of the same series. However, it is evident that if we are not to end up in a vicious circle or an infinite regress, there must exists a "first" member upon which the existence of all the members of the series—including itself—depend. The capacity to grasp this immanence-cum-transcendence, to perceive the presence of the universal in the particular, the infinite in the finite, the "extimity"[16] of the zero, the mana, the object *x* of perception, and so on, is essential to the functioning of each mode of symbolic consciousness.

Deleuze cites several examples of this Object = *x*, one of which is Frege's zero.[17] Frege does not figure prominently in either *Substance and Function* or the *Philosophy of Symbolic Forms*. Nevertheless, in both we find an interesting discussion of the function the zero. The process of counting is not possible without the ability to fuse at least two series of numbers, where the condition of possibility of this fusion is the number zero. In order to add, for example, 7 + 3, it is necessary to count to seven, and then to count three more positions further along the same system of numbers. However, this is possible only if one sets up a second and parallel system linked to the first by means of the zero in which one moves forward three steps. At the number seven one must begin again: one (which is eight), two (which is nine), three (which is ten). The movement forward demands the juxtaposition (and in a sense even the superimposition) of the two systems. An analogous operation is performed in the inverse process of subtraction. Both are graphically represent by Cassirer in the following diagram:

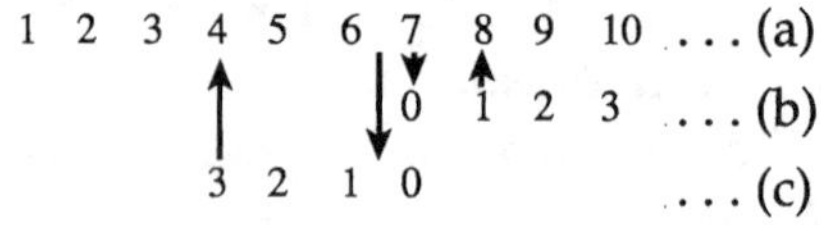

The zero is thus the point in a symbolic series from which all other points are determined and organized into an organic unity of elements. It is also the point at which different systems of symbols intersect. As we shall see, the sacred will prove to be the zero point par excellence of culture, a point from which all cultural meaning radiates.

The Structural Subject of Praxis and the "Futurality" of the Symbolic

> The *subject* is precisely the agency which follows the empty place: as Lacan says, he is less a subject than subjected—subjected to the empty place.[18]

The symbolic is not only inseparable from its effects, but it is inseparable from a certain activity from which it has emerged, and whose objective expression it thus constitutes. When Cassirer speaks of the different "energies of spirit," he is speaking above all about the different activities of spirit. Language, myth, religion, science, art are above all else activities: one speaks a language, on lives a myth, one practices a religion, one constructs a science, one creates and contemplates a work of art. On a more profound level the presence of the symbolic, as a sensuous image impregnated with meaning, is the product of the "productive imagination."[19] This is why Cassirer writes that

> the symbol hastens ahead of reality, as it were, showing it the way and clearing its path. It does not merely look back upon reality as existing and having become [i.e., as something already finished], but becomes a moment and motif of its very becoming. It is this form of the symbolic vision (*Schauen*) that specifically distinguishes the spiritual, the historical will from the mere "will to live," mere vital instinct. (*PSF*, III, p. 182/212)

In a passage that could easily have been taken from a passage of *Sein und Zeit*, Cassirer goes on to explain that the knowledge that Spirit can acquire of itself, can only be produced in a temporal structure where the past and the present interpenetrate in the light of the future: this knowledge "only arises, insofar as [Spirit] preserves its history in its pure presence and anticipates its future in a formative process (*es entsteht erst, indem er in seiner reinen Gegenwart seine Geschichte bewahrt und seine Zukunft gestaltend vorwegnimmt*)" (*PSF*, III, p. 188/219). Thus "only a being who wills and acts, who reaches into the future and determines the future by his will, can have a 'history'; [only such a being] can *know* of history because and insofar as he continually *produces* it" (*PSF*, III, p. 182/211). Evidently, this "historical will" is not possible without the activity of the "productive imagination" that "*projects*" before consciousness a sensuous image pregnant with meaning:

> This "representation" of the future characterizes all human action. We must place something not yet existing before ourselves in "images," in order, then, to proceed from this "possibility" to the "reality," from potency to act. (*Logic*, p. 26)

As we shall see there is no subject prior to culture. The subject is both the *terminus a quo* and the *terminus ad quem* of the symbolic process of culture. Each symbolic forms constitutes a specific mode of "vision" by which spirit sees the world. To see the world is to see it through the eyes of sprit. The subject, and especially the mythical subject, is thus subjected to the power of the symbolic image that hastens ahead into the real opening up the reality of the world. It is, as Lacan says, more subjected to the symbolic function than the subject of the symbolic.

A Grammar and Topography of the Symbolic Function

The basic structure of the symbolic function having been established, we can now move on to the more daunting task of working out the specific nature of the different symbolic forms and their relation to each other in the whole of culture. It is often asked how many symbolic forms there are. There are no shortage of answers to this question. Cassirer himself never explicitly addresses the problem. What is more, Cassirer seems to just assume that the different symbolic forms that he does treat are in fact symbolic forms, without ever explaining why. However, he does seems to suggest how we are to go about determining the different forms. We must establish, through a systematic survey of the various cultural expression of spirit, the "universal characteristic" of the symbolic form.

> We should then possess a kind of grammar of the symbolic function as such, which would encompass and generally help to define its special terms and idioms as we encounter them in language and art, in myth and religion. The idea of such a grammar im-

> plies a broadening of the traditional and historical concept of idealism. Idealism has always aimed at juxtaposing to the *mundus sensibilis* another cosmos, the *mundus intelligibilis*, and at defining the boundary between these two worlds. . . . *[T]his* opposition is no longer irreconcilable and exclusive. For the senses and the spirit are now joined in a new form of reciprocity and correlation. Their metaphysical dualism seems bridged, since it can be shown that precisely the pure *function* of the spirit itself must seek its concrete fulfillment in the sensory world. (*PSF*, I, p. 86 f./19)

But we have already seen that the symbolic function at once distinguishes and unites a signifier and a signified or, in other terms, an intuitive sensuous image and a nonintuitive meaning. Each symbolic form *qua* symbolic form possesses this structure. What distinguishes one cultural form from another is the logic or law (φ) that determines the nature of the relation between the signifier (S) and the signified (s). It is the relation between the two elements of the symbol that determine the specific mode of presence of meaning, and thus the specific mode of "seeing" that each constitutes. There is a limited number of logical possibilities which constitute the fundamental ways in which the signifier and the signified can be related, and these logical possibilities provide, as we shall see, the ideal models for the constitution of the infrastructure into which the symbolic system differentiates itself. We can quickly consider these logical possibilities here.

The two constitutive elements of the symbolic function can logically be imagined to exist at a stage of indistinction or complete identity; a stage where the difference between the signifier and the signified though determined nevertheless remains unrecognized, and thus the signifier is taken *for* the signified. The signifier is, as it were, totally "transparent" and is therefore in a relationship of complete immediacy with the signified (cf. "The Problem of the Symbol," p. 417). Subsequently, in this realm the signifier holds a logical primacy over the signified. Let us symbolize this logical possibility by collapsing "S" for the signifier and "s" for the signified into one another: φ(**S**). Cassirer calls this most basic dimension of the symbolic, which constitutes a kind of *Urphänomen* (cf. *PSF*, III, p. 99/116), "expression" (*Ausdruck*).

A second structure into which the symbolic can logically differentiate itself is a relationship in which the signifier and the signifier are differentiated in such a way that the signifier stands for or indicates a signified which is itself assumed to be accessible and to exist independently of its representation, as an "objective state of affairs" (cf. "The Problem of the Symbol," p. 418)—be it an object, a subject, or a relation of some sort. Cassirer terms this signifier/signified relationship "representation" (*Darstellung*). We can use the following classical algorithm to visualize this ideal possibility: $\varphi(\frac{S}{s})$.

A third logical possibility has two branches. On the one hand, the reality of the signified can be suspended and the signifier recognized to signify nothing more than a position in a chain of signifiers—a position that the signifier in occupying actualizes. There is, therefore, no signified as such—the real "is relegated entirely to the sphere of the unknowable and becomes a mere 'X' " (*PSF*, I, p. 76/7). Such a position knowingly "renounces its aspiration and its claim to an 'immediate' grasp and communication of reality" (*PSF*, I, p. 76/7). In our algorithm of signifier over signified, the signified is therefore crossed out: $\varphi(\frac{S}{X})$. Here we find ourselves in the domain of pure ideal representation. On the other hand, it is also possible that the signifier is suspended, so that nothing but the signified remains, which can only be approached directly, "without the mediation of an image" (*PSF*, II, p. 249/298). This logical possibility could be schematized as follows: $\varphi(\frac{X}{s})$. Here we enter into the domain of pure expression beyond all representation. Both $\varphi(\frac{S}{X})$ and $\varphi(\frac{X}{s})$ lead us into the domain of what Cassirer calls "pure signification" (*reine Bedeutung*).

A final logical possibility remains. It is not only conceivable but, as we shall see in our the course of our analyses, necessary for the dynamics of the symbolic structure, that there exists a stage in which the expression and the representation are in perfect harmony; where, in other words, the difference between the signifier and the signified is not, as in expression, merely submerged in an imaginary identity; where it is neither, as in representation, left in a state of irreducible opposition; where, finally, the identity is not achieved by the crossing out of one or the other of the two poles. The whole structure of the symbolic will prove to originate from, pass through, and return to an ideal pole in which the difference and identity between the signifier and the signified coexist in such a way that the one is not the other, and the other is not the one and, nevertheless, they are the same: in which there is revelation and concealment of the signified in and through the signifier: where the signifier signifies only itself in all its sensibility.

The Moments within the Structure of Meaning

Throughout our study of the principal cultural forms we will encounter again and again each of the these different mode of the symbolic function. Each cultural form constitutes its own system of signification according to a specific structural law of formation. Each one of these "cardinal directions" is defined by its place and specific function within the interior of the structure of signification itself. However, insofar as signification is for Cassirer always understood as a process, each symbolic form must be thought of as a moment within the dynamic structure of the process of signification. In fact, within every simple presence of meaning each of these symbolic forms is found. Only through their collective work, and their interaction with one another, does meaning come about. Every awareness of meaning, and thus every consciousness of the world properly speaking, contains these five moments or elements of meaning. Without the expressive dimension of meaning our awareness of the world would loose the concreteness of a lived experience of the world.[20] The dimension of representation provides the distance from the immediately given necessary to permit it to become meaningful and thus something that is given to consciousness. Without the force of representation we would remain imprisoned within the world of things. The two movements toward pure signification are already found in the simultaneous movement away and back to the concrete givenness of expression. But only insofar as the two forces are in harmony does anything that can be rigorously called a presence come about. At the same time, insofar as each cultural form proves to be a unique "spiritual energy" each is a moment within the interior of spirit. In this context Cassirer quotes Hegel:

> The life of the actual spirit . . . is a cycle of stages which on the one hand still subsist side by side and only on the other hand *appear* as past. The moments which the spirit seems to have left behind it are also present in its depths.[21]

Three

Language: The "Genesis" of Signification and the *Aufbau* of the Objective World

In the Beginning Was the Word . . .

Everything begins with language. For Cassirer man is, and is man, only insofar as he speaks, and to speak is always to speak a language. Language arises only in and through a free act of speech, and yet this spontaneous act is always already animated and limited from within by something that transcends it. Language possesses a central and primordial place in the system of symbolic forms. One is even tempted to say that there is nothing but language. Cassirer himself cedes at one point to this temptation and speaks of the other symbolic forms as different forms of language.[1] It is, of course, against the basic principles of the philosophy of symbolic forms to reduce the different cultural forms to one particular form. Nevertheless, it would not be going too far to say that without language there would be no culture, and that the other cultural forms are the direct or indirect consequence or effect of the presence of language, or at the very least dependent upon it in one way or another for their existence. Consequently, "language stands in a focus of cultural life, a point at which rays of quite diverse origin converge and from which lines of influence radiate to every sphere of culture. [However,] if language should be shown to be a truly original and independent energy of the human spirit, it must take its place in the totality of these forms, but it must not be thought to coincide with any of the others" (*PSF*, I, p. 175 f./122).

At first, nothing could be more familiar to us than the presence of language, and nothing more natural than speaking a language. Language is just there, it has always been there. And yet our naive everyday view of language quickly shows itself wholly inadequate to account for the presence of language itself. There is a certain inherent paradox in speaking about language, in bringing language to language as language through language. But can language in fact be brought to itself? Can it be made to show itself while at the same time remaining itself? And if language can be brought to language, can it be done in any other way than through language itself? We will encounter this same basic paradox in our consideration of other symbolic forms. However, it will only be in the conclusion of our study that we will be able to consider this paradoxical task of the philosophy of symbolic forms in more detail. For now, we must content ourselves with the hypothesis that speaking about language, the very tentative to bring language to language as language through language, is not only the condition of possibility of the *presence* of language, but of language as such: language, in other words, exists and is language, only in the moment of its own self-showing.

The *Differentia Specifica* of Language as a Symbolic Form

Strictly speaking, for Cassirer "in the beginning is the act" (*Logic*, p. 51), the act as mythical ritual around the revelation of the sacred, the act as aesthetic comportment towards the world, and the act as linguistic designation. "Myth, language and art begin as a concrete, undivided unity, which is only gradually resolved into a triad of independent modes of spiritual creativity" (*LM*, p. 98/156). The centripetal force of myth and the centrifugal force of language interpenetrate and form one another in the harmony of expression and representation that characterizes for Cassirer the aesthetic image. Although each of these spiritual forces will come to be distinguished from the others, they nevertheless remain entangled with one another: wherever and whenever one finds man, one finds that mythical creature who speaks and comports himself toward the world in a poetic way through his relation to the sensuous figure of his god.

If language possesses a privileged position in the structure of culture, it is due to the paradoxical position in which it places us vis-à-vis speaking about the other symbolic forms, and not to any intrinsic hierarchical status or ontological priority: for to speak about something it is necessary to reduce it to language. In a certain sense mythical thought "is" only to the degree that we can speak about it, to the extent that we can objectivize it into language: this is equally true of the objects of the aesthetic imagination, the concepts of scientific theory, of religious vision, and, so it would seem, of language as the process of designation and differentiation itself. Language therefore "is" only insofar as it reveals itself to be language—insofar as it names itself. Thus, whenever we "find" mythical gods or demons, aesthetic figures, religious symbols, pure scientific equations, or the linguistic signifier itself, we "find" language, for the simple reason that it is the linguistic form which "provides the possibility of 'finding-again' (*Wiederfinden*) and of recognition" (*PSF*, III, p. 108/126).

What is the *differentia specifica* of language as a cultural form? In a word: "The aim of repetition lies in identity—the aim of linguistic designation lies in difference" (*PSF*, I, p. 189/137). Language constructs or structures the real by introducing difference, it is the process of differentiation in the literal sense of the word. Language is the system of real differentiations that determine the self-identity of sameness that provides the objective world with the stability of a perceived presence.

> Both [perception and intuition] become "objective" (*gegenständlich*) inasmuch as the energy of language succeeds in clarifying, differentiating, and organizing the mute and undifferentiated chaos of simple subjective states of mind. . . . A life in "meanings" supplants the life of mere impulses, of being absorbed by the immediate impression and into the various needs. These meanings are repeatable and recurring; something that does not cling to the bare here-and-now, but which comes to be meant and understood as something identical with itself in countless life-moments and in the appropriation and use by countless different subjects. By virtue of this identity of intention, which rises above the multifariousness and diversity of momentary impressions, there emerges, gradually, and by stages, a determined "state," a "common cosmos." (*Logic*, p. 14 f.)

A Structural "Myth" of the "Genesis" of the Symbolic Function of Language

In order to work through Cassirer's theory of language and determine its specific function as a spiritual energy, it is necessary to begin at the beginning, and consider, as it were, "the genesis of the articulated sound," the dynamic process of " 'the noise rounding itself into a tone'—as Goethe puts it" (*PSF*, I, p. 186/134). As we shall see, this process by which "man spins language out of himself and himself into language" (*PSF*, III, p. 15/19), as Cassirer often says, represents the genesis of the "symbolic function" itself, and thus the birth of culture and man. "Here the universal *symbolic* function appears through the particularity of the linguistic function, as it unfolds in accordance with immanent laws, in art, in the mythical-religious consciousness, in language and in knowledge" (ibid.). We cannot, of course, ever elucidate the genesis of language by means of a "genetic" or causal explanation. Because language is perpetually oscillating between objectivity and subjectivity, we cannot explain the formation of language as either an imitation of objective reality, or as an expression of simple subjective emotions. Both the "interjectional" theory and "onomatopoetic" theory of language beg the question rather than solve it (*Essay*, p. 141). They assume the presence of the objective world and the perceiving and linguistic subject, and thus also the presence of language. Strictly speaking, we can never speak about a "before" or "beyond" language, and thus about the origins of language. We are always already before language and in language. For this reason most linguists have today abandoned the question of the genesis of language altogether as being ill formed. What follows, therefore, must be understood as essentially a "myth" of the "genesis" of language and the symbolic function. A myth that seeks to reveal the structural move from "nature" to "culture": the point where the "spark jumps the gap," as Cassirer repeatedly puts it.

The Animal and the *Animal Symbolicum*

The structural movement from the animal world (nature or life) into the human world (spirit or culture), from simple consciousness to self-consciousness, represents the point at which a "life in 'meanings' supplants the life of mere impulses, of being absorbed by the immediate impression and into the various needs" (*Logic*, p. 14). The animal possesses an immediate and purposeful engagement in and with the world. Cassirer is more than willing to grant animals a certain level of consciousness of both their "interior" and "exterior" "worlds." He goes as far as to acknowledge in animals the ability to manipulate its world in a manner that would normally be considered as technological, that is, with tools fabricated to achieve a specific goal. It is also seems necessary to recognize in animals a certain level of self-expression and communication, and thus a certain level of social organization and even politics (cf. *Essay*, p. 29 f.). In defining man as an *animal rationale*, as a technological animal, or a social or political animal, we do not capture the *differentia specifica* of the human mode of being. Wherein lies the difference? For Cassirer the essential difference is that the structure in which the animal finds itself is a merely formal and biological structure, whereas the structure in which man finds himself is a symbolic structure of his own creation. "In short, we may say that the animal possesses a practical imagination and intelligence whereas man alone has developed a new form: a *symbolic imagination and intelligence*" (*Essay*, p. 33). In other terms, man becomes man at the moment he steps back from the immediate needs of his practical engagement in and with the concrete reality around him and dares to venture out into a virtual reality, that is to say, a realm of pure ideal possibility. In both the problems it confronts and the solutions that it implements, the animal is limited to the concrete, to concrete problems and concrete solutions. As a species it develops the technical mastery of the world and passes it on through a process of imitation—the present is charged with the past and one could even say dominated by it. The animal repeats that which was because that is all there is. From the perspective of "nature" "things are as they are because they were as they were."[2] The animal, individually or collectively, is unable to change its "habits." Change or evolution comes about slowly, and is orchestrated by chance rather than by "de*sign*," and is preserved in the species through the mechanism of "adaptations"—a term too vague to do any real justice to the complexity of the phenomenon at hand—rather than through active repetition and appropriation.

From Animal Desire to the Image of the Future: *"Le signifiant passe à l'étage du signifié"*

The animal is aroused by objects in which it "sees" something "desirable," something of "vital" importance. In its perception of the object the animal senses, recognizes even, its own negativity. That is to say, it perceives in the object its own felt need, and becomes absorbed in and by the presence of this object to the point of loosing itself in the object. The animal, we could say, is subjected to the object of its desire. The animal's whole world condenses into the perception of this one object, and radiates out from it. That in which it does not recognize its own vital need possesses little or no importance. Even its awareness of its own being is absorbed into its obsession with this object. In this state it is not uncommon that an animal will pursue the object of its desire with seemingly little regard for its own life. However, the powerful instinct for self-preservation that is inherent in all forms of life is not disregarded here, as it might first appear, but in fact provides the driving force behind the animal's relentless and often fatal pursuit: for though the animal's consciousness of itself has been absorbed by this effective state of desire, it is only, paradoxically, in the moment of its affection that its "self-awareness" is first awakened. Although its desire has found an "objective expression" in the presence of the object of desire, this presence is experienced by the animal in its flesh, and thus as yet possesses no alterity as such. The animal's very being is indistinguishable from the object of its desire, so much so that we may say that it is constituted by it.

The structure of animal desire in many ways prefigures the structure of human desire, and the difference between them is found not so much in the structure of desire itself as in the nature of the object that is desired:[3] the animal peruses something that is simply concrete, whereas man pursues something that is essentially virtual, that is to say, something ideal. The animal is determined by its needs, which are in turn determined by the blueprint or structural plan (*Bauplan*) of its species. "Each animal species is firmly bound, as it were, to the circuit of its needs and drives (*Triebe*); it has no other world than that which is prescribed for it by its instincts" (*Logic*, p. 27 f.). When the animal pursues an object, and thus seems to act toward a determined goal located in the future, in reality it is only reacting, according to its instincts, to its own felt need and the overwhelming desire or hunger for this or that object. "Action is subject to an impulse from behind that drives and propels it into the future; it is not determined by this future and its the ideal 'anticipation' " (*PSF*, III, p. 276/323). The animal is driven forward by its biological and vital impulses, by an instinctive reflex forward. "As soon as the excitation abates, and the drive (*Trieb*) is clamed, Being and the world of perception (*Vorstellungswelt*) collapse together again" (*LM*, p. 38/107).

Furthermore, the animal never stops to question its choice of objects, or its denial of others. The animal cannot sublimate its desire for an object by substituting one object for another. There is only this one object, this immediate and concrete presence of felt need, which, for better or worse, it must "accept" as such. However, "compared to animals, who always say 'Yes' to whatever happens to be (*Wirklichsein*), even when they are repelled and are running away, man is 'the being who is able to say No' (*'Neinsagenkönner'*) . . . 'the ascetic of Life,' the everlasting protest against sheer reality"[4] (" 'Spirit' and 'Life,' " p. 863/38). The animal's acceptance, however, is an implicit acceptance. For in the end it does not really have a choice. Certainly, the animal can choose between advancing or retreating, between engaging an enemy or evading it (cf. *MS*, p. 44), but it cannot, as it were, change the rules of the game by considering the possibility of something that as yet does not exist, and as such advance toward or retreat from this imaginary and as yet nonexistent being.

> Here nature acts wholly as an outward stimulus which must be sensuously present in order to arouse the sensation corresponding to it; it does not enter into the relationship of the pure image, which is designed by the power of the imagination (*das in der Vorstellungskraft entworfen*), and which in a sense anticipates the existence of the object. (*PSF*, III, p. 111/130)

For some time consciousness remains enslaved to the tyranny of its own internal negativity, to that emotional force of its momentary self-affectivity that determines its very being. However, at a certain moment an opposition to this tyranny of emotions manifests itself, a resistance against the overwhelming presence of sheer reality begins to make its appearance. Torn between the desire for something and the horror of the sheer reality of its presence, the emotional conflict seeks a solution, a resolution to the conflict, a way to "control the situation" (*Aufbau*, p. 53) and establish a harmony between the two tensions. The torment leads in the end to an expression of protest *designed* to put an end to this despotism. From the depths of its being arises an explosive rejection of the present situation, a cry of opposition, a sound impregnated with meaning, a sound that intends to "say" something . . . "ah!!"—that is to say, "enough is enough, things could be otherwise than they are, or at least they should be." In the brief instance that follows this initial outburst there arises a first fleeting moment of awareness . . . a moment forming itself out of the lingering silence of the resonating echo of this primordial "ejaculation" (*Essay*, p. 114), a moment of self-awareness and astonishment, a moment of waiting for the world to respond to our objection. In this moment we find the genesis of the symbolic function.

> When mere bestial terror becomes an astonishment moving in a twofold direction, composed of opposite emotions—fear and hope, awe and admiration—when sensory agitation thus seeks for the first time an issue and an *expression*, man stands on the threshold of a new spirituality. (*PSF*, II, p. 78/99)

In this first expression the sensuous presence, through which the animal sensed the negativity of its biological needs, whose existence was thus purely subjective, becomes an object (*Gegenstand*) standing over against consciousness, and thus becomes something objectively present.

> In its most charged state, the I (*Ich*) turns towards [the] *One* (*Eine*), lives in it and forgets (*vergißt*) itself in it. Thus, we find here, instead of a widening of intuition (*Anschauung*) its most extreme narrowing; instead of an expansion which gradually leads it through ever new spheres of being, a drive (*Trieb*) towards concentration; instead of an extensive diffusion an intensive compression. This focusing of all forces upon a *single* point is the prerequisite for all mythical thought and all mythical formation. When the I (*Ich*) is, on the one hand, completely given up to a momentary impression and "possessed" by it and, on the other hand, there is the utmost tension between [the I] and the outside world, when the external reality (*Sein*) is not simply contemplated and perceived, but suddenly overcomes man in its sheer immediacy, with the affect of fear or hope, terror or wish fulfillment, then, as it were, the spark jumps across, the tension finds a release, in that the subjective excitement objectifies itself, and presents itself to man as a god or demon. Here we stand before [the] mythico-religious *Urphänomen*. (*LM*, p. 33/103; my trans.)

> As soon as the spark has jumped across, as soon as the tension and affect (*Affekt*) of the moment has found its discharge in the word or the mythical image (*Bild*), a turning-point (*Peripetie*) is introduced into spirit: the excitement as a merely subjective con-

> dition is extinguished, to be absorbed into the structure (*Gebilde*) of myth or the structure of language.[5] (*LM*, p. 36/105; my trans.)

And so we have it, a first indicative expression that designates something that is desired or rejected. "It is one of the first steps by which the perceiving and desiring I removes a perceived and desired content from himself and so forms it into an 'object,' an 'objective' content" (*PSF*, I, p. 181/128): and with this, a symbol is created, and with it "a life in 'meanings' supplants the life of mere impulse"; or as Jacques Lacan writes, *"le signifiant passe à l'étage du signifié."*[6]

The Futuricity of the Symbolic Function

In this moment, in this object, the "future" has become "an image, a prospect" (*LM*, p. 38/107). No longer something that can be approached immediately, as is the case with all the objects of the animal world, it has become something that exists only as an ideal possibility, as something to come, something to be anticipated. Only with this prospect, and with the anticipatory preparations for it, is the way open to overcoming the tyranny of emotion.

> The general trend of language formation has been disclosed in the transition from the mere sensuous sound of excitement to the *cry*. The cry, e.g., of fear or pain, may remain entirely within the sphere of the mere interjection; and yet it already means more than that, in so far as it is not the mere reflex following instantly upon a sense impression, but is rather the expression of a definite and conscious intent. For now consciousness no longer stands in the sign of mere reproduction, but enters the sphere of anticipation (*Antizipation*): it no longer clings to what is given (*Gegebenes*) and present (*Gegenwärtiges*), but reaches out to represent futurity (*greift auf die Vorstellung eines Künftigen über*). (*PSF*, I, p. 286/258)

> Instead of being moved immediately by an actual stimulus, [man] looks to "possible" needs, to the satisfaction of which he prepares the means in advance. . . . The impulse does not originate only from the spur of the present, but belongs also to the future, which must in some way be "anticipated" in order to become effective

> in this manner. This "representation" of the future characterizes all human action. We must place something not yet existing before ourselves in "images," in order, then, to proceed from this "possibility" to the "reality," from potency to act. (*Logic*, p. 26)

The cry is no longer a physical reaction, an instinctive expression, but a call, a demand, an act of speech employing symbols. The effective presence of the sensuous image is no longer a "signal" that triggers a vital instinct, a preprogrammed "chain of actions." It has become a "symbol" that possesses a signification that must be "contemplated" (cf. *Essay*, p. 32). The mere sign of the animal world remains firmly planted in the physical present. However, as we have seen, the symbol does not represent what is, but what could be. It is this orientation toward a future possibility, or more precisely, it is this orientation toward the image of a future possibility, that defines all human intentionality. The symbol rushes into the real, splitting it and internally forming it, and subsequently opening up reality in its path. We thus see that the intentionality toward the future, toward the image of the future, and thus the process of history are inherent to human existence. It is the history of creating the symbol that opens up the world, this process of constructing the internal form of being, that defines human spirit.

> [T]he symbol hastens ahead of reality, as it were, showing it the way and clearing its path. It does not merely look back upon reality as existing and having become [i.e., as something already finished], but becomes a moment and motif of its very becoming. It is this form of the symbolic vision (*Schauen*) that specifically distinguishes the spiritual, the historical will from the mere "will to live," mere "vital instinct." (*PSF*, III, p. 182/212)

Spirit exists only insofar as it preserves its history in the presence and anticipates its future in and through the formative process of creating it. Thus "only a being who wills and acts, who reaches into the future and determines the future by his will, can have a 'history'; [only such a being] can *know* of history because and insofar as he continually *produces* it" (*PSF*, III, p. 182/211).

However, it is important to insists that the future has not only become an "image," it has become an "ideal" (*Essay*, p. 54). The futuricity of the symbolic function is more than a simple foreseeing of needs. It is above all an ethical ideal, possessing both theoretical and religious signification. For Cassirer, ethics is present from the beginning as part of what it is to be human. To be human is to be orientated toward an "ideal future" that goes beyond the present state of affairs and beyond our finite existence.

The Subject of History

The movement from the passive form of consciousness of the animal to the active intentionality toward the world and toward the future implies at the same time the creation of a subject of consciousness and the self-consciousness of the subject. Consciousness comes to recognize itself in its own activity. It discovers itself in and through the act of rising up in protest. In its spontaneous and explosive rejection consciousness becomes aware of something standing over against itself, of an 'object' in the etymological sense of the German *Gegenstand*, and subsequently in the mirror of its activity it becomes aware of itself as the source of this activity. Thus, all human "consciousness is a consciousness of objects insofar as it is a self-consciousness—and it is self-consciousness only in and by the virtue of the fact that it is a consciousness of objects" (*PSF*, IV, p. 66/64). The echo of its own expression, still fully subjective in nature, returns to the subject as something essentially other, as something objective. As such, it is thus at once something familiar and yet foreign to the subject.

> The intellectual aspiration breaking itself a path through the lips in speech, its product returns to the ear of the subject. The representation is transferred to real objectivity, without being deprived of subjectivity. This language alone can do; and without this transposition into an objectivity which returns to the subject—a transposition which, where language plays a role, always happens implicitly—the formation of the concept, and hence all true thinking, is impossible.[7]

The explosive discharge of emotion into expression, the primordial cry of rage against sheer reality, establishes its own "otherness" to itself. Throughout Cassirer's work we see again and again that "the road 'outward' becomes at the same time a 'road inward.' For it is only as its outward intuition becomes more determined, that its inner intuition can truly unfold" (*PSF*, I, p. 213/167). In other words, consciousness becomes self-consciousness in the alterity of the objective "manifestation of the voice" (*Aufbau*, p. 135 f.).

> This consciousness of self is not something readily present from the beginning, but rather must be spiritually won and produced—and, in this production, the "transfer into an objectivity returning to the subject" carried out by language is indispensable. The I only gets itself into focus (*Blickpunkt*), as it were, when it succeeds in grasping itself in this manner in the mirror of its own external expression. For all manifestation (*Äußerung*) of the mere states of the I (*bloße Zuständlichkeiten des Ich*) is now accompanied by a new way of listening (*Hören*), a certain manner of becoming aware of them (*Gewahrwerdens derselben*) and of "listening" ("*Horchen*"). And this mode of listening leads gradually to a form of "obedience" (*Gehorsam*) which is far removed from the mere subjection, the unconditional sway to emotion (*Affekt*). (*Aufbau*, p. 136)

The Binary Structure of the Real

Throughout Cassirer's theory of culture we find that everything returns again and again to a binary structure of opposing directions of meaning. As must already be clear, the discharge of emotion realizes itself primarily in the articulation of phonetic sounds that we can represent by the two sounds ā and ō. As we shall see, the whole cultural life of spirit is caught up in the interplay between these two sounds, or more precisely between the two fundamental directions of intentionality represented by them. However, Cassirer's language also suggests a literal trusting away of that which is rejected, and a drawing closer of that which is desired. Cassirer seems to argue for a hierarchical order of the senses. Smell and touch are considered as the most basic, as the existence of that which they encounter is limited by their presence to the body. The " 'objective' content stops, as it were, at the limits of our own body, instead of becoming a true 'other' ('*Gegenüber*'), instead of moving into an ideal *distance*. Such a distance is achieved only in the highest, objective senses, in hearing and vision" (*PSF*, III, p. 130/151). The binary opposition of conflicting emotions, desire and rejection, of awe and horror, which forms the essence of the essential structure of the initial conflict and which finds its release in the rejection of the sheer actuality, first constitutes itself either through a physical thrusting away or drawing towards of the as yet nameless real. This physical gesture is accompanied by, and perhaps even aided by, certain vocal expressions that Cassirer calls "vocal gestures" (*PSF*, I, p. 202/153). The "yes" and "no" of the child do not initially represent a logical distinction, but rather an "expression of affective attitude, a desire or rejection" (*PSF*, III, p. 109/128). The initial polarity of oppositions is preserved and stabilized into fixed directions in the "phonetization" of the structure.

> To the tendency, the desire, the affect which goes directly to the things, language always opposes another direction, affected, as it were, by an opposite sign. In it there always co-exist attraction and repulsion, which remain in a sort of ideal equilibrium, for the need to immediately attract the things to the self, and to simply englobe them into its sphere of the I is opposed here by another need, namely, to distance them from the I, in order to posit them in front of the I (*vorstelligmachen*) and render them objective in this act of positing. The force of "attraction" is balanced by the force of "abstraction." The conversion towards the thing which is accomplished in language is at the same time a way of returning from them. The interaction and concrete conjugation of these two processes condition and render possible this sort of intellectual appropriation of the world which is the essential and characteristic trait of language. (*Aufbau*, p. 139)

The "Phonetic Metaphors"

The process of differentiation effected by language thus realizes itself in the progressive process of phonetization. The phonetic sounds being at once spiritual and material, they represent the most primordial materialization of spirit as well as the most primordial spiritualization of matter. We are no longer dealing here with mere sounds, but with elementary units of meaning. The cry of the animal, although it expresses pain and joy, remains in the final analysis as silent and voiceless as any other merely physical thing. The emotional interjections of the animal "say nothing," for they possess no intention to say (*PSF*, I, p. 206/42). The ejaculation of emotion only takes on meaning and says something once it has passed into a "coherently ordered phonetic sequence, in which the context and order of the activity are reflected" (*PSF*, I, p. 185/134). We have already seen that the meaning of a symbol is its place in a symbolic system. The meaning of a word is thus always another word, its place within a language as a system of meanings. Long before language achieves its full and complete expression its spiritual force remains embodied in a system of "phonetic metaphors" ("*Lautmetaphern*") (*PSF*, I, p. 201/153). Nevertheless, these first linguistic units of meaning are ordered into a phonetic sequence that represents the binary structure of desire and rejection.

> In the very first babblings of children a sharp distinction is evident between sound groups of essentially "centripetal" and essentially "centrifugal" tendency. The *m* and *n* clearly reveal the inward direction, while the explosive sounds *p* and *b*, *t* and *d* reveal the opposite trend. In the one case the sound indicates a striving back to the subject; in the other, a relation to the "outside world," a pointing or rejection. The one corresponds to the gesture of grasping, of attempting to draw closer, the other to the gesture of showing or thrusting away. (*PSF*, I, p. 201/153)

Differences in Meaning Do Not Equal Ontological Differences

The "system" of phonetic metaphors functions as the basic "framework" in which all subsequent differentiations will be situated. Before we consider the basic lines of this process of differentiation it is important to emphasis here that these distinctions do not copy already existing distinctions, but rather function to differentiate and fix our perception, intuitions, and thoughts of the world and ourselves.

> The function of "naming" becomes the starting point and vehicle for the function of defining objects—or, to put it a better way, for the function of establishing objects. In naming a content, it then

> becomes ripe for perceiving and observing as an object. With the name, it acquires a constancy, a persistence, and a permanence that is denied to the fleeting contents of experience that are given no names. (*PSF*, IV, p. 72/70)

Language does not begin from an already given world of objects. The objective world that we find before us is the product of the linguistic process. We might say that where there is no word, there is no thing. "The unity serves as a point of crystallization for the multiplicity of representations; the as such heterogeneous phenomena become homogenous and uniform through their relation to a common center. And by virtue of this relation, they become the phenomena of one and the same 'object' " (*Aufbau*, p. 130). The name functions as a common *center of reference*, which gives the content a new unity of essence. The spiritual force of language is not exterior to the objective reality it shows. The word is not a label of identification that is attached to an already existing objective presence, but rather functions as the rule of progression by which consciousness groups a series of elements that is called a thing, an action, a relation, and so on. Language thus establishes the lines of differentiation within the interior of consciousness itself. "Language does not enter into a world of already finished objective intuition only to adjoin to the already given and clearly reciprocally delimited individual objects 'names' as purely external and arbitrary signs—rather, it is itself the means of the formation of objects" (*Aufbau*, p. 126). "The construction (*Aufbau*) of the intuitive reality begins, . . . when the continuous flow of sensuous phenomena beings to divide" (*PSF*, III, p. 142/165). "What happens here is not that existing distinctions, given to consciousness by sensation or perception, are simply stabilized and provided with a certain phonetic sign as a kind of trademark, but rather that dividing lines are drawn within consciousness as a whole" (*PSF*, I, p. 288/261). Language introduces the lines of relation that structure our intuition of the world, insofar as all consciousness is a consciousness of relation. Each word condenses and concentrates the whole into a part, and subsequently constitutes the part as a part of the whole. Only in this state of "pregnance" where the part is seen as a part of the whole, is it possible "to find again in the simple, as it were, punctual 'here' and 'now' of present experience an other, a 'not-here' and a 'not-now.' Everything that we call the 'identity' of concepts and signification, or the 'constancy' of things and attributes, is rooted in this fundamental act of finding-again" (*PSF*, III, p. 114/133). It is thus necessary to "resist the temptation of seeking to make the differences of meaning and signification intelligible by tracing them back to ontologically real differences (*ontisch-reale Differenzen*)—of explaining them through realistic assumptions concerning the condition and the structure of the world of things or the world of simple sensation" (*PSF*, III, p. 122 f./ 142 f.).

The Three Stages of Language

As we have seen, the "aim of linguistic designation lies in difference." Language is that symbolic form that constructs the objective world by differentiating it through phonetic designation. Like every symbolic forms, language passes through three stages in the progress toward its full and complete expression: namely, "mimetic," "analogical," and "truly symbolic" (cf. *PSF*, I, p. 190/139). By "virtue of this movement [it] is able to attain its own area of being and meaning. Thereby it reaches its completion and internal limits" ("The Problem of the Symbol," p. 419). In the first *mimetic* stage, the force of language clings to concrete reality, the "signifier" and the "signified" are fused together into an undifferentiated concrete reality. Long before the phonetic metaphors come to provide a means of communication, these "concrete names" function to construct our intuition of the objective world. Because language does not yet explicitly distinguish between the sign and the thing, the logic of things is equivalent to the logic of signs. The analogical stage remains close to the mimetic level, insofar as the pure function of signification remains fused with its sensuous image. The key difference seems to be that language now begins to combine the phonetic metaphors in the phenomenon of "reduplication" in order to indicate aspects of the reality that clearly go beyond its simple "presence," for example its relation to the past or future (cf. *PSF*, I, p. 195 f./ 146 f.). In the final symbolic stage, language "strives to extend and finally to surpass its limits. It makes a virtue of necessity, that is, of the ambiguity inevitable in the linguistic sign. For this very ambiguity will not permit the sign to remain a mere individual sign; it compels the spirit to take the decisive step from the concrete function of 'designation' to the universal and universally valid function of 'signification' " (*PSF*, I, p. 197/148). This final moment in the self-unfolding of language brings language to its "internal limits" and the threshold of science. However, language can never cross this frontier without ceasing to be a spoken and lived language, without ceasing to be itself: "All linguistic concepts remain in the zone between action and reflection, between doing and contemplation" (*PSF*, I, p. 285/257). This is why the objective world that is constituted by language is always a lived world. Even where language seems to be wholly concerned with the differentiation and construction of the world of intuitive objects, these objects are always characterized in terms of the subject that perceives them, and thus the objectivity that is established by language is always a subjective reality. "For the word is not a copy of the object as such, but reflects the soul's image of the object" (*PSF*, I, p. 284/256). In a certain sense, when we turn to speak about language, when we are consciousness of the presence of language, we have already left language behind, we have already left the lived world that it has constituted. The transition from language to science demands the negation of this subjective dimension of language. We will consider the relation between language and science, and the transition from the one to the other, in more detail below in the chapter devoted to science.

The Construction of the Objective World

Having established the specific function of language as a symbolic forms, Cassirer goes on in volume one of the *Philosophy of Symbolic Forms* to illustrate the long path by which language has come to differentiate the objective world. Although we cannot enter here into all the details of the extensive historical and anthropological evidence compiled by Cassirer to support his analysis, it is important to consider the basic lines of this development.

As we have seen, the differentiation of the objective world possesses a logical primacy in the development of the self-consciousness of spirit. It is no doubt for this reason that Cassirer begins by considering the construction of the objective world. It is from the "body," or more precisely the "image of the body," as "an original set of co-ordinates" (*PSF*, I, p. 206 f./159), that language begins to " 'set out' or isolate *existere*" giving it the form of an "independent 'existence' ('*Existenz*')" (*PSF*, I, p. 204/156). "In three diverse, but closely related phases, language develops the three basic intuitions of space, time and number and so creates the indispensable condition for all intellectual mastery of phenomena and for every synthesis of these phenomena into the unity of a 'world concept' " (*PSF*, I, p. 226/183). It becomes clear in the course of reading the *Philosophy of Symbolic Forms* that each symbolic form is understood by Cassirer to move through the same three phases in its particular construction of the world. What is more, it also seem that Cassirer associated a certain symbolic form with each one of these phases. Language, as we shall see, is essentially spatial in its orientation, whereas myth proves to be more temporal. Art, science, and religion seem to be a part of the domain of number. Though Cassirer seems to draw this analogy he does not explain it, nor does he develop it in any explicit way.

Each symbolic forms possess its own "schema" according to which it orders the world. In the case of language the world is differentiated and constructed according to the schematism of space (cf. *PSF*, I, p. 215/159). "For language, the precise differentiation of spatial *positions* and spatial *distances* represents a point of departure from which it proceeds in the construction of objective reality and in the determinations of objects. The differentiation (*Differenzierung*) of place serves as a basis for the differentiation of content" (*PSF*, I, p. 203/155). As we have already seen, the original framework of phonetic metaphors introduces a first primordial distinction within consciousness between, on the one hand, a centrifugal movement outward (expressed by explosive sounds such as *p* and *d*) and, on the other hand, a centripetal movement inward (expressed by soft sounds such as *m* and *n*). "For the most part, the soft vowels express the place of the person addressed, the 'there,' while the place of the speaker is indicated by a sharper vowel" (*PSF*, I, p. 202/154). In this way, the *ō* designates the "there" toward which the action of expression is directed, and inversely the *ā* designates the "here" as the source of action. At the same time, the "*ā* designates the temporally present," while the "*ō* designates the temporally absent"—at this point there is as yet no distinction between the "future" and the "past" (*PSF*, I, p. 202/175). In differentiating time language must move to a "higher dimension" of activity than in the case of the differentiation of space. The differentiation of space establishes a heterogeneous coexistence of the two elements: here and there. However, "the elements of time exists as such only because consciousness 'runs through' them and in so doing differentiates them" (*PSF*, I, p. 215/170). In the differentiation of time, language must establish a homogenous succession of mutually exclusive elements that follow each other in a determined sequence, an *"order in progression"* (*PSF*, I, p, 231/190). Thus, whereas here can become there, and there can become here, the "directions from past to the future and from the future to past are not interchangeable" (*PSF*, I, p. 217/172). It is through the differentiation of action that language comes to be able to differentiate and represent time. As we saw, language begins this by applying the spatial designation of here and there to indicate that which is present and that which is not-present. However, insofar as language has only distinguished between the now and not-now, "only the relatively small segment of consciousness that is immediately illumined by the light of the now, can truly exist.... Hence the whole of an action cannot be apprehended either in thought or language unless consciousness literally 'actualizes' it in all its detail thrusting each of its stages, one after another, into the light of the now" (*PSF*, I, p. 222/178). The action is thus dissected into small pieces. Language must establish the ideal moments of an action and subsequently unite all the different pieces into a "teleological *whole*" (*PSF*, I, p. 222/179). In the final analysis, language achieves its differentiation of time only by conceiving it in terms of heterogeneous parts, that is to say, in terms of space.

In turning to the representation of number, language arrives at the limit of its ability. "Though language prepares the way for these symbols [the symbols of mathematical number], it cannot pursue this road to its end.... For language cannot take the decisive step which mathematical thought demands of numerical concepts, namely their characteristic detachment and emancipation from the foundations of intuition and the intuitive representation" (*PSF*, I, p. 228/186). Again language can only determine the heterogeneity of elements. Even where it determines, as in the case of its representation of time, a homogeneity of elements, this homogeneity remains relatively simple and expresses more an ordered sequence of separate moments. "Through the differentiation of spatial objects, language arrives at its concept of collective multiplicity—through the differentiation of temporal acts, it arrives at its expression of particularity and separation" (*PSF*, I, p. 239/199). It perceives, therefore, either multiplicity or unity, the many or the one, but it is unable to perceive the one in the many, or the many in the one—it is unable, in other words, to unite into a truly differentiated unity the coexistence and heterogeneity of space and the regulated succession and homogeneity of time.

The Construction of the Subjective World

The spatial differentiation of place also serves as the foundation for the differentiation of the contents of the I, Thou, and He (cf. *PSF*, I, p. 203/155). "It is the same half-mimetic, half-linguistic act of indication, the same fundamental forms of 'deixis,' which give rise to the opposition of here, there and over there and to that of 'I,' 'thou' and 'he' " (*PSF*, I, p. 213/168). "Here" is the place where I always find myself, and despite wherever I might be, I can always say that I am at this moment here. And, by consequence, the there is the place where the other is always found. In this way, "Japanese has created a word for 'I' from a local adverb whose proper meaning is 'center' and a word for 'he' from another word meaning 'there' or 'over there' " (*PSF*, I, p. 215/169). Language places the I as the subject who speaks at the center of the world, and the thou as the person to whom the subject speaks at its circumference.

Here too everything begins from the body: "the first concrete feeling of self (*konkrete Selbstgefühl*) is entirely bound up with the concrete intuition of one's own body (*Leibes*) and limbs" (*PSF*, I, p. 251/215). As in the construction of the objective world it is the "image of his own body (*Körpers*)" (*PSF*, I, p. 206/159) that provides the individual with the original model of itself. Cassirer does not elaborate on the precise nature of this "concrete feeling of self." We will return to this question at the end of the next chapter on myth. For now, we might say that this "concrete feeling of self" is the self-affectivity of the living and existing being vis-à-vis itself. Defined in this way, it would seem necessary to attribute this "concrete feeling of self" also to the animal world and in the final analysis to all living, organic existence. And, in fact, when we turn to consider the behavior of animals it would seen rather evident that there must be some sort of "feeling of self" by which the animal distinguishes its own existence from that of the world's, from which it coordinates all its actions. The Cartesian thesis by which the animal world is nothing by an elaborate mechanical mechanism goes against all the observable evidence. The animal does not, however, apprehend itself as such. It never becomes an object of knowledge, and thus is never self-conscious. The subject "sees itself, one might say, in the image of the object which it acquires as 'its own' " (*PSF*, I, p. 260/226). The subject recognizes itself in the "mirror of its own expression," in the "mirror of its own activity," in "the image of its own body" . . . we see that the metaphor of the mirror plays an important role in the thought of Cassirer. Even in *The Logic of the Cultural Sciences* Cassirer will maintain that it is only in "in the mirror of his culture" that man can come to know himself (*Logic*, p. 102). As in animal desire, man sees in the image of his own felt need, his own self-affectivity. As we shall see, there are two basic attitudes that will be adopted toward this mirror image: (1) Spirit can recognizes itself in its image and in this way form an imaginary identification with it. As we shall see, this misrecognition will form the basis of mythical consciousness. (2) Spirit can recognize the image to be just an image, and as we shall see there are a number of different ways spirit can react to this revelation.

Language and the Ethical Norm

Now, we have seen that the emergence of self-consciousness is "accompanied by a new way of listening (*Hören*), a certain manner of becoming aware of . . . (*Gewahrwerdens*) and of 'listening' ('*Horchen*'). And this mode of listening leads gradually to a form of 'obedience' ('*Gehorsam*') which is far removed from the mere subjection (*Unterwerfung*), the unconditional sway to emotion (*Affekt*)" (*Aufbau*, p. 136). The symbolic function was born to put an end to the tyranny of emotion. Cassirer illustrates this through an example of a young child who is overcome by fear every time he encounters an "unknown face." The young boy begins to repeat to himself the words "no fear" each time he encounters a stranger, and in this way "mastered the situation" (*Aufbau*, p. 136 f.). The child is thus able to calm and control the sudden outbursts of expressive emotion. The emotional dimension of the subject, the subject's self-affectivity, is now subordinated to the "jurisdiction of language" (cf. *Aufbau*, p. 138). The subject is subjected to the law of language and to its normative practices. The dimension of ethics is thus implicitly present from the very beginning. To be human, to speak a language, is to become an ethical agent subjected to the law and order of logos (cf. ibid.). The entrance into language "implies that the sensory drive, instead of preceding directly towards its object, instead of satisfying itself and losing itself in the object, encounters a kind of inhibition and reversal, in which a new *consciousness* of this drive is born" (*PSF*, I, p. 180/126). "Through the inhibition of direct outbreaks into gestures and inarticulate cries an inner measure, a movement within sensuous desire and representations is achieved" (*PSF*, I, p. 186/134).

Language as *Weltanschauung*

As one knows, Cassirer's theory of language owes much to Wilhelm von Humboldt. It would not be going too far to suggest that Cassirer has only rendered explicit what was already implicit in the method and work of Humboldt. However it would be an oversimplification that would overlook an essential difference between their respective views to maintain, as it is often done, that Humboldt's concept of the "inner form of language" is without qualification the same as Cassirer's concept of the symbolic form of language. It might be said that much of what Humboldt says about language, Cassirer says about each of the symbolic forms. For both prove to be an "organic form" and a system of "differentiations" (*PSF*, I, p. 155). As for Humboldt, language is for Cassirer a system of "classifications" that subsume reality under a system of concepts, thus giving it structure and form. Thus, language is not work (*ergon*) but an activity or energy (*energeia*) of spirit.[8]

The real difference between diverse languages is not a difference in sounds that "describe the same mass of independent present-at-hand (*vorhanden*) objects and concepts" (*Aufbau*, p. 123), but rather a difference in world perspectives. Each language is characterized by the *Weltanschauung* that it forms (cf. *Essay*, p. 120). As one knows, Humboldt coined the term "inner form" to designate the specific law of formation by which each language creates a specific *Weltanschauung*. Now it is necessary to distinguish, as Cassirer does, between the world perspective created by language and the perspective of language *qua* language. "For while languages differ in their 'perspective of the world,' there is a perspective of language itself that distinguishes it from the other spiritual forms" (*PSF*, I, p. 285/257). When Humboldt refers to the "inner form of language" he is referring principally to the perspective of the world created by language and not to the perspective particular to language as such (cf. *PSF*, I, p. 284). However, when Cassirer refers to the "inner form of language" as a symbolic form, he is referring to the morphological structure of language as such, and thus to the universal form of the perspective belonging to language *qua* language. Cassirer does not clearly elaborate this distinction. We see in *The*

Logic of the Cultural Sciences that when Cassirer speaks about the way in which the cultural sciences subordinate the particular under the universal it is necessary for him to introduce the concept of "style" in order to account for the difference between the universal structure of the symbolic form of language, which is the same for every language, and the specific nature that distinguishes one language from another. We will return to consider in more detail Cassirer's concept of "style" when we turn to consider science as a symbolic form.

Four

Myth as the Other of Logos or the Texture of the Real: The Presence of Meaning as the Meaning of Presence

A Philosophy of μῦθος?

Philosophy desires to be self-conscious logos (λόγος), it desires to speak and know the truth of being as the being of logos. What need, then, does philosophy have of a critique of myth (μῦθος)? For myth is nothing if it is not a chaotic madness, a *hiatus irrationalis*, an irreducible irrationality within the real, within the very fabric of reason itself: in other words, myth is nothing if it is not the other of logos. From its very beginning philosophy's sole raison d'être has been to overcome the irrationality of myth and do away with its phantasms and visions, to discover beyond the appearance of things the truth of things. However, just as philosophy believes that it has finally unveiled the truth, just as it is about to grasp and speak the truth, just as it is about to realize its most deep-rooted desire, myth reappears—once again, that which was taken to be *the* truth reveals itself to be nothing more than another mirage, another myth. Thus, the history of the becoming, or the self-realization of logos is indistinguishable from the history of the being and eternal return of myth. Unable to give up its conviction that the "real is rational and the rational is real," and unwilling to resign itself to the limitations of finite reason, philosophy continues on its holy quest for the eternal and universal reason of things, for the truth. However, the inability of reason, λόγος, to liberate itself from the presence of μῦθος has slowly brought about the recognition that this irrationality, this mad belief in illusions, in some way belongs to the essence of rationality itself, that within the very fabric of reason this unreason has its proper place and specific function. It is perhaps not by hazard that our century has given rise to psychoanalysis as the science of madness, and witnessed the development of the mathematical theorems of fractal structures as a "theory of chaos." Nor by hazard that philosophy has come to see truth as the interplay between unconcealment (ἀλήθεια) and concealment (λήθη), and thus critiqued the tradition as a metaphysics of presence that perpetually falls victim to the "myth of the given." Nor, finally, is it by hazard that it is also during this same period that philosophy has come to recognize in a new and more profound way the essential role played by myth in human existence: for the problem of myth stands at the heart of this general direction of thought as its object of study touches upon all of them. Of course, from its very beginning, as Cassirer himself points out, philosophy has attempted to explain or, more to the point, to explain away the presence of myth; and by doing so, defined itself in opposition to myth. But up to now it has, as we shall see, perpetually reduced myth to something other than itself. Cassirer's critical phenomenology of myth is a bold attempt to determine the specific function of myth as a cultural form within the interior of logos as that which is other than logos, without reducing it to logos.

Myth as a Symbolic Form . . . a Reading

Cassirer's theory of myth is perhaps the most original part of his philosophy of symbolic forms, and no doubt precisely for this reason the most in need of clarification and interpretation. Paradoxes, if not contradictions are abundantly presence throughout Cassirer's treatment of myth. On the one hand, for example, myth is to be seen as an independent and permanent structural dimension of spirit possessing its own specific function within culture, and thus as having an equal status as a symbolic form. Nevertheless, Cassirer consistently speaks of myth as an "adversary" that must be overcome. In the end, seemingly against the tenets of his own theory of myth, Cassirer was unable, or perhaps unwilling, to abandon the tacit assumption of the Enlightenment, and to a degree of all philosophy since Parmenides, that once the movement from mythos to logos has been made there can be, or at least should be, no going back. Any return of myth must be viewed as a regression to a more primitive stage resulting from a failure of rationality.[1] And indeed, there seems to have been no attempt by Cassirer to analysis the mythical structures of his own culture and times. Cassirer's analysis of myth limits itself to examples taken from early humanity. The only example of the contemporary presence of myths considered by Cassirer seems to have been those created by the architects of German National Socialism, and even these are immediately qualified as being "artificial" and thus are clearly not to be understood as genuine myths (cf. *MS*, p. 82ff.). It is thus not difficult to appreciate Heidegger's reproach, even if one does not fully share it, that "such a rich and accommodating presentation of the phenomenon of spirit . . . is not yet philosophy."[2] However, Cassirer himself stresses that his study is "by no means . . . conclusive" but rather "at most a beginning" (*PSF*, II, p. xvii/xii).

The difficulties involved in understanding Cassirer's conception of myth, and the problems inherent in that conception, can only be overcome through a careful reading of the second volume of the *Philosophy of Symbolic Forms,* which provides Cassirer's most extensive treated of myth as a symbolic form. The structure of the present chapter thus follows closely that of this truly groundbreaking work on myth. However, as closely as our reading is, it diverts from Cassirer's original presentation of the problem in at least one important respect. For reasons that will become clearer in the next chapter, Cassirer treats myth and religion together in the same volume. As we shall see, the contents of myth and religion are the same, though their spiritual forms are very different. Thus, there is a close dialectical relation between the two, such that they are always found together. In my treatment of myth and religion I have, however, elected to separate them and deal with each individually in order to render more explicit their specific natures and functions. This is, in fact, in keeping with the basic tenets of Cassirer's own philosophy and methodology: for although each symbolic form is defined by its place in the whole and its relation to each of the other symbolic form, each symbolic form must nevertheless be understood according to the criteria particular to its specific mode of symbolic meaning. This chapter thus deals exclusively with that realm of spirit that Cassirer calls the "*magical mythical* world view," as opposed to the "truly *religious* world view," which will be treated in the next chapter (*PSF*, II, p. 25/32).

The *Differentia Specifica* of Myth as a Symbolic Form

The Hazard and Paradox of a "Philosophy of Myth"

"A 'critique of mythical consciousness,' " Cassirer writes in the first sentence to the second volume, "cannot but seem hazardous and even paradoxical" (*PSF*, II, p. xii/vii). But in what way "hazardous" and why "paradoxical"? Paradoxical, certainly because, as Cassirer continues to explain, since Kant "critique has presupposed the reality of a fact toward which the philosophical question is directed. . . . But is the world of myth a fact of this kind?" (*PSF*, II, p. xii/vii). Presumably not. The extension of the transcendental method to other domains of culture, such as language, art, and science, proves to be less problematic than in the case of myth. For myth, almost by definition, belongs exclusively to the sphere of illusion and non-being (μὴ ὄν), and ever since Parmenides philosophy has maintained that only that which *is* can be made the object of philosophical investigation: οὔτε γὰρ ἂν γνοίης τό γε μὴ ἐόν (οὐ γὰρ ἀνυστόν) οὔτε φράσεις ("for you could not know what is not [that cannot be done] nor indicate it") says the goddess.[3] "Once philosophical idealism arrived at its own concept, once it saw the idea of 'being' as its original and fundamental problem, the whole of myth was relegated to the realm of non-being" (*PSF*, II, p. viii/vii). A critique of mythical consciousness is therefore paradoxical, because it inquires into that which is not: or more specifically, that which is not present to the transcendental subject of the theoretical and speculative consciousness—or when it is present, takes the form of a meaningless chaotic madness, an irrational and emotive belief in illusions. A philosophy of myth therefore seeks to determine the lawfulness of a domain that appears to be lawless (*PSF*, II, p. 4/6).

But in what way is this "hazardous"? First of all it is hazardous to philosophy, for to take up a critique of mythical consciousness as a positive mode of spiritual formation, is at the same time to put into question the self-identity of philosophy since Parmenides. The question is whether or not philosophy can successfully engage in a "philosophy of myth" without at the same time ceasing to be philosophy, or whether it must not transform itself into something Heidegger has vaguely called thinking. And, in fact, the precise status of philosophy within the philosophy of symbolic forms, and its place within the system of culture, is not entirely clear and even proves to be thoroughly problematic. We shall return to this in the conclusion when we consider Cassirer's theory of the "*Urphänome*" (cf. below p. 210).

It is, however, above all hazardous for myth itself. Cassirer is more than aware of the difficulties and dangers inherent in undertaking a "philosophy of myth." The quotations marks in the title of the introduction to the second volume of the *Philosophy of Symbolic Forms* indicate not only the paradoxical nature of such a project, but also that what is at stake there is precisely the question of methodology. For Cassirer every mythology is a sort of theory of myth.[4] What is interesting to note is that in the final analysis every theory of myth reveals itself to be nothing more than a sort of myth of theory. Every theory of myth ends by projecting its own self-image onto the concrete presence of myth, and thus sees in myth nothing other than its own objective reflection.

> Every scholar [has] found in myth those objects with which he was most familiar. At bottom the different schools saw in the magic mirror of myth only their own faces. The linguist found in it a world of words and names—the philosopher found a "primitive philosophy"—the psychiatrist a highly complicated and interesting neurotic phenomenon. (*MS*, p. 6)

The theoretical attitude can perceive and understand myth only by "reducing it to something *other* than what it immediately is and signifies" (*PSF*, II, p. 12/17), only by transforming it into a theory of myth and recognizing in this "magic mirror" its own image of itself. The process by which theoretical consciousness recognizes in myth its own theoretical structures is thus a process of misrecognition, or of *méconnaissance* as Lacan would say: which is interesting, as it is precisely this type of misrecognition or *méconnaissance* that characterizes mythical consciousness.

But is not the philosophy of symbolic forms also menaced by this tendency of theory to misrecognize in myth only its own theoretical identity? Does it not, after all, only see in the "magic mirror" of myth another symbolic form? Does it not also confirm its own theoretical identity in a sort of myth of myths? Almost certainly it is and does. Cassirer is, however, aware of the "danger":

> [T]hough a subordination of myth to a general system of "symbolic forms" seems imperative, it presents a certain danger. For

> if a comparison of the mythical form with other cultural forms is taken in a purely *objective* sense, i.e., based on purely objective parallels and connections, it may well lead to a leveling of the intrinsic form of myth. And indeed there has been no lack of attempts to explain myth by *reducing* it to another form of cultural life, whether knowledge, art, or language. (*PSF*, II, p. 21/28)

Cassirer hopes to avoid this danger by means of his concept of the symbolic function, which expresses itself differently in each of the cultural forms. Cassirer's transcendental phenomenological approach thus aims to establish not the unity of the contents of each of the cultural forms, but rather the unity of its structure: "it is not enough to demonstrate [the unity of culture and each of its "original forms"] through the phenomena [i.e., their content]; we must explain it through the unity of a specific 'structural form' ('*Strukturform*') of spirit" (*PSF*, II, p. 11/15). The aim of a philosophy of myth is thus to determine its universal "structural form." However, this task is rendered all the more difficult as the distinction between content and structure that critical analysis must make is wholly foreign to the mythical attitude itself. Here, the ideal structure and the content that this structure creates are indistinguishable from one another (cf. *PSF*, II, p. 20/26). Again the paradox and the danger! For in order to understand myth for what it is, it is necessary to enter into its own worldview, but to enter into its worldview is to abandon the theoretical perspective from which an analysis of the structure of this worldview would be possible. "The world views of myth and of theoretical knowledge cannot coexist in the same area of thought. They are mutually exclusive: the beginning of one is equivalent to the end of the other" (*PSF*, III, p. 78/91). Unfortunately Cassirer says little about his method of treating myth. In *The Logic of the Cultural Sciences* he only indicates that it involves a "highly difficult and complex 'hermeneutics' " without elaborating further about the nature of this hermeneutics (*Logic*, p. 97). We find ourselves before the same problem that was encountered in the tentative to speak about language. As in the case of language, it would seem that myth can only be myth insofar as it denounces itself, and thus to a certain extent ceases to be myth. Myth can only be approached through a myth of myth. Again we will have to postpone our consideration of the meaning of this until the conclusion.

Like all symbolic forms, myth proves to be a specific structural form of spirit. However, as we shall see, myth is in fact the structural form par excellence. In a number of places Cassirer even speaks of mythical thought as "structural thinking" or of mythical space as "structural space" and so on: an expression that he does not apply to the other symbolic forms. As we shall see, lived myth appears to consciousness not as a historically and culturally determined meaning, but rather as the very meaning of life itself. Once we have begun to see in myth a culturally and historically determined signification, we have already left the perspective of myth itself. It is for this reason that it is easier to undertake a study of myth through the analysis of the myths of another culture and another age other than our own. The myths of our own culture and our own times are too close to us to be placed at an ideal distance and analyzed. In two footnotes in the third volume of the *Philosophy of Symbolic Forms* Cassirer defines his philosophical project in the following Heideggerian terms: it seeks the conditions of possibility necessary to effect the transition from the "existence of '*Dasein*' " to the "objective meaning of 'logos,' " from the "stage of the '*Zuhandenen*' " to the "form of the *Vorhandenen*" and this through the "domain of *symbolic* formation" of representation and signification (*PSF*, III, pp. 149/173, 163/190). The mythical world is this initial domain of existential meaning that is lived by spirit as the meaning of its own existence, it is the "meaning of the being of *Dasein*" (*Seinssinn des* Daseins).

The Presence of Meaning as the Meaning of Lived Presence and the Texture of the Real

Now, in order to determine more clearly the *differentia specifica* of myth as a symbolic form it is necessary to turn, as does Cassirer, to a consideration of the link between "the problem of signification" and "the problem of designation" (*PSF*, II, p. 23/30). As we have seen, all presence is always already mediated by the presence of the symbol, and every symbol is comprised of a sensuous presence and a nonintuitive meaning.

> For no content of consciousness is in itself merely "present" ("*präsent*"), or in itself merely "representative" ("*repräsentativ*"); rather, every actual experience indissolubly embraces both factors. Everything present (*Gegenwärtige*) *functions* in the sense of representing (*Vergegenwärtigung*), just as all representation (*Verge-*

> *genwärtigung*) demands a link with something present (*Gegenwärtiges*) in consciousness. (*PSF*, III, p. 199/232)

Thus, as we saw in the final section of chapter 2, every symbolic form is determined by the nature of the rapport that it establishes between the signifier and the signified. It is this relation that determines the mode of presence of meaning or the mode of "seeing" that is constituted by this symbolic form. All theoretical forms of seeing the world are, for example, characterized by the fact that the distinction between the two is explicitly and consciously posited. The presence of the sign represents something other than itself. Both the words of language and the symbols of science, as a spoken and thought logos, accomplish this task according to different degrees of ideality. Here, the sign is always taken as secondary to the reality that is represented. The sign is only a "re-presentation" (*Vergegenwärtigung*), a means of rendering present a more original and authentic presentation (*Gegenwärtigung*).[5] This is why the system of signs constructed by theoretical consciousness possesses a certain circularity, reversibility, and thus a certain relativity of meaning that is necessary to this particular mode of representation and signification. In contrast, mythical intuition is always the awareness of an absolutely unique and concrete presence and reality. Here, there is no distinction between the sensuous image and its nonintuitive meaning. The mythical image stands before us as the concrete incarnation of the meaning it represents. It is so woven into our intuition of reality as to be indistinguishable from it. Insofar as the mythical image represents the immediate and concrete presence of spiritual signification—and thus the signification of immediate and concrete presence—it constitutes what we can call the *texture* of the real. Here "to be effective" (*wirksam sein*) *is* "to be real" (*wirklich sein*) (*PSF*, II, p. 37/49).

> [Here] the essence does not recede behind the appearance (*Erscheinung*) but is manifested in it; it does not cloak itself in the appearance but in the appearance is given to itself. Here the phenomenon as it is given in any moment never has a character of mere representation, it is one of authentic presence (*echte Präsenz*): a being and a reality is fully *present* (*Gegenwart*) in it, rather than only being mediately "rendered present" through the phenomenon (*ein Seiendes und Wirkliches steht in ihm in voller*

> *Gegenwart da, statt sich nur mittelbar durch dasselbe zu "vergegenwärtigen"*). (*PSF*, III, p. 68/79)

But how are we to reconcile the idea that "the basic mythical drive (*Trieb*) is a drive towards animation, i.e. towards the concrete *intuitive* apprehension and representation of all elements of *Dasein*" with the fact that this "drive is directed with particular intensity towards what is most 'unreal' and lifeless, that the shadow realm of words, images, and signs exerts so substantial a power over the mythical consciousness?" (*PSF*, II, p. 24/31). To formulate the question in this way is, for Cassirer, to have misunderstood the nature and function of the givenness of concrete presence. Traditional metaphysics errs not so much in positing the existence of something beyond the representative sign that must ultimately be understood as the real, but in assuming that this reality can every be rendered present independently of the sign, on the one hand, and in attempting to speak about this ultimate reality in terms of that which is present to consciousness (and thus which is constituted by this reality), on the other. And for this reason it has continually overlooked the nature and structure of the givenness of presence. For Cassirer, that which lies beyond the sign cannot be known or experienced; it has never been, nor will it ever become the "object" of consciousness—this of course does not mean that it cannot be posited, nor that it cannot be present through its absence, nor does it mean that it cannot play an important role in the structure of spiritual meaning and life. Rather to the contrary. As we shall see in the next chapter, religion is defined precisely by that intuition of an ultimate reality beyond the sign. What is more, without this intuition of something beyond the sign, the sign itself could not function.

When Cassirer writes that all "representation, as presence, is at the same time *Vergegenwärtigung*," how are we to understand this term *Vergegenwärtigen*? The precise translation would be "re-presentation" in the sense of a recollection of something. We have already seen that for Cassirer everything present (*Gegenwärtiges*) functions as a *Vergenwärtigen*, just as every *Vergenwärtigen* requires something present (*Gegenwärtiges*). In the case of theoretical knowledge we saw that the sign is secondary to that which is re-presented. The sign thus functions, as we said, to re-represent some original and authentic presentation. When we want to directly approach this presentation, we find that it too represents something else, and so on. In the end, pure theoretical thought recognizes that the meaning of any signifier is only its position in the system of signifiers that it has itself constructed. In the case of mythical consciousness, however, presence does not point beyond itself to another more original reality, but rather re-presents itself as a self-referential concrete presence. This does not mean that the distinction between the signifier and signified does not exist, only that it has not been explicitly posited.

> The mythical world is "concrete," not because it has to do with sensuous objective contents, not because it excludes and repels from itself all merely "abstract" factors—everything which is solely meaning and sign; it is concrete because in it the two factors, the factor of thing and the factor of meaning, are indiscriminately taken up (*aufgehen*) into each other, because they have grown together into an immediate and "concretized" unity. (*PSF*, II, p. 24/32)

Here, the image is not taken to re-present a meaning, but rather is the presence of meaning itself. In the mythical worldview, "every appearance is always and essentially an incarnation" (*PSF*, III, p. 88/79). The means of representation cannot be separated or distinguished from that which is represented. In the experience of lived concrete presence, in the authentic effective presence that we take to be the real, the moments of *Gegenwärtigung* and *Vergegenwärtigung* are fused together into a single undifferentiated reality. Thus, although myth "signifies one of the first steps beyond the 'given,' its product at once resumes the form of the given" (*PSF*, II, p. 24/31). The domain of myth is thus the realm of the *imago,* which is ruled by a fusional logic of imaginary identification and misrecognition.

> [In fact] from this point of view the relation between "image" (*Bild*) and "thing" (*Sache*) insofar as the two are differentiated must actually be reversed. The image must assert a peculiar primacy over the thing. For what "is" in the object in its expressive character is not taken up and destroyed in the image; on the contrary, it is set in high relief and intensified. The image frees this expressive reality from all merely accidental determinants and concentrates it in a single focus. (*PSF*, III, p. 69/81)

In the context of myth a more faithful translation of *Vergegenwärtigung* might be "actualization" in the sense of rendering something present. Insofar as the mythical figure refers back to a previous past, this past is absolute and does not refer beyond itself. Here "we cannot describe recollection as a *simple* return of an event, as a fait image or copy of former impression. It is not *simply* a repetition but rather a rebirth of the past" (*Essay*, p. 51; my emphasis).

Myth as the Feeling of Life

The *differentia specifica* of myth can also be defined in terms of the dialectical interplay between life and spirit that runs throughout Cassirer's work. Myth is often equated with that dimension of meaning that Cassirer calls "expression." Strictly speaking the domain of expression prefigures culture and myth as their source.

> [The] meaning and content of the purely expressive function cannot be *accounted* for by way of a *single* sphere of spiritual formation, because as a truly universal and as it were world-encompassing function it precedes differentiation (*Differenzierung*) into the various spheres of meaning, it precedes the divergence of myth and theory, of logical reflection and aesthetic intuition. Its certainty and its "truth"' are, in a manner of speaking, pre-mythical, pre-logical and pre-aesthetic; it forms the common soil from which all these formations have in some way sprouted and to which they remain attached. (*PSF*, III, p. 81/95)

It is clear that for Cassirer the expressive dimension of meaning is also found in the animal world, and ultimately in life as such. In fact, what is apprehended in pure expression is, in the final analysis, the "unitary life stream" (*ein einheitlicher Lebensstrom*) (*PSF*, III, 86/101).

> Insofar as myth condenses into lasting configuration, insofar as it sets before us the stable outlines of an objective world of forms, the significance of this world becomes intelligible to us only if behind it we can feel the dynamic of the feeling of life (*Lebensgefühls*) from which it originally grew. (*PSF*, II, p. 69/89)

But how are we to understand this "feeling of life"? Cassirer seems to have two things in mind here. First this awareness of life is the feeling of *a* life, that is to say, the intuitive awareness of the organic unity that provides the identity of a specific living organism and determines the world in which this organism finds itself. All organisms possess a certain self-awareness and intuitive knowledge of the form of their existence. It is necessary, for example, to be able to distinguish the members of the same species from other species for the purposes of matting, hunting, defense, and other such vital activities. Each organism has its own rhythm of life, and thus a certain biological sense of time. There is a time for everything, and everything has its time. The animal must also have a sense of its spatial world, a biological geography if you will. We are too quick to think of the biological world in merely physical terms, as a mechanical mechanism of chemicals and forces. For Cassirer each animal perceives and reacts to the "world" of its species. "In the world of a fly," Cassirer writes quoting Uexhüll, "we find only 'fly things'; in the world of a sea urchin we find only 'sea urchin things' " (*Essay*, p. 23). Of course, in its world the animal's life remains a life of impulses. Its "instincts" are nothing other than a "fixed chain of actions" and the animal cannot but play out this "melody of impulses" determined for it by the nature of its species (*Logic*, p. 26). The animal fuses together with its world in such a way as to be one with it. It is this same sense of identity, this same feeling of life that is found in mythical thought. Here too the historical and conventional meaning of culture is immediately lived by spirit in such a way as to be one with it. In the same way that the biological organism lives out its structural plan (*Bauplan*), the spiritual organism lives out its life in the structural differentiation of language. As we shall see, Cassirer even characterizes the mythical world as a "biological" one (cf. for example *PSF*, II, pp. 109/135 and 148/179).

On a more profound level, this "feeling of life" implies an awareness of life itself. It is here that myth and religion part company. For myth is never able to distinguish this awareness of life itself from its feeling of the form that life takes in actualizing itself. As we shall see, this intuition of life that animates the form of life is the beginning and end, the alpha and omega, of the pure religious intuition. We will return this distinction when we treat religion as a symbolic form.

The Structure of the Mythical World

A Critique of μῦθος

The first step in applying the approach of critical philosophy to the various cultural forms is to establish the laws and categories governing each of the different modes of intentionality that constitute the life of spirit. Evidently we cannot directly inquire into the life of pure consciousness, but rather must begin from its objective manifestations and laboriously work our way back toward their conditions of possibility. This process of "reconstruction" (cf. *PSF*, III, p. 53/63) already presents a considerable challenge in the case of empirical perception, where the reality from which we are to begin is more or less objectively "experienced." In the case of mythical consciousness, as we have already indicated, the task is made all the more difficult by the fact that "myth lives entirely by the presence of its object—by the intensity with which it seizes and takes possession of consciousness in a specific moment (*Augenblick*)" (*PSF*, II, p. 35/47). Through an analysis of the nature of the presence of the mythical object to consciousness, and in contrast to the nature of the theoretical and empirical object, Cassirer takes on this arduous task of reconstructing the general laws and categories of mythical consciousness. We need not follow Cassirer's analysis here in all its historical and anthropological detail, but it is nevertheless interesting and important to consider *grosso modo* the essential dynamic and structural characteristics of mythical thought. Throughout our considerations here it should be kept in mind that what is essentially being presented here is the universal structure of the emotional and effective life of spirit. It is thus necessary to see beyond the examples taken from early humanity and try to see the basic structures at work in our everyday lives today. For in the final analysis, nothing could prove to be closer to our existence, to the meaning of our existence (the meaning of the being of *Dasein* as Cassirer says), than our mythical worldview.

The General Structural Law of Myth

The "*law of concrescence or coincidence of the members of a relation*" (*PSF*, II, p. 64/82) is the most general expression of the law that governs and structures all mythical thought. From this basic structural law all the characteristic qualities of mythical consciousness, the mode of presence of its object, and the logic that underlies its judgments and actions are derived. In contrast to theoretical consciousness, which forms a synthetic and heterogeneous unity of ideal differences, mythical consciousness forms a synthetic unity in which all difference is reduced to the homogeneous and undifferentiated unity of real identity.

> Only the observers who no longer live in [myth] but reflect on it read such distinction into myth. Where we see mere "representation," myth, insofar as it has not yet deviated from its fundamental and original form, sees real *identity*. The "image" (*Bild*) does not represent the "thing" (*Sache*); it *is* the thing; it does not merely stand for the object, but has the same actuality, so that it replaces the thing's immediate presence. (*PSF*, II, p. 38/51)

We have already seen that this "identity thinking" (*PSF*, II, p. 66) "possesses neither the impulsion nor the means to correct or criticize what is given here and now, to limit its objectively by *measuring* it against something not given, something past or future. . . . All 'truth' and reality dissolve into the mere presence of the content, all phenomena are situated on a single plan" (*PSF*, II, p. 36/47). Thus, from the perspective of mythical consciousness there can be no "hidden meaning" (*PSF*, II, p. 38/50), no distinguishing between illusion and reality, between the image and the thing, the means of representation and that which is represented, between cause and effect.

When and where mythical consciousness encounters difference, it negates this difference by identifying one content of consciousness with another, so that the difference "concresces" into a single configuration of consciousness. When the difference becomes so great that it takes on the form of a binary opposition, and thus can no longer be synthesized into a single configuration based upon resemblance however small and fleeting, mythical consciousness "hypostatizes" (*PSF*, II, p. 165 f. n23/198 n1) each of the antithetical positions as a concrete being existing independently of the other. "The *substantial*, mythical mode of thought either makes the many into one or the one into the many. Here there is only concrescence or divergence; there is not that characteristic union of different things which is effected in the purely intellectual syntheses of consciousness and in its specific logical form of unity, in the 'transcendental unity of apperception' " (ibid.). As a result of this attitude of "material indifference," there is for mythical consciousness "but one dimension of relation, one single 'plan of being' ('*Seinsebene*'). In cognition the pure relational concept comes, as it were, *between* the elements which it links. For it is not of the same world as these elements—it has no material *existence* comparable to theirs, but only an ideal *signification*" (*PSF*, II, p. 63/82).

The Characteristic Traits of Mythical Thought

From this general structural law of mythical and imaginary fusion, a number of characteristic features of mythical consciousness directly or indirectly follow. The first among these is that the contents of mythical consciousness are always in a constant state of "metamorphosis." Contrary to theoretical consciousness, which understands all specific events or happenings as the lawful manifestation of a universal rule of progression, mythical consciousness sees each particular event as the direct result of an equally specific and equally determined cause. Because myth continually reduces all difference to identity, "anything can *come from* anything, . . . anything can stand in temporal or spatial contact with anything. Whereas empirical thinking speaks of 'change' and seeks to understand it on the basis of universal rule, mythical thinking knows only a simple metamorphosis" (*PSF*, II, p. 46/61). The curious result is that, whereas the theoretical attitude is able to account for accidents brought about by any number of uncontrollable and essentially unimportant factors as exceptions to the general governing rule, such "accidents" are unthinkable for mythical thought. Every effect is understood by myth as resulting not from a "cause" (*Ursache*) in the theoretical sense, but rather from a specific "original object" (*Ur-Sache*) (*PSF*, II, p. 54/70). As we shall see, this concept of the *Ur-Sache* plays an important and central role in the construction of the mythical worldview. As a result, everything comes from something, everything has a reason why, and thus there are no mere accidents. "Death in particular never occurs 'of itself' but is always brought about by magic influence" (*PSF*, II, p. 47 f./63). Death, as the end of life, is totally alien to the mythical worldview, which knows nothing but the feeling of life. Death is thus seen as simply a transition from one life form into another in the continuous metamorphosis of life as a whole.

Whereas science aims to understand the "how" of things, myth seeks to explain the "why" of things. Theoretical consciousness explains a particular event only insofar as it functions as an expression of a universal law that governs it. Science "subordinates" the particular phenomenon "to that universal complex of conditions which we call 'nature.' A phenomenon such as the death of a man is understood if we succeed in assigning a place to it within this complex—if we can recognize it as necessary on the basis of the physiological conditions of life" (*PSF*, II, p. 49/64). Bound as it is to the concrete here and now of that which is immediate and sensuously present, mythical thinking is unable to distinguish the particular from the universal rule and see in the particular nothing other than a concrete example of some universal transcendental principle. Myth's drive to explain "the death of precisely *this* man, at *this* particular time" (*PSF*, II, p. 49/64) cannot be appeased by an abstract theoretical explanation of this death in terms of the general physiological conditions of the human anatomy. Theoretical consciousness is content once it can say that the apple fell in accordance with the laws of gravity that apply to every physical object. The mythical worldview is satisfied only once it knows why this particular apple fell and not another, and why it fell when it did rather than earlier or later. In keeping with its general outlook, myth will attribute the cause of this event to an equally specific and concrete existence. Again we find ourselves before the mythical concept of the *Ur-Sache*.

Another significant characteristic of mythical thought that follows from the general law of mythical thinking is the relation it posits between the whole and the part: the principle of *pars pro toto*. "For our empirical apprehension the whole *consists* of its parts; for the logic of natural science, for the logic of the analytical-scientific concept of causality, it *results* from them; for the mythical view neither of these propositions applies; here there prevails a true indifference, both in thought and practice, between the whole and its part. The whole does not 'have' parts and does not break down into them; the part *is* immediately the whole and functions as such" (*PSF*, II, p. 49 f./65). The part does not simply represent the whole, nor is it merely taken as the whole—rather, the whole dwells in its wholeness in each part. For this reason the fate of any one of the elements of the whole is intertwined with the destiny of the whole. Insofar as everything is a part of the whole, the fate of everything is connected to the fate of everything else. It is this interwovenness of everything with everything, this primordial "belonging together" of all the members of a mythical relation, that is at the root of the purely mythical worldview. Thus, through the "sympathetic" bond they possess with the "whole" any two things, regardless of their spatial or temporal differences, can be fused together into a concrete relation based upon any superficial likeness between them. It is curious that this fundamental conviction of mythical thought, along with other characteristic of this worldview, seems to be confirmed by the new science of fractals and chaos theory. Here too the whole is said to be found in every part.

Unable to form a differentiated unity based upon the application of a rule of progression that establishes the sequence of order, mythical thinking establishes the teleological unity of the whole by positing the absolute beginning point and end point to this order. Again we return to the *Ur-Sache*, for myth traces the origins of the whole back to a "simple and original thing (*Ur- und Anfangssache*)" (*PSF*, II, p. 54/70). In the final analysis, this *Ur-Sache* is nothing other than the mythical image of life itself. As for the mythical worldview everything comes from life and returns to life, this *Ur-Sache* proves to be both the beginning and end, the alpha and omega, of everything that is.

The reduction performed by mythical consciousness results in a substantialization of meaning into a concrete and material manifestation. "The mythical fantasy drives toward animation, toward a complete 'spiritualization' of the cosmos; but the mythical *form of thought*, which attaches all qualities and activities, all states and relations to a solid foundation, leads to the opposite extreme: a kind of materialization of spiritual content" (*PSF*, II, p. 55/71 f.). This is why spirit is originally understood as "substance" and only in the course of its unfolding comes to understand itself also as "subject." However, it is important to emphasis that for Cassirer this materialization of spirit is not a secondary and essentially accidental factor in the process of the realization of spirit, but rather it is only by means of this mechanism of physical "transference" that spirit is able to achieve its visibility if not its reality. As we saw above, at the level of mythical signification the sensuous is completely impregnated and fused together with a spiritual meaning, and thus it signifies something that it is. The concrete life world of spirit is therefore wholly sensuous, and for this reason lived in the flesh more than in the mind—if such distinctions have any meaning here.

Myth as the Concrete Life World of Spirit

The mythical world is, however, more than a mode of thinking or a mode of presence. It is above all a form of action and even a series of actions that constitute a life. The fantastic stories and unreal images are only the "outer shell of myth" and have their roots in the cults and rituals of a myth.

> In the cult and the rite the mythic is itself still something lived; it is put into living action. In the legend it then becomes something enunciated and through this enunciation it attains a new objective distance. (*PSF*, IV, p. 91/88)

Cassirer distinguished between two dimension of myth. At first sight myth manifests itself in the form of a legend or fable that is repeated and acted out by a people. This "narrative" dimension of myth is only the external manifestation of the true heart of myth, it is only "a mediate interpretation of the part which resides immediately in the activity of man and in his feelings and will" (*PSF*, II, p. 39/51). This more profound dimension of mythical reality is not so much thought as performed.

> Seen in this light, rites are not originally "allegorical"; they do not have a merely copy or representative meaning but rather an absolutely *real* meaning (*realer Sinn*); they are so woven into the reality of action (*Realität des Wirkens*) as to form an indispensable part of it. . . . The cult is the true instrument by which man subjects the world, not so much in a spiritual as in a purely physical sense. (*PSF*, II, p. 39/51)

It is through such ritual action that spirit constitutes its concrete life world as an objective expression of that feeling of life which determines its own form of life. Again these actions are not so much something that mythical spirit does, but is; they form the very meaning of being alive.

The Templum of the Sacred

Although all the content of mythical consciousness is always in a state of constant "metamorphosis," there must nevertheless be one point that remains constant, a point from which this metamorphosis derives its unity and around which the various mythical rituals organize themselves. At the heart of these ritual activities and the mythical worldview is found the presence of the "sacred." The sacred, or more precisely the mythical image of the sacred, forms the structural schema according to which mythical consciousness organizes and constructs its world. It is the zero point of the emotive and effective life world of spirit. "All reality and all events are projected into the fundamental opposition between the 'sacred' and the 'profane,' and in this projection they assume a new meaning, one which they do not simply 'have' from the very beginning but which they acquire in this form of contemplation, one might say in this mythical 'illumination' " (*PSF*, II, p. 75/97). The sacred functions as the zero point from which the whole mythical world is hallowed. It is the Object x the image of which furnishes the schema that forms the life of spirit. The sacred is the *templum* that delimits the whole and internally differentiates it. The "*templum* (Greek τέμενος) goes back to the root τεμ, 'to cut,' and thus signifies that which is cut out, delimited" (*PSF*, II, p. 100/123). "The basic word τέμενος (*tempus*), *templum* signified nothing other than bisection, intersection: according to the terminology of the later carpenters two crossing rafters or beams still constituted a *templum*."[6] Through the *templum*, or more specifically the world that is opened up through its "contemplation," the god, the community, and the individual "make themselves at home (*heimisch*)" (*PSF*, II, p. 101/124). In this "homeland" (*Heimat*)—to employ Heidegger's term—the finite human being stands before the mythical figure of the sacred, and thus in the proximity of the "origins" of what "is," the life stream.[7] The sacred image is the "archetypal image" (*Ur-bild*) that constitutes the presence of the primordial cause (*Ur-Sache*) of everything, the source from which it has sprung. The world, which has been sanctified and constructed according to *templum*'s image, is thus the *temple* that houses the *templum*. And as the whole is in the part, the whole mythical world is found in the *temple* as the temple is the whole world.

The original source of mythical consciousness is the immediate awareness of the universality and fundamental identity of a unitary life stream. In its most rudimentary form, this life stream does not take on the form of a personal existence, it is not delimited and determined by a specific identity, as *a* life, but rather stands before consciousness as a "nameless presence" (*LM*, p. 71/134 f.), as the presence of the *mana*. The overwhelming nature of this presence to consciousness threatens to absorb consciousness into it (cf. *PSF*, III, p. 90/106). As what awakens consciousness, it fills it in such a way that the distinction between what is received in consciousness, the presencing of this nameless presence, and the receiving consciousness cannot be made. In this way, consciousness finds itself entangled in the fundamental paradox that shall forever determine it: for, on the one hand, it cannot stand before this nameless presence without at the same time losing itself in it, without fusing into an undifferentiated oneness with it, and thus ceasing to "be." Consciousness must therefore turn away from it and impose a "barrier" (*Schranke*) between itself and the sheer immediacy of the "unitary life stream" (*einheitlicher Lebensstrom*) (cf. " 'Spirit' and 'Life,' " p. 870/47). And yet on the other hand, it is only in the moment that it stands before this nameless presence that consciousness is awakened to the presence of the alterity of "something" that stands over against it, which is essentially different from it, and through this conscious awareness of the alterity of that which is given becomes self-conscious. It must, therefore, return to this nameless presence by overcoming the barrier that it itself has established, which divides and separates it form its origins. For only in this way can it rejuvenate itself. In mythical consciousness we witness the first "turning inward (*Innen-Wendung*) and becoming aware (*Inne-Werdung*)," which is essential to the emergence of self-consciousness (*PSF*, III, p. 90/106).

Now, etymologically the term μῦθος has its roots in the expression of "protest" or emotion, as the utterance of a "sobbing."[8] But a "protest" against what? What tragedy has brought about this "sobbing"? What primordial "experience" has awakened consciousness to itself, and given rise to the mythical figure and thus to the constitution of spirit as such? Death . . . or more precisely the anticipation and experience of death: "the whole of mythical thought may be interpreted as a constant and obstinate negation of the phenomenon of death" (*Essay*, p. 84). Consciousness is awakened to itself by a vital need. In the case of animals once this vital need has been fulfilled, consciousness returns again into the nothingness from which it arose—and with this all feeling of self and of the world collapses. In the case of human consciousness, however, these "elementary mythical experiences which rise up out of nothing and dissolve into nothing" are, as we have seen, conjoined with another force, the force of the image, of representation, and this image provides this experience with the stability or "unity of a *character*" (*PSF*, III, p. 91/107). Consciousness is thus not only awakened, but has become conscious of its own awakening, its own "*char-*

acter," its own existence, and subsequently of its own pending destruction—it anticipates and then, as it were, lives through its own death, and this experience is relived again and again. "The primary mythical 'condition' (*'Gegebenheit'*) is man divided and torn" (*PSF*, III, p. 90/106). On the one hand, consciousness is separated from its immediacy in the stream of life (*Lebensstrom*), and only in this way does it become something determined and enduring. On the other hand, isolated as it is from the stream of life, its existence is a lifeless one. It must reestablish its unity with life, rejuvenate itself in its origins. This, however, entails the paradoxical destruction of its determined and enduring "existence"—without which it is nothing. Consciousness, therefore, is caught up in an endless cycle of birth and death; a perpetual turning away and returning to its original source; an incessant construction and destruction of the life of consciousness. Mythical consciousness is unable to "reconcile" itself with death, with the "destruction of [its] personal existence." Death is thus "denied and 'explained away' by myth." "In mythical thought the mystery of death is 'turned into an image'—and by this transformation, death ceases being a hard unbearable physical fact; it becomes understandable and supportable" (*MS*, p. 49)—but only because it has been repressed. What mythical consciousness opposes to "the fact of death" is its "confidence in the solidarity, the unbroken and indestructible unity of life" (*Essay*, p. 86).

The tension is thus resolved, if only temporarily, through the differentiation and mediation of the mythical figure, in which the two poles are *aufgehoben*, sublated, taken up into a single concrete image, from which they also emerge. The presence of expression insofar as it is objectified into the mythical image contains "a revelation and at the same time retains a kind of *mystery*; it is this interpenetration, this revelation which both reveals and conceals, that gives the mythical-religious content its basic trait, its character of 'holiness' (*Heiligkeit*)" (*PSF*, II, p. 74/95; my emphasis). For this reason, that which possesses the character of "holiness (*Heiligkeit*) always appears *at once* as the distant and the near, as the familiar and protective but at the same time absolutely inaccessible, as the *mysterium tremendum* and the *mysterium fascinosum*" (*PSF*, II, p. 78/99). It is at once worldly and otherworldly—everything and yet nothing. It is from the presence of the mythical figure that the life world is "hallowed."

> That which is hallowed (*Geheiligte*) in a mythical and religious sense has thereby become forbidden, an object of awe, hence

> "unclean." This double meaning, this peculiar "ambivalence" is still expressed in the Latin "*sacer*" and the Greek ἅγιος, ἅζεσθαι, for these terms designate both the holy (*das Heilige*) and the accursed or forbidden, but in both cases something "consecrated" and set apart. (*PSF*, II, p. 79/100)

In the face of the concrete presence of the figure that represents the presence of that nameless presence which awakens consciousness to itself, everything is determined as being either sacred or profane, as consecrated or unconsecrated.

The Mythical Intuition of Space

"Just as space, time and number can be shown to be basic instruments and stages in the process of *objectivization*, so they also represent the three essential phases in the process of mythical 'apperception' " (*PSF*, II, pp. 81 f./103). Space is the first phase as it is through the spatial differentiation of language that the mythical world is first established. Mythical intuition is orientated toward the life stream, however this feeling of life only gains its concrete form through the representational force of language. From a certain perspective we can say that myth is the effect of language, insofar as it is through language that the entrance into "a life in meanings" is brought about and myth is precisely this life in meanings.

In keeping with its fusional logic of identity "the distinction between 'position' and 'content,' underlying the construction of 'pure' geometric space, has not yet been made and cannot be made" within the mythical worldview (*PSF*, II, p. 84/105). Everything has its place and in a sense is its place. "For mythical thinking the relation between what a thing 'is' and the place in which it is situated is never purely 'external' and accidental; the place is itself a part of the thing's being, the place confers very specific inner *relationships* upon the thing" (*PSF*, II, p. 92/115). The meaning of a mythical object is the place it occupies in the whole of the mythical world as an expression of its proximity to the sacred. The spatial world of myth proves to be thoroughly "*structural*, . . . regardless of how far we divide, we find in each part the form, the structure, of the whole" (*PSF*, II, p. 88 f./110). The whole dwells, we might say, in its holiness as a whole in each of the parts. Thus, one finds the structure of the whole cosmos is reflected in the structure of the city, in the structure of the home, and even in the structure of the dinner table. We may graphically represent this by way of the three images in figure 4.1.[9]

Figure 4.1

The first of the three images represents, if you will, the basic "model" or "structural law" of the spatial dimension of mythical consciousness as it is embodied in the whole of the cosmos. This structure is comprised of eight boxes that are arranged together in a square to form the whole, a unitary figure of a square in a square, an open courtyard. If in each of these parts there dwells the whole, then upon closer examination we will find that each of the original eight boxes making up the whole is itself comprised of eight boxes, which are, again, joined together in a square so as to form the unity of the model figure (a square in a square): this is represented in the second image, and again in the third . . . the process is, at least in theory, endless. The structure internally differentiates itself through its own repetition. Any one of the three images can represent either the structure of the cosmos as a whole or the structure of a single garden. The reader might object, however, that this simple geometrical figure falls short of the complexity of the real. The image is too symmetrical, too simple. And that perhaps a more adequate representation of the real might be an image such as that in figure 4.2.

Figure 4.2

In this image of a tree we discover a complexity of elements and movement that is closer to the complexity of nature and culture. Certainly the figure in figure 4.1 is simple, but it is not too simple, for it is from an equally simple configuration that the image in figure 4.2 has been generated.[10] Mythical space its created by means of the same repetition of one basic structure, which "manifest itself to us on an enlarged or reduced scale, but which, large or small remains the same" (*PSF*, II, p. 89/110).

> The primary spatial difference, which in the more complex mythical configurations is merely repeated over and over and increasingly sublimated, is this difference between two *provinces* of being: a common, general accessible province and another, sacred, precinct which seems to be raised out of its surroundings, hedged around and guarded against them. (*PSF*, II, p. 85/106)

The schema for this spatial structure comes form the mythical image of the sacred. In the same way that the human body is a three-dimensional spatial expression of its DNA structure, the mythical world proves to be a three-dimensional spatial expression of its unique feeling of life. The mythical world is thus only a "spatial projection of [a] general totemic view" (*PSF*, II, p. 87/110). Like the worker bee, we begin from the moment of birth to construct and order the world according to a given worldview that is given to us as a member of this or that culture.

The Temporal Structure of Myth

As important as these spatial differentiations are to the structure of the mythical worldview, we must go beyond its "mythical geography" (*PSF*, II, p. 93) to consider the true "interior" of this world, namely its intuition of time. For "myth seems to penetrate more deeply than language into time: it seems able to dwell in the original form of time, for it takes the world not as rigid being but as constant change; not as a finished form, but as an ever renewed metamorphosis" (*PSF*, III, p. 164/191). However, in keeping with its spiritual orientation, myth "can apprehend time only in the image of life, and consequently it must transpose and dissolve everything which moves in time, everything which comes and goes in set rhythm, into the form of life" (*PSF*, II, p. 110/136). Because mythical intuition knows nothing of the distinction between culture and nature, between the image of life and life itself, "mythical time is always conceived as the time both of the natural processes and of the events of human life: it is a biological-cosmic time" (*PSF*, II, p. 148/179). This "biological time" (cf. also *PSF*, II, p. 109/135) manifests itself in a "feeling of phases" that is punctuated by a basic motif that repeats itself in the same way that a motif repeats itself in a piece of music. "The 'holy days,' the times of festival, interrupt the uniform flow of life and introduce distinct lines of demarcation" (*PSF*, II, p. 108/134). Once again, we see that everything begins by the presence of the *templum* as the archetypal image of the whole of life. "The Latin *tempus* [time], to which corresponds the Greek τέμςνος and τέμςνος (preserved in the plural τέμπεα), grew out of the idea and designation of the *templum*" (*PSF*, II, p. 107/131). Thus here too it is through the repetition of a certain basic "temporal *Gestalt*" (*PSF*, II, p. 108/132)—namely, the *Gestalt* of the *templum*—that the uniform flow of time or life is punctuated and internally differentiated. The whole of mythical life is absorbed in, and in a sense springs from, the anticipation of these holy events and is *consecrated* to their preparation. The passage from one stage of this holy calendar to the next is governed by sacred rituals and "rites of passage."

Because mythical consciousness reduces all difference to identity, it continually reduces the past, the present, and the future into the simple moment of the "magical 'now' ": "The magical 'now' is . . . , to quote Leibniz, '*chargé du passé et gros de l'avenir*'—laden with the past and pregnant with the future" (*PSF*, II, p. 111/137). From a certain perspective mythical consciousness proves to be a " 'timeless' consciousness" (*PSF*, II, p. 106/131) for it possesses no explicit awareness of the passage from one well-determined moment to another. What is, is what is genuinely and fully present. Although mythical consciousness dwells in the magical moment of the present, there nevertheless remains a certain primacy of the past insofar as the event becomes holy only by being posited in a "superhistorical" institution of the past (*PSF*, II, p. 6/9). This past is an "absolute past" whose effect is lived in the present as the sacred and original meaning of the present. "The past itself has no 'why': it *is* the why of things" (*PSF*, II, p. 106/130). Everything that we call history, is nothing but the unfolding and rebirth of this original event; every historical event is only one stage in the retelling of the sacred story of the beginning as it was written in the beginning. Of course, this retelling of this history of the beginning "is not simply a repetition but rather a rebirth of the past: it implies a creative and constructive process" (*Essay*, p. 51).[11] Thus we see that "in the relationship between myth and history myth proves to be the primary, history the secondary and derived, factor. It is not by its history that the mythology of a nation is determined but, conversely, its history is determined by its mythology—or rather, the mythology of a people does not *determine* but *is* its fate, its destiny as decreed from the very beginning" (*PSF*, II, p. 5/8).

The Sacred Numbers

"Beside space and time, the third formal motif dominating the structure of the mythical world is *number*" (*PSF*, II, p. 140/169). However, when myth turns to the expression of numeric properties, it comes, like language, to the internal limits of its proper mode of expression and thus to the threshold of a new spiritual force: "in mythical thinking [number] appears as a vehicle of specifically religious *interpretation*" (*PSF*, II, p. 143/173). The positing of number brings out the contradiction inherent within the mythical worldview. For, on the one hand, in keeping with its basic character it reduces all similarity to identity. Everything that possesses the same number is understood to be essentially "the same," thus seeing the differences between the objects as only a difference in appearance (cf. *PSF*, II, p. 142/172). However, on the other hand, in recognizing the number of a thing to be its "truth" transcending its "appearances," myth has broken with its own worldview. For now something that is present is measured by something that is not.

> Mythical number stands then at a spiritual turning point—it too strives to escape from the narrowness and confinement of the immediate sensuous material world view to a freer, more universal view. . . . [I]t is like Plato's Eros, the "great intermediary," by which the earthly and divine, the mortal and immortal, communicate with each other and are composed into the unity of a world order (*durch den Irdisches und Göttliches, Sterbliches und Unsterbliches miteinander verkehrt und sich zur Einheit einer Weltordnung zusammenfaßt*). (*PSF*, II, p. 144/174)

Once again it is important to remember that as yet there is no distinguishing between the human world and life as such. Here too, each number possesses a specific holy character that reflects its place in the whole process of life. The numbers are limited to a few basic whole numbers. Let us consider the first few elementary numbers.

> For one, two, and three we everywhere find examples of such hypostases, not only in the thinking of primitive people but also in the great cultural religions. The problem of the unity (*Einheit*) [the number 1], which emerges from itself, which becomes "another" ("*andere*") second entity [the number 2], and is ultimately reunited with itself in a third [the number 3]—this problem [these three numbers] belongs to the common cultural heritage of mankind. (*PSF*, II, p. 145/174)

That all reality is triadic, nothing could be more self-evident to the Western mind. The history of spirit, if not its very being, is for Cassirer, as it was for Hegel, a history by which spirit comes to know itself. Everything begins when that which is in-itself (*an-sich*) differentiates and becomes other, an object for-itself (*für-sich*), in order to then recognize itself in and by the alterity of its own difference to itself and thus become consciousness of itself as a differentiated reality, that is to say, something in and for itself (*an-und-für-sich*). The primordial structure of "history" for Cassirer, as for Hegel can be schematized as in figure 4.3.

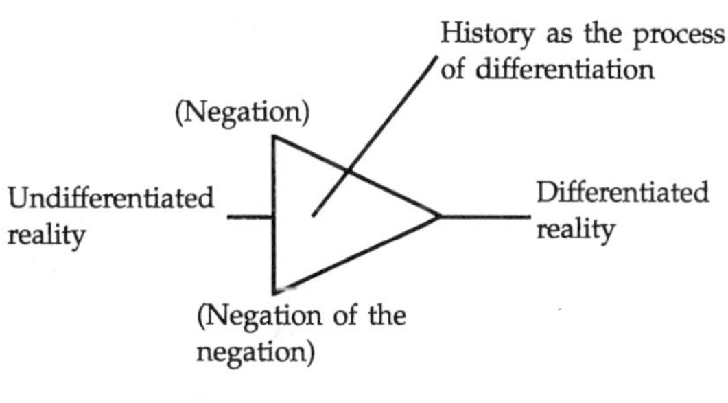

Figure 4.3

It is, however, above all the number four which proves to be "the 'sacred number' par excellence: for in it is expressed precisely this relation between every particular reality and the fundamental form of the universe" (*PSF*, II, p. 147/177). Everything within the mythical world possesses a "fourfold (*vierfältige*) organization": man stands on the earth, as a mortal, beneath the celestial heavens before the immortals (cf. *PSF*, III, p. 164/192, and *PSF*, II, p. 144/174). The space between the earth and heaven is divided into four cardinal directions of north, south, east, and west; to each direction there corresponds one of the four elements from which everything is composed and one of the four seasons of the year: "To the north belongs the air, to the south fire, and to the east earth, to the west water; the north is the home of winter, the south of summer, the east of autumn, the west of spring" (*PSF*, II, p. 87/108). The "veneration of the number four is expressed in the worship of the form of the cross, which is attested as one of the oldest religious symbols" (*PSF*, II, p. 147/177). Once again, we find ourselves before the *templum* which, as we said, originally "signified nothing other than bisection" or "two crossing rafters or beams." In Christianity, for example, each end of the cross represents one of the "four zones of Heaven, [and is] equated with certain phases of the Christian story of salvation" (*PSF*, II, p. 148/178).

It is not difficult to be reminded here of Heidegger's concept of the fourfold.[12] As Heidegger writes: "Out of the fourfold, the simple onefold of the four is ventured. This appropriating mirror-play of the simple onefold of earth and sky, divinities and mortals, we call the world."[13] The primordial structure of the "world" for Cassirer as for Heidegger can be schematized as in figure 4.4.[14]

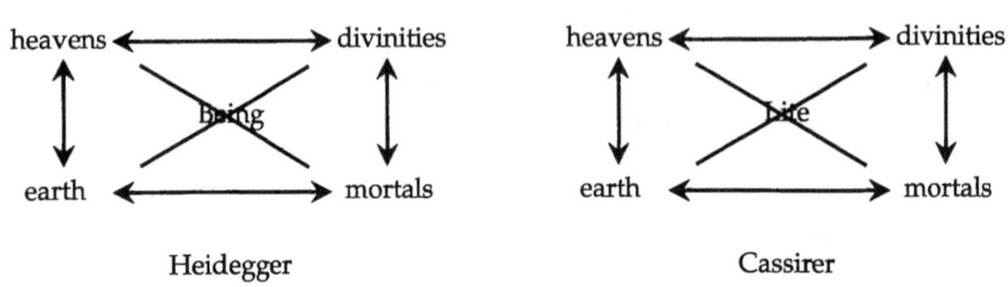

Figure 4.4

We need not enter here into the rich anthropological detail of Cassirer to demonstrate this structure. However, it should be asked whether or not this similarity in structure is not rather an accidental and illusory coincidence of content? Cassirer seems to argue that this is not:

> The fact that similar systems are found all over the world shows that what we have here is not an isolated offshoot of mythical thinking but one of its typical fundamental intuitions—not a mere content of mythical thinking but one of its determining factors. (*PSF*, II, p. 87 n3/109 n1)

The Subject of Myth as the Myth of the Subject

"It would not be possible to speak of a *discovery* of the subjective reality in myth if the widespread view that the concept of the I and the soul were the *beginning* of all mythical thinking were justified" (*PSF*, II, p. 155/185). In other words, the personal subject, the I, is not the source of myth but its result. Man is not born with an ego, but acquires one in and through the cultural process and in this myth plays a major role. The subject of myth will prove to be the myth of the subject. It is through the imaginary identity with the *Ur-Sache* that the subject acquires a place, or better inscribes itself within the system of cultural meaning, and thus the unity of an enduring and meaningful existence.

We can perhaps already ask ourselves in what way the mythical subject is different from the animal. From a certain perspective there is no difference. We have already seen that Cassirer characterizes the mythical world as a biological one. Although the movement from the animal world of nature to the human world of meaning involves the transition from the "circle of action" to the "circle of vision," we have already seen that the mythical world remains intrinsically a world of action and performance. The difference is found in the fact that "the animal *performs* these actions, but it does not stand apart from them and is not able to regard them objectively, either individually or as a whole" (*PSF*, IV, p. 76/74), whereas man objectively reflects upon his actions—man, but not mythical man. Mythical consciousness places the emphasis on the performance of action, and not on the contemplation of the nature of action as such. The mythical subject is, as Lacan would say, "less subject than subjected"—subjected to the empty place, that is to say, to the presence of the sacred (cf. above, p. 55). Where then is the difference between the two found? In all its actions the animal is never anything more than a concrete expression of its species. It sees the world and reacts to the world in a way typical of its species, according to the program that is inscribed in its flesh. Certainly, each animal possesses a certain feeling of self, but this self-affectivity remains bound to its general feeling of life, and never develops the idea of self that constitutes an ego. Each animal is a little different from every other, but the differences in their nature are accidental and thus of little importance. Its will is always the will of the species applied to a given situation. The animal can never transcend its immanent being-in-the-world and thus can never become self-conscious of its self. This feeling of self, this self-affectivity that is the most basic characteristic of consciousness—understood in the most general sense of the word—becomes self-consciousness only at the moment that it not only becomes an object for itself, but recognizes in this object its own self-affectivity, its own feeling of self. For it is only at this moment that the whole is in the part and the part in the whole: for it is only now that there stands before consciousness a presence that not only represents the concrete expression of the unity of consciousness, over against which it stands as something present, but which its itself self-conscious. "Thus consciousness is a consciousness of objects insofar as it is self-consciousness—and it is self-consciousness only in and by virtue of the fact that it is a consciousness of objects" (*PSF*, IV, p. 66/64). The whole cultural process represents nothing other than this movement from the concrete feeling of self or the concrete self-affectivity of the living entity, to the self-consciousness existence of the individual. The mythical process is but the first step in this movement. Here we might say that the subject acquires its identity in the "mirror of culture" without yet being able to distinguish its image from itself.

Cassirer's Reading of Freud's Theory of the Oedipus

Cassirer's theory of subject of myth is, in the final analysis, a theory of the affectivity and emotions. In *The Myth of the State* Cassirer considers the general theory of emotions developed by Freud—and, it should be said, with some favor. His reading of Freud is, however, a critical and interpretative one. As one knows, for Freud the "source of the totemistic system was the dread of incest" (*MS*, p. 32). Freud draws an analogy between the two fundamental commandments of all totemism—namely, the taboo against killing the totem animal and the taboo against sexual relations with women of the same totem—and the crimes of Oedipus who killed his father and married his mother. Thus, for Freud culture is only the "eternal story of man's sexual life" (*MS*, p. 35).

> For prehistoric times to the present man was always haunted by the same two fundamental wishes. The wishes to kill one's father and to marry one's mother appear in the childhood of the human race just as it appears, in the strangest disguises and transformations, in the life of every individual child. (*MS*, p. 35 f.)

Cassirer's critique of Freud is twofold. The essential critique concerns Freud's methodology. Freud falls victim to the myth of the given, insofar as he focuses upon the content of myth rather than upon its structural form and function. It is "not enough simply to know the *subject-matter* of myth in order to understand its character and nature" (*MS*, p. 33). The content of a myth does not give us its meaning, but rather it is only through an interpretation of this content that we can arrive at an understanding of the function of myth and thus at its true meaning. Freud takes the facts as given, but facts are meaningless without interpretation. Thus, Freud understands the myth of Oedipus too literally, reading it to mean that we desire to kill our actual father and sleep with our actual mother. Freud understands the event of Oedipus as a real event—which is itself a mythical perspective. We have already seen how the theory of myth is in the final analysis a myth of theory—"after a few decades," concludes Cassirer, "the sex myths will share the fate of the solar or lunar myths" (*MS*, p. 35). Cassirer's second critique concerns the facts of Freud's theory themselves. For according to the anthropological studies of such anthropologists as Frazer, Spencer, and Gillen not only are the institutions of totemism and exogamy distinguishable and separable, but "the evidence of the tradition seems even to point back to a time when a man always married a women of his own totem."[15]

Upon rereading Cassirer's critique of Freud and the analysis of the function of myth in the life of spirit that follows, it would seem that Cassirer nevertheless develops his own theory of Oedipus. For Cassirer the myth, the narrative part of the myth, is not a mere work of fantasy, a fiction without truth. Rather to the contrary, "the legend is not a mere fairy tale. It has a *fundamentum in re*; it refers to a certain 'reality.' But this reality is neither physical nor historical; it is *ritual* [and thus, we might add, symbolic]. What is *seen* in the . . . cult is *explained* in the myth" (*MS*, p. 42). The question, then, is what is "*explained*" in the myth of Oedipus? Insofar as myth is the concrete expression of structure, the myth of Oedipus explains the nature of the relation of the particular, living, and concrete subject to the structural law of culture that constitutes this subject as subject. It explains, as we have seen again and again in this chapter, the origins of "culture" as the "process of the framing (*Gestaltung*) and forming (*Bildung*) [which] removes us more and more from the originality of life" (*PSF*, I, p. 113/59)—and this in and through the "archetypal image" (*Ur-bild*) (*PSF*, II, p. 240/287) that "imprints" itself in consciousness (cf. *PSF*, II, p. 75/95) through its "anticipation" in the future (*PSF*, III, p. 276/323) and thus "pre-forms" (*vor-bilden*) it (*Logic*, p. 30).[16] It is the question of the "transition" from "life" to "culture," or from the life of nature to the life of spirit, and the formation of the person or subject of culture that this transformation assumes. In the following, one can read in the "margins"[17] the presence of the Freudian theory of Oedipus.[18]

The Birth of the Subject . . .

"The birth of man is a mythical not a physical act" (*MS*, p. 38). That is to say, it is a symbolic act that constitutes the meaning of the subject's existence. It is from the act of intentionality de*sign*ed to achieve a *desired* affect, or better from the "rule of this action" that the spiritual formation of reality, and thus the constitution of a subject of action, first arises (cf. *PSF*, II, p. 201/224). And although it is, as we shall see, desire that entices action, it is above all the sacred action of the ritual, and more specifically the structural law determining this action prescribed by the *Ur-Sache* that gives desire its concrete form: for the "form is always, not the desire for action, but action itself."[19] In the last chapter we have already seen that everything begins from desire, and that the essential difference between animal desire and human desire is found in the nature of the object that is desired.

> The first energy by which man places himself as an independent being in opposition to things is that of *desire* (*Wunsch*). In desire he no longer simply accepts the world and the reality of things but builds (*aufbauen*) them up for himself. It is man's first and most primitive consciousness of his ability to *form* (*Fähigkeit zur Gestaltung*) reality that moves itself in desire (*das sich im Wunsche regt*). And since this consciousness permeates all "inward" as well as "outward" intuition, all reality seems subjected to it. There is

> no existing thing and no occurrence which must not ultimately submit to the "omnipotence of thought" [quoted from Freud, *Totem and Taboo*] and the omnipotence of desire. Thus, in the magical world view the I exerts almost unlimited sway over reality; it takes all reality back into itself. But precisely this immediate equating (*In-Eins-Setzung*) of I and reality involves a peculiar dialectic in which the original relation is reversed. The enhanced feeling of self (*Selbstgefühl*) which seems to express itself in the magical world view indicates actually that at this stage there is as yet no true self (*Selbst*). Through the magical omnipotence of the will the I seeks to seize upon all things and bend them to its purpose; but precisely in this attempt it shows itself still totally dominated, totally "possessed," by things. (*PSF*, II, p. 157 f./ 187 f.)

Strictly speaking, however, mythical consciousness is not "totally 'possessed' by things," but by a very specific *thing* (*Sache*), by the sacred figure of the *Ur-Sache,* which represents the presence of the mana, and which constitutes the structural law that opens up the worldview of myth and provides it with its center. And more precisely still, it is not the *Ur-Sache* itself, but rather its "image" that overcomes mythical consciousness. We have already seen that in the mythical intuition "the image . . . asserts a peculiar primacy over the thing (*Sache*)" (*PSF*, II, p. 240/287): "in the image [mythical consciousness] possesses the essence, the soul, of the object" (*PSF*, III, p. 69/81). In mythical consciousness there is "no difference between the 'archetype' (*Urbild*) and the 'image' (*Abbild*) as such" (*PSF*, II, p. 240/287). Thus, in the final analysis, that which "possesses" mythical consciousness is not so much the *Ur-Sache* as the *Ur-Bild,* which constitutes the mythical image of the *Ur-Sache,* thus providing it with its presence and above all its form. Everything that possesses mythical significance, which has been raised up from the common everyday world to take on a meaning, does so through its proximity to this original and primordial figure, the *Ur-Bild*—of course from the perspective of mythical consciousness the *Ur-Bild* is taken for the *Ur-Sache,* and thus what is "seen" is simply the concrete presence of the *Ur-Sache.* The mythical figure (*Gestalt*) of the sacred serves two essential functions, and it is important that they be clearly distinguished. On the one hand, it functions to represent the nameless presence of the life stream out of which everything arises and back into which everything must return. In the sacred figure the subject recognizes its own self-affectivity, its own feeling of life, and through this the life stream. On the other hand, the mythical figure provides the "structural law" that gives life its form and thus renders this feeling of life into the intuition of a life form. The former is, if you will, the object of desire, whereas the latter is the law of desire insofar as it is the structural law or "rule of action" that determines the general direction or attitude of our sacred action and thus our active relation to the sacred *Ur-Sache*.

The Sacred *Ur-Sache* as the Object and Law of Desire

Desire is the first energy by which spirit organizes reality, but what is desired? And what is the relation between desire and this *Ur-Sache*? We have already seen that the structure of animal desire prefigures that of human desire. The animal's "feeling of self" (*Selbstgefühl*) is aroused by the presence of an object that signifies for it some vital need. The object stands over against the animal as the exteriorization of an internal *disorder*. However, once this essentially biological need has been fulfilled through the interiorization of its external representation, the disorder is overcome and its feeling of self returns into the nothingness from which it arose, and with this the animal's awareness of itself and its world once again collapses into an undifferentiated unity of simple existence, into the "immediate unity which . . . units 'observing' (*Bemerken*) and 'effecting' (*Bewirken*)" (" 'Spirit' and 'Life,' " p. 869/45). As we have just seen, consciousness becomes self-consciousness in the moment that it rejects this return into the undifferentiated unity with the life stream, the nameless presence of self-affectivity, the nothingness from which it arose—in other words, in and through its rejection of its imminent death in absolute immanence. Man is that being who *says* no (*'Neinsagenkönner'*) to the overwhelming presence of life—who negates it by crossing it out, ~~Life~~. However, man is also that being who "is" only by turning upon himself and negating its ~~self~~ in a reciprocal return to life (cf. " 'Spirit' and 'Life,' " p. 877/55)—of course, the negation or thrusting away of life is the condition of possibility of any return. Within the makeup of self-consciousness there exists a certain paradoxical tension between the demand to establish a "barrier" (" 'Spirit' and 'Life,' " p. 870/47) between itself and the sheer reality of the life stream, on the one hand, and the need to overcome this barrier and reestablish the immediate unity with it, on the other. Human desire originates from the conflict between the two demands, between the centrifugal force of thrusting away that establishes distance and thus the alterity of difference, on the one hand, and the centripetal force of return that establishes the unity of identity, on the other. The tension finds its solution in the mythical image. The mythical figure gives the feeling of life its objective form, and thus determines the specific attitude that will characterize a particular culture, a particular *Weltanschauung*. Thus, what is desired is unity: "It is a deep and ardent desire of the individuals to identify themselves with the life of the community and with the life of nature" (*MS*, p. 38). The mythical figure represents the objectification of this desire. It is *"le désir collectif personnifié"* (the collective desire personified). And it is through the imaginary identification with this personification of desire that the individual subject gains its "alter ego" (*PSF*, II, p. 42/56), its *persona* in the etymological sense of the word that goes back to the mask of the actor. However, at this first stage "the *feeling of self* is immediately fused with the *feeling of community*. The I feels and knows itself only insofar as it takes itself as a member of a community, insofar as it sees itself grouped with others into the unity of a family, a tribe, a social organism" (*PSF*, II, p. 175/209). And as there is no distinction between the natural order of life and the cultural domain of historical meaning, this identity is felt and lived as the very meaning of *Dasein*. Between spirit and being, culture and life, there exists an organic unity in which the two are fused together by the "sympathy of the Whole," by the "sameness" of their "real identity" (*Essay*, p. 94).

The Mother: The Object of Desire

It is necessary to consider the way in which the object of desire manifests itself in myth. Again we return to the structural moment of the transition from nature to culture.

> The cries of discomfort, of pain and hunger, of fear or fright, which we find throughout the organic world begin to assume a new shape. They are no longer simple instinctive reactions, for they are employed in a more conscious and deliberate way. When left alone

> the child demands by more or less articulate sounds the presence of its nurse or mother, and it becomes aware that these demands have the desired effect. Primitive man transfers this first elementary social experience to the totality of nature. (*Essay*, p. 110)

The mythical figure, the *Ur-Sache* represents the stream of life from which all things arise, and into which all things return. At this point, nature—coming from the Latin *nasci*, "to be born"—as that which is essentially other to consciousness, appears as the "great and benign mother, the divine lap from which all life originates" (*Essay*, p. 100). It is in and through the sacred action of the ritual that individual consciousness overcomes the separation and "immerses itself in the stream of universal life, . . . to be absorbed in the whole of nature" (*MS*, p. 41). The feeling of the natural and magical solidarity of all life has won over that which separates and isolates the individual from the source of life, from "*Mother Earth*" ("*Mutter Erde*") (*PSF*, II, p. 190/227). There is a primordial "fusion" (*Verschmelzung*) among the parts into a whole, as each individual in the tribe is the concrete expression of the mythical figure, the totem, which constitutes the tribe as a whole through the determination of their real identity (cf. *PSF*, II, p. 181/216). Through the presence of the mythical figure, mythical consciousness is given an "idea of life" (*PSF*, II, p. 188/225) and this image functions to condense and objectify its feeling of life (*Lebensgefühl*) to the point that the particular self-consciousness is freed from its "*particularity*" and is able to return to the stream of life. "This liberation is achieved in wild, orgiastic dances which restore man's identity with the original source of life. Here we have no mere mythical-religious *interpretation* of the natural process but an immediate union with it, an authentic drama which the . . . subject experiences in himself. The mythical *narrative* is for the most part merely an outward reflection of this inner process, a light veil behind which this drama is apparent" (*PSF*, II, p. 189/225 f.; cf. also *MS*, p. 41). Through the sacred ritual the particular overcomes the separation between itself and the universal by fusing together with it, by identifying itself with it and becoming it. The ritual act is no mere make-believe. In the enacting of the drama the dancer does not represent the mythical figure, the totem, the god of the clan, but rather *becomes* the god.[20]

> This basic sense of identity, of identification, is manifested most particularly in fertility rites celebrating the death and resurrection

> of the god. What happens in these rites . . . is no mere imitative *representation* (*Darstellung*) of an event but is the *event* itself and its immediate *execution*. (*PSF*, II, p. 39/52)

The Father: As the Law of Desire . . .

Thus, "by a first act of identification man asserts his fundamental unity with his human or animal ancestors—by a second act he identifies his own life with the life of nature. As a matter of fact there can be no sharp distinction between the two realms" (*MS*, p. 38 f.). In the preceding section it is the unity of the individual with the source of life, with the symbolic mother, that has been emphasized. But what of the unity of the individual with the ancestors, or forefathers of the tribe? What is the function of the father? If the earth is the mother, and this is so even for Plato,[21] then according to the fourfold structure of the mythical world, it would seem that the father, as the counterpart of the mother would be the heaven. And in fact, in a great many religions we find that " 'Mother Earth' (*'Muttter Erde'*) is juxtaposed to 'Father Heaven' (*'Vater Himmel'*)" (*PSF*, II, p. 191/228). The reason why the mother and the earth should be conjoined together into the mythical figure that symbolizes the *mana*, the source of life from which everything is born and grows, is rather obvious.[22] The presence and function of the Father in the birth of man is, however, less obvious, for the simple reason that at this stage in the development of mythical thought, "the laws of sexual procreation are unknown. Birth is, therefore, always regarded as a sort of reincarnation" (*MS*, p. 39; cf. also *PSF*, II, p. 180/215). What is "reincarnated" in the act of birth is the totem that constitutes the real identity between the individual and the tribe, and the tribe and the original source of life. Each member of the tribe is a descendant of the totem (cf. *Essay*, p. 82 f.). However, the emphasis here is on the relationship and bond that is established between the part and the whole as the expression of the identity of the whole, rather than on the process of descendance as such.

> [T]he unity of a particular totemic group does not rest on the way in which the members of the group are reproduced; rather, the process of generation presupposes this unity of the group. For

> the totemic spirits enter into such women as they have recognized as essentially akin to them. (*PSF*, II, p. 183 n15/219 n1)

This identification between the tribe and its totem should not be seen as representing a general phenomenon of identification between the clan and nature in general, but rather as representing a specific identification between a specific clan and a specific totem. Each *particular* clan, as a particular clan, possesses its own *particular* totem—within each clan, the subdivision into different classes of activities (warriors, hunters, farmers, . . .) will be differentiated through the system of totems, each subdivision possesses its own totem.

> [In] the choice of a totem animal . . . a specific life attitude and spiritual attitude is represented and objectified . . . the relationship between the clan itself and its totem animal is so close that it is hard to decide whether the clan chooses a particular totem animal according to its own character or whether it has not rather molded itself according to the character of the animal; warlike clans and occupations correspond to wild, powerful animals and peaceful clans and occupations to tame animals. It would seem as though the clan saw itself objectively in its totem animal, as though it recognized its nature, its particularity, its basic trend of action in the animal. (*PSF*, II, p. 186/222 f.)

The emphasis here is on the *"basic trend of action."* It is the nature of the action that constitutes the relation of the clan to its totem. As with the animal that must interiorize the object of its desire so as to restore its unity and thus revitalize itself, the clan must also regularly consume its totem. Though the consumption of the totem animal brings about its physical destruction, it is reincarnated in and through the members of the clan. In fact, it is only in the ritual destruction of the physical existence of the totem, that its spiritual meaning arises: "the spiritualization of the sensuous through the act of sacrifice results directly in a sensualization of the spiritual. The sensuous is destroyed in its existence and physical being (*Das Sinnliche wird seiner Existenz, seinem physischen Dasein nach vernichtet*). . . . Only by being slain and eaten is the sacrificial animal enabled to serve as an 'intermediary' (*Mittler*) between the individual and his clan and between the clan and its god" (*PSF*, II, p. 228/273). Whereas the animal consumes the object of its desire in order to restore its own individual life, in the case of self-consciousness "the true accent of the sacral act is on the performance by the community as a *whole*. In the eating of the flesh of the totem animal the unity of the clan, its relationship with its totemic ancestor, is restored as a sensuous and corporeal unity; we may say that in this feast it is restored forever anew" (*PSF*, II, p. 227/271 f.). Through this "communion" with its god, the totem "who passes as the father of the clan," the unity of the whole which determines its identity as a whole is established (*PSF*, II, p. 227/272). It is the simultaneous and harmonized obedience of all the particulars of the whole to the law of the totem that determines the order of things, and thus determines the whole of which the particulars are only the immediate concrete expression, establishes their belonging together as one. The structural law of the ritual act, its "rule of action," brings together, as it differentiates the members of the whole. Here, nature, as that which is brought about in and through the lawful "communion" with the totem, is "seen" as the "sphere of law and lawfulness. And by this feature alone it proves its divine origin" (*Essay*, p. 100). As Hegel writes:

> To realize this unity, the reconciliation, restoration of the subject, and his self-consciousness, to bring about a positive feeling of participation in that absolute and a unity with it—this transcendence of the separation constitutes the sphere of the cult.[23]

The Law of the Taboo and the Reign of Fear

The "rule of action" imposed by the taboo upon the individual is absolute. What counts in the mythical world is the unquestioned, unwavering obedience to the law. It must be remembered that the law is not seen as a historically contingent social convention, but rather as belonging to the natural order of things. To fail to adhere to the law through the execution of rite can only result, as the myth of Oedipus clearly shows, in the destruction of the natural order.[24] "The very survival of the world depends upon the correct execution of rites" (*PSF*, II, p. 39/51). The taboo governs through fear, the fear of the end of the world, the fear of death. Every aspect of social life is governed by taboos whose sovereignty is absolute and unquestionable. The individual accepts this situation because this is the way things are and have been from the beginning, as it was decreed in the beginning. It is the destiny of things and of the individual: for "the whole of a man's life is contained and decided in its beginning, in the constellation of the hour of his birth" (*PSF*, II, p. 89/111). More precisely, in the moment of initiation into the tribe, which marks the death of the natural entity and the birth of a spiritual one, an event brought about and marked by the ritual of receiving of one's name. The transformation from the biological to the social realm that "seemed to free the spirit from the fetters of things becomes a new fetter which is all the stronger since it is not a mere physical force but a spiritual one" (*PSF*, II, p. 24/32). However, "the taboo system threatens to make the life of man a burden that in the end becomes unbearable. Man's whole existence, physical and moral, is smothered under the continual pressure of this system. It is here that religion intervenes" (*Essay*, p. 108). The taboo system at the heart of myth brings about its own "disavowal." Mythical consciousness comes to its logical conclusion, in the moment of its own self-negation, its own internal transformation: within its own essence are found "the immanent conditions for its own future sublation (*Aufhebung*); it contains the potentiality of a spiritual process of liberation which is indeed effected in the progress from the *magicalmythical* world view to the truly *religious* view" (*PSF*, II, p. 25 f./32).

Five

Religion: The "Logic of Absurdity" and the Intuition of the ~~Real~~

"Credo quia abusrdem"

"Religion" as a Symbolic Form

In the context of the philosophy of symbolic forms, "religion" is to be understood exclusively in terms of its *differentia specifica* as a symbolic form. We are not concerned, therefore, with the content of any particular historical manifestation, but rather only with determining the structural law that constitutes the unique perspective and specific function of religion within the whole of culture. In the case of language we began from the implicit agreement that although there exists a number of different languages, each constituting its own particular perspective of the world, there nevertheless remains a perspective particular to language as such; and subsequently, that every language, insofar as it provides a concrete expression of the universal form of language, possesses equal dignity as a language. However, insofar as "religion" is concerned with the revelation of *the* truth, it would seem that there can only be one true religion, for there is only one truth. The truth of religious consciousness is by its very nature absolute and unique, and therefore exclusive—all other religions, apart from the "one" true religion, must by definition be denounced as primitive superstition or at the very least qualified as a preparatory stage in the unfolding of the one true religion, and thus lacking in some respect. To undertake a philosophy of religion, certainly in the context of the philosophy of symbolic forms, is to a certain degree to relativize the uniqueness and exclusivity of the religious perspective. For we begin, as we did in the case of language, from the presupposition that there are a number of different religions, and that each of these historical manifestations, insofar as it provides an authentic concrete expression of the universal structure of religious consciousness, possesses equal dignity as a true religion: there is not, therefore, one true religion, but rather many. There remains, nevertheless, only one truth, for the truth is the whole. Let us, therefore, not be too eager here to pay homage to the plurality of difference. Admittedly it is tempting in our intellectual epoch to acknowledge the individual autonomy of different religions, to respect the uniqueness and difference of the other, and thus to relativize their unique claim to *the* truth. However, religion is not a question of personal taste, but rather of "life or death" (*MS*, p. 48), "to be or not to be, that is the question," the existential question that lies at the heart of religious consciousness—the truth of religion, therefore, cannot be relativized without at the same time being destroyed. Religion truthfully speaks the truth, or it is nothing. However, as we shall see, "not the whole truth, because there's no way to say it all. Saying it all is literally impossible: words fail. Yet it's through this very impossibility that the truth holds onto the real."[1] Thus, we are not interested here in establishing any one specific religion as the ideal and true religion, nor are we interested in undertaking a comparative study of the contents of different religions. Rather, as has already been said, our aim is to establish the structure and function of religion as a symbolic form. On the one hand, it is accepted that there is a plurality of religions, each of which must be considered as an authentic expression of religious consciousness. On the other, it is equally acknowledged that in its concrete expression the truth of religion is, and must be universal, and therefore exclusive. Here I can only present Cassirer's theory of religion as a symbolic form. As to whether or not the theory corresponds to the reality of religious experience, this I must leave to the reader's own religious sensibility—in the end this seems to me to be the only viable approach to a "philosophy of religion."[2]

Cassirer's "Philosophy of Religion"?

Cassirer's treatment of religion is closely integrated with his treatment of myth. In fact, so closely that at first sight it would seem that religious consciousness is for Cassirer nothing more than an extension and final stage of mythical consciousness possessing no autonomy as a symbolic form. Although we find numerous references to "mythical-religious" or "religious" consciousness throughout Cassirer's writings, and especially in the second volume of the *Philosophy of Symbolic Forms*, we find no single work explicitly devoted to religion as a symbolic form. In *An Essay on Man* myth and religion are also treated together in the same chapter. Cassirer's most extensive and explicit analysis of religion appears in the final part of the second volume devoted to myth and is entitled *"Die Dialektik des mythischen Bewusstseins"* ("The Dialectic of Mythical Consciousness").[3] As there is no work exclusively devoted to religion as a symbolic form, we are forced to decipher the meaning of religion through a reading of these texts that primarily deal with myth.

The chapter is divided into three parts. The first section, "The *Differentia Specifica* of Religion as a Symbolic Form," sets out to determine the basic synchronic structure and function of religion as a symbolic form. The second section, "The Diachronic Unfolding of Religion," follows religion in its diachronic unfolding as it struggles to free itself from its mythical foundations and come to its full realization and expression. The third section, "The Sacrifice: 'From Spell to Prayer,' " considers, if you will, the mechanism of this transformation from myth to religion from the perspective of the concrete activity that constitutes it.

The *Differentia Specifica* of Religion as a Symbolic Form

The *Differentia Specifica* of Religion

Religion embodies both a "theoretical" and a "practical" dimension. "It contains a cosmology and an anthropology; it answers the question of the origin of the world and the origin of human society. And from this origin it derives man's duties and obligations" (*Essay*, p. 94). These different elements are "fused together" into a basic intuition of the natural order of things and of man's place in this order, which gives expression to the fundamental religious belief in the "sympathy of the Whole" (*Essay*, p. 95). However, myth also provides us with an answer to the question of the origin (*Ur-Sache*) of the world and of man; myth too derives from this origin the dutiful activity of the individual; myth too is grounded in a belief in the "sympathy of the Whole." Both prove to be expressions of the same primordial "awareness of the unity and fundamental identity of life" (*MS*, p. 37), the intuitive insight that the whole dwells in each of its parts. Wherein lies, then, the *differentia specifica* of religion as a symbolic form? The essential difference between the two lies in the fact that the intuition of the individuality of particular self-consciousness is in myth fused together with the intuition of the universal, with the intrinsic "unity and fundamental identity of life"; whereas in religious consciousness it transcends and thus stands over against the intuition of the intrinsic "unity and fundamental identity of life." As we have seen, in myth the individual "subject" is understood exclusively in terms of its position in the whole as an expression of the structural law of the whole, as a "link in the chain of life as a whole" (*PSF*, II, p. 194/233). Here, "the I feels and knows itself only insofar as it takes itself as a member of a community" and "only in and through this social organism does it possess itself; every manifestation of its own personal existence and life is linked . . . with the life of the totality around it" (*PSF*, II, p. 175/209). Religious sympathy, on the other hand, "gives scope for a new feeling, that of individuality" (*Essay*, p. 96). The move from a "*mythical-magical* world view to the truly *religious* world view" marks the self-awakening and "liberation" of spirit (*PSF*, II, p. 25/32), or in more Hegelian terms, the transition by which "spiritual reality" is no longer apprehended and expressed as "substance" but " 'equally as subject' " (*PSF*, II, p. 26/34). It involves the discovery of the individuality of particular self-consciousness, the discovery of the individual's true self, the I, standing over against the whole. And thus, it marks the transition "from mythos to ethos" (*PSF*, II, p. 168/200): for "man achieves his true I through the idea of self-responsibility" (*PSF*, II, p. 173/206). "Only when man's vision passes beyond the sphere of life to that of ethical action, beyond the biological to the ethical sphere, does the unity of the I gain primacy over the substantial or semisubstantial notion of the soul" (*PSF*, II, p. 166/198). And, as we shall see, the discovery of the true self involves the recognition of the alterity of the other, the thou, and most specifically of the Divine Other, "for the I, man's true 'self,' finds itself only through the detour of the divine I" (*PSF*, II, p. 205/245), through the recognition of a power that transcends the magical influence of the omnipotence of the desire and thought (cf. *PSF*, II, p. 223/267). Religion, therefore, marks the spirit's recognition of the real beyond its own subjective sphere. It is the moment in which spirit turns back on itself and negates its own objective expression in order to realize its true essence.

The Antinomy of Religious Thought

In the opposition between the religious intuition of the unity and identity of life and the universal sympathy of the Whole, on the one hand, and its awareness of the determined "individuality" of *a* particular life, on the other, there is found the essential paradox, if not contradiction, that constitutes the basic essence of religious consciousness: for the feeling of "individuality" that is postulated here implies at the same time "a negation or at least a restriction of that universality of feeling that is postulated by religion: *omnis determinatio est negatio*. It means finite existence—and as long as we do not break the barrier of this finite existence we cannot grasp the infinite" (*Essay*, p. 96). This irreconcilable opposition, this fundamental antinomy between the finite, temporal existence of the individual, on the one hand, and the infinite, eternal existence of the Absolute, on the other, constitutes the *terminus a quo* and *terminus ad quem* of religious consciousness. In terms of the ethical language of religion it is a question of what Christianity, for example, understands in terms of our "original sin," as the inevitable "fall" into the finitude of the temporality of the world, and of our "redemption" from this fallen existence. Religion recounts the story of our "falling away"[4] from an immediate proximity to the Absolute, from an authentic mode of existence (*Dasein*) into the inauthentic mode of worldly existence (*Dasein*) in which we always already find ourselves, and of our eternal sacred quest to return to this lost authentic proximity, to that lost paradise that never was and never will be.

The Aim of Religion

It would be wrong to assume that the way to redemption advocated by religion ever actually delivers us from the binary oppositions of this fundamental antinomy of worldly existence, or even that this is in fact its true goal—rather to the contrary, the aim of the religious prospect of redemption is not to resolve the basic antinomy of our existence, but rather to unveil it, to dwell in it, and through this unveiling-dwelling to constitute it as such. It is only from the perspective of redemption that sin first acquires its meaning; and inversely, it is only from the recognition of the radical finitude of our worldly existence that our awareness of the mystery of the Absolute is awoken, and subsequently that redemption as a return to the "proximity" of the Absolute acquires its meaning. The primary function of religion is to reveal the impossibility, and thus absurdity of human existence, an existence located somewhere between the Absolute of the eternal and the virtual nothingness of the finite.[5] The truth of man's nature is that "man has no 'nature'—no simple or homogeneous being. He is a strange mixture of being and non-being. His place is between these two opposite poles" (*Essay*, p. 11). Religion does not answer the question of existence, it awakens it—and insofar as it awakens it in us, it awakens us to ourselves, for "as the being who alone is capable of questioning, man is also the being who is and remains to himself thoroughly problematical, the being eternally *worthy* of questioning" ("'Spirit' and 'Life,'" p. 877/55). The myth of the original sin,[6] of the ahistorical fall from the authentic proximity to the Absolute is not meant to resolve the irreducible antinomy of human existence, but rather to teach us to discover in ourselves the truth of our being, to see our existence for what it is: divided, fallen and thus essentially mysterious—*we who would know all as yet know nothing of ourselves.*

> Religion, therefore, never pretends to clarify the mystery of man. It confirms and deepens this mystery. The god of whom it speaks is a *Deus absconditus*, a hidden God. Hence even his image, man, cannot be other than mysterious. Man also remains a *homo absconditus*. Religion is no "theory" of God and man and of their mutual relation. The only answer that we receive from religion is that it is the will of God to conceal himself. . . . Religion is, therefore, . . . a logic of absurdity; for only thus can it grasp the absurdity, the inner contradiction, the chimerical being of man. (*Essay*, p. 12)

Religion: The *Aufhebung* of Myth and of the Real

Religion constitutes itself in and through the "sublation" (*Aufhebung*) of the mythical image world (cf. *PSF*, II, p. 24/32)—that is to say, in and through the simultaneous negation and preservation of the reality of mythical consciousness. As we have seen, mythical consciousness proves to be completely "homogeneous and undifferentiated" (*PSF*, II, p. 37/49) lacking any sense of "depth" and therefore unable to differentiate between "foreground and background," between "that which is grounded (*Grund*)" and that which " 'grounds' (*Begründetes*)" (*PSF*, II, p. 36/48). Here, there is no distinction between the "ideal" and the "real," between "existence" and "meaning," between the "image" as a copy (*Abbild*) and the "image" as a prototype (*Urbild*), between the *Ur-Bild* and the *Ur-Sache*. The mythical image is so woven into our immediate intuition of reality as to be indistinguishable from it. In fact, we might even say that the mythical image, insofar as it represents the concrete and immediate presence of spiritual meaning—and thus the meaning of immediate concrete presence—constitutes the concrete texture of the real insofar as it is what is "fully *present* (*volle Gegenwart*)" (*PSF*, III, p. 68/79).

> Where it first appears the mythical image is by no means taken *as* an image, as a spiritual expression. Rather, it is so deeply embedded in man's intuition of the world of things, of "objective" reality and the objective process, as to appear an integral part of it. (*PSF*, II, p. 238/285)

Evidently mythical consciousness is constructed upon a fundamental "illusion"—a *méconnaissance*, Lacan would say. For it mistakenly takes the material presence of the representative image, the signifier, for the concrete presence of the "thing" represented, the signified. In mythical consciousness the signifier thus possesses a certain primacy over the signified, determining its objective representation to consciousness. Although it is true that, from the perspective of analytical and theoretical consciousness, the reality of the mythical image world must be recognized as essentially "fictitious, it is an unconscious, not a conscious fiction" (*Essay*, p. 74). It is this basic *méconnaissance*, this "naive indifference of 'image' ('*Bild*') and 'thing' ('*Sache*')" and "the immanence of both" (*PSF*, II, p. 252/301) that constitutes the "immanent condition for its own future sublation, [for] the potentiality of a spiritual process of liberation which is indeed effected in the progress from the *magical-mythical* world view to the truly *religious* world view" (*PSF*, II, p. 24 f./ 32). Religion is the spiritual force or vision that grasps, through a recognition of this "inner contradiction, the chimerical being of man" (*Essay*, p. 12).

> Religion takes the decisive step that is essentially alien to myth: in its use of sensuous images and signs it *recognizes* them as such—a means of expression which, though they reveal a determinate meaning, must necessarily remain inadequate to it, which "point" to (*"hinweisen"*) this meaning but never wholly exhaust it. (*PSF*, II, p. 239/286)

However, insofar as the mythical image is not recognized as a mere image, insofar as it is not seen as what represents the real but rather as the authentic and full presence of the real itself, religious consciousness "cannot complete its peculiar critique of the image world without drawing real existence into it. Precisely because at this stage there is still no detached 'objective' reality in the sense understood by analytical theoretical cognition" (*PSF*, II, p. 239/286).

The "Logic of Absurdity"?

Religious consciousness thus constitutes itself through the recognition of the opposition between "meaning" and "existence," between the *UrBild* and the *Ur-Sache* that is essentially alien to mythical consciousness. But why call this "a logic of absurdity"? If this is not already clear it is perhaps because we are too quick to accept the distinctions of religion as given and self-evident, and therefore fail to appreciate the true immensity of the task that stands before religious consciousness—and thus why it must be considered as a "logic of absurdity." It is not enough to accept as given the distinctions introduced by the religious attitude, rather we must enter into the process by which myth gives way to religion and by which religion struggles to free itself from its mythical foundations.

The "Inner" Transformation of Myth

From a certain perspective, the distinction between the *Ur-Bild* and the *Ur-Sache* already exists within mythical consciousness, though in the form of an implicit "contradiction" (*PSF*, II, p. 235/281). Thus, essentially the emergence of religion represents the point where the principle governing myth becomes problematic to itself, and forces mythical consciousness to recognize its own "manifestation as something 'external' (*'Äußerliches'*) [and thus] not wholly adequate to its own drive for expression" (*PSF*, II, p. 236/282). The turning upon itself of the mythical consciousness marks a transformation "from within" of both its *"contents"* and its " 'inner form' " (*PSF*, II, p. 235/281). The alterity of its own difference to itself, to its own image world, a difference that mythical consciousness represses in its negation and transformation of all difference into a real and homogeneous identity, returns; and it returns not despite the force of mythical consciousness or its particular structural law, but rather as a paradoxical expression of its final logical conclusion. As with every cultural form, the inner "contradiction" of myth provides the catalyst for its diachronic unfolding (cf. *PSF*, II, p. 235/281; cf. also " 'Spirit' and 'Life,' " p. 880/58). Thus, as with all the other symbolic forms, myth progresses through the same three ideal stages of development—mimetic, analogical, and symbolic—toward its final and full expression (cf. *PSF*, II, p. 237/284). However, in its final stage of development, "in this turn [upon itself] mythical consciousness remains within itself. It does not move out of its sphere or pass into a totally different 'principle,' but in completing its own cycle it ends by breaking through it. This fulfillment, which is at the same time a transcendence, results from the relation of myth toward its own *image world* (*Bildwelt*)" (*PSF*, II, p. 235 f./282). The final "symbolic" stage of myth, in which myth comes to its "internal limits" by recognizing the alterity of its own difference to itself, marks therefore the threshold of a new spiritual force destined to go beyond it, namely the first "mimetic" stage of religious consciousness.

"Idolatry": The Constitutive Factor of Religion

Although mythical consciousness proves to be an instrument of its own overcoming, it is nevertheless the religious attitude as such that "must inject into the mythical consciousness an alien tension, an opposition it does not know as such, in order to disintegrate and destroy it from within" (*PSF*, II, p. 241/288). It must expose the mythical image for what it is, an image. It must reveal the effective presence of the mythical god to be only a material representation, a "molten image," an "idol" that as such is itself void of meaning:

> Be not afraid of them, for they cannot do evil, neither also is it in them to do good . . . his molten image is falsehood, and there is no breath in them. They are vanity, and the work of errors. (Jeremiah 10:5 ff. cited: *PSF*, II, p. 244; cf. also Isaiah 44:10 ff.)

The "idol"—the mythical image world—is an expression of "vanity"—of the spirit's narcissistic relation to its own mirror image returning to itself as other—and results from "errors"—from the *méconnaissance* of spirit, insofar as it takes its own image to be the real, to be the *Ur-Sache*. In religion spirit thus seeks to overcome its own narcissistic relation of *méconnaissance* to its own image world. The "constitutive factor" of religious consciousness, therefore, is the "prohibition of *idolatry* (*Bilderdienst*)" (*PSF*, II, p. 240/287).

"Idolatry" Is a *Petitio Principii*

It is important to keep in mind, however, that from the perspective of mythical consciousness the image is never seen as an image and subsequently "taken" for a god, but rather is experienced and felt as the immediate and concrete presence of the god itself. Thus, with the introduction into consciousness of the distinction between the *Ur-Bild* and the *Ur-Sache* "it is as though a chasm unknown to the unreflecting, 'naive' mythical consciousness had suddenly been opened. The representational world (*Vorstellungswelt*) of polytheism, the 'pagan' vision (*Grundansicht*) combated by the Prophets, was not guilty of worshipping a mere 'image' of the divine, since for this view there was no difference between the 'archetype' (*Urbild*) and 'image' (*Abbild*) as such. In its images of the divine this representational world (*Vorstellungswelt*) still held immediate possession of the divine itself—precisely because it took these images never as *mere* signs but always as concrete-sensuous revelations" (*PSF*, II, p. 240/287). The essential factor here is not the movement from a polytheistic worldview to a monotheistic one. Certainly the transition from polytheism to monotheism plays an important role in the development of religious consciousness, it is however not what essentially determines the structure of religious thought as such. Rather, the essential factor concerns the change in attitude of consciousness toward that which is immediately and concretely given, and the meaning that is represented through it. Because mythical consciousness does not distinguish between the means of representation and the meaning of representation, between the signifier and the signified, that which is concretely present to consciousness, insofar as it is "seen" by mythical consciousness, is "perceived" as the concrete "texture" of the immediate presence of the real.

The "Texture" of the Real . . .

By "texture" I mean to designate that elusive quality of resistance or effective presence that announces to consciousness from within it the presence of an existence that is other than itself and thus transcends it, and through this effective presence constitutes consciousness insofar as consciousness is always an awareness of. . . . The effective presence represents the return of consciousness to itself through its encounter with a "limit" or "barrier" that stands over against it as essentially other. This "otherness" is received as affect and determines the awareness of consciousness. And in fact even the self-awareness of consciousness itself is made possible only by means of this effective presence that constitutes it. The effect, however, is not that which is truly other, but only the alterity of consciousness' own difference to itself, which represents the presence of the other to consciousness as its limit and thus constitutes consciousness as such. Insofar as consciousness mistakenly takes the effective presence for the authentic presence of that which constitutes it, that is, the other, we have that dimension of meaning that Cassirer understands as mythical consciousness. The mythical world is the "sphere of efficacy (*Wirksamkeit*)" (*PSF*, II, p. 26/34). Once again, within mythical consciousness "to be real" (*wirklich sein*) is "to be effective" (*wirksam sein*). Consciousness takes its own difference to itself, its own self-affectivity to be that which is other than itself, and thus as the measure of the real.

Mythical consciousness is that dimension of awareness that results from the immediate concrete presence of the texture of consciousness as the affect of structure, and for this reason it is clear that the charge of idolatry proves to be "a kind of *petitio principii*, for it imputes to this view a conception which is not inherent in it but is brought to it only through a new perspective in which it is placed" (*PSF*, II, p. 240/287).

Religion as Rereading (*Relegere*) of the *Text*ure of the Real

The religious attitude toward the presence of that which is present to consciousness thus takes up the effective presence of the mythical image and transforms it into a "means of expression" that represents something beyond itself in the same way that the material letter of the text is no longer taken as a simple sensuous design but rather as a sign that possesses a meaning that transcends it. It recognizes that which consciousness takes to be real as only the "manifestation" of its own effective presence returning to itself from the barrier that determines it—that which is really real lies beyond this and only appears to consciousness in and through its effective affect upon it. The sensuous-empirical presence of that which is present to consciousness is no longer taken as the texture of the real itself, as the immediate effective presence of the real to consciousness, as that which is truly other, but rather, if you will, it is now taken as the *text*ure of the real, as that which concretely represents the real—the real now understood in terms of the "*Ur-Sache*," the cause or original thing, which grounds the effective presence of consciousness, as that which is truly other (cf. *PSF*, II, p. 237/284). The real is now seen to be other than its immediate concrete presence. The religious attitude transforms the real into a sign, into a text, which reveals a determined meaning, which " 'points' ('*hinweisen*') to this meaning but never wholly exhaust[s] it" (*PSF*, II, p. 239/286). The "immediately given reality of 'things' is transformed by the religious view into a world of 'signs.' . . . Things and events do not now simply signify themselves but have become an indication of something 'other' ('*Anderes*'), something 'transcendent' ('*Jenseitiges*')" (*PSF*, II, p. 252/301). Thus, as in the mysticism of Eckhart, all reality becomes a text, "the 'speech of God,' . . . all creation, all natural as well as spiritual and historical events, become a continuous *speaking* of the creator to the creature through the creature"[7] (*PSF*, II, p. 253/302). Religion, therefore, is a question of transforming the texture of the real into a "*hiero*glyphic," a "sacred image,"[8] that both reveals and conceals the meaning of the real in and through its concrete presence as the *text*ure of the real; it is a question of bringing out the spirit of the text in and through the most "scrupulous attention" (*religio*) to the material letter of the text, to the effective presence to consciousness of creation; in a word, it is a question of interpretation, and thus a question of "rereading" (*relegere*).[9]

The Necessity of the Text

The purest manifestation of the essence of religion, as we shall see, is found in "mysticism" and the "method of 'negative theology' " (*PSF*, II, p. 250/298). It is "mysticism which attempts to arrive at the pure meaning of religion as such, free from all encumbrance with the 'otherness' of empirical-sensuous existence and of the sensuous image and representations (*Vorstellungswelt*)" (*PSF*, II, p. 249/298). In the course of the unfolding of religious consciousness "the mythical world gradually sinks into nothingness" (*PSF*, II, p. 245/293). However, religious consciousness is never able to liberate itself completely from the presence of myth without at the same time destroying the very foundation of its own specific mode of consciousness: the history of religion thus proves to be a history of "bondage and liberation" (*PSF*, II, p. 25/33) possessing no final redemption or deliverance from the force of the mythical worldview. "By its very nature religion can never escape from the sphere of the 'image,' the sphere of intuition and fantasy. From them it derives its peculiar power; it would wither away and die were it not continuously nourished from this soil" (*PK*, p. 295/299). Thus, the history of religion shows that religious consciousness "remains indissolubly connected and penetrated with mythical elements" (*Essay*, p. 87).

> In religious consciousness . . . the conflict between the pure meaning it embraces and the image in which it is expressed is never resolved but bursts forth anew in every phase of its development. A reconciliation between these two extremes is continuously sought but never fully achieved. The striving beyond the mythical image world and an indissoluble attachment to this same world constitutes a basic factor of the religious process itself. Even the highest spiritual sublimation (*Sublimierung*) of religion does not cause this opposition to disappear but only makes it increasingly clear and *understands* it in its immanent necessity. (*PSF*, II, p. 251 f./300 f.)

Dogma as Idolatry

We must not be lured into thinking that what religion critiques in the mythical image is simply its "materiality." Rather, as should by now be clear, it is a certain attitude toward this concrete "material" presence—or simply, the material of consciousness—that is overthrown. "Negative theology" should be understood quite literally as a "negation of theology," and more specifically as the negation of the historically contingent dogma of theology. By "dogma" Cassirer means "the form assumed by pure religious meaning when men seek to express it in terms of objective representations" (*PSF*, II, p. 249/298). From the perspective of the pure religious attitude, the "dogma" of religious thought is as much an idol as is the sensuous-empirical figure of the "golden calf."

> Accordingly, mysticism rejects both the mythical and the historical elements of faith. It strives to overcome dogma because in dogma, even when expressed in purely intellectual terms, the factor of imagery is still predominant. For all dogma isolates and limits: it seeks to transform what is meaningful only in the dynamic of religious life to the determinacy of *representation* and its static "productions" ("*Gebilde*"). Thus, from the standpoint of mysticism, image and dogma—the "concrete" and "abstract" expression of religion—amount to the same thing. (*PSF*, II, p. 249/298)

A "Mixed Religion"

At the same time, however, the mystic must "speak not only the language of God but the language of man" (*Essay*, p. 103). In other words, the negative theology of the mystic requires as its means of expression the "imagery" of the positive theology that it negates as idolatry. There exists between the two a relationship of co-constitutionality not unlike the one we have already seen between thought and language. Both exist only in the dynamical process by which they continually revitalize themselves by turning upon themselves, and by virtue of this transcending from within transform each other into something new.[10] Again, we find that the "productive is in constant opposition to the traditional. . . . The tendencies that are directed toward preservation are no less significant and indispensable than those that are directed at renewal, because renewal realizes itself only upon the basis of permanence, and because the permanent can only exist by virtue of a constant self-renewal" (*Logic*, p. 113 f.).[11] Mysticism must begin from the content of a historically contingent dogma that it reveals to be mere idolatry. At the same time, however, it needs this historical representation as a means of expression, for without it the meaning that it opens up through its destruction would remain essentially meaningless and would in fact threaten to engulf consciousness in its own nothingness. With the absolute negation of the effective presence that announces within consciousness the presence of the other, there remains "nothing." Not the nothingness of the darkness, which is essentially an experience of absence, insofar as the darkness is nothing more than the presence of the absence of light, and thus still meaningful and thus still a form an awareness of. . . . Rather, the nothingness that follows is the absolute nothingness of the nothingness of the Absolute in which there is no longer even the presence of absence, there is nothing . . . no, there is not even nothing, for this "nothing" is completely without meaning for us and therefore is not—beyond the effective presence that constitutes the texture of consciousness there lies a nothingness so absolute that it absorbs and negates even itself, and thus can never, directly or indirectly, become the object of consciousness—let us designate this absolute nothingness of the Absolute quite arbitrarily by the figure X and call it the real, or better the ~~*Real*~~ as it is the "nameless nothingness" that stands beyond anything and everything we dare imagine it to be.[12] The mystic "is threatened by the constant danger that this nothingness and meaninglessness will seize not only upon being but upon the I as well" (*PSF*, II, p. 250/299). "Mysticism reveals to us, or rather would reveal to us, if we actually willed it, a marvelous prospect; but we do not, and in most cases we could not, will it; we should collapse under the strain. Therefore we remain with a mixed religion" (*Essay*, p. 102). In its concrete manifestation, then, religion is always comprised of a negative and positive element, of a negation and affirmation of the effective presence that constitutes consciousness, a negative and a positive theology.

In the same way that Cassirer objected to the artificial separation and juxtaposing of thought and language, so he objects to any attempt to establish a static opposition between negative and positive theology, between religion and myth. In *An Essay on Man* Cassirer critiques Bergson for positing an "irreconcilable opposition between what he describes as 'Static Religion' and 'Dynamic Religion' " (*Essay*, p. 87). It becomes clear in reading Cassirer's critique that he parallels his own distinction between mythical consciousness and religious consciousness with the one made by Bergson (cf. *Essay*, p. 102). For Bergson "Static Religion" aims at "maintaining and making eternal the present state of affairs" while "Dynamic Religion" seeks ever "new forms of human life which never existed before" (*Essay*, p. 89). As with Cassirer's distinction between myth and religion, the former seeks the construction and preservation of the life world of spirit, whereas the latter seeks its renewal through destruction.

> To the continuous *building up* (*Aufbau*) of the mythical world there corresponds a continuous drive to *surpass* it, but in such a way that both the position and negation belong to the form of the mythical-religious consciousness itself and in it join to constitute a single indivisible act. The process of destruction proves on closer scrutiny to be a process of self-assertion; conversely, the latter can only be effected on the basis of the former, and it is only in their permanent co-operation that the two together produce the true essence and meaning of the mythical-religious form. (*PSF*, II, p. 237/283)

The "Mythical-Religious Form"

From this it becomes clear why Cassirer deals with myth and religion together, and why he often speaks of the "mythical-religious" consciousness: for, strictly speaking, in their concrete historical manifestation the two represent, if you will, *the externalized interior of the other*. Mythical consciousness represents the moment of immanence in the meaning constituted by the symbolic function, whereas religious consciousness represents the moment of transcendence. But, as we have seen time and again, the symbolic relation is always "an immanence in transcendence and a transcendence in immanence." Thus we find myth in the interior of religion, and religion in the interior of myth. Myth and religion are therefore inseparable in their concrete historical manifestation. Throughout Cassirer's analysis we find that when he wants to refer specifically to myth as a cultural form, as opposed to religion, he speaks of the "*magical-mythical*" worldview, or of "magical" consciousness, to distinguish it from the "truly *religious* worldview" of religious consciousness.[13] Thus, as with language and myth—which are, in their concrete manifestation, always fused together and co-constitutive—we are nevertheless able to speak in abstraction about the specific force of mythical consciousness, on the one hand, and that of the "truly *religious*" consciousness, on the other.

From "Idol" to "Icon" and the *Schein* of the Truth

It also becomes clear why, for example, "there is scarcely a single feature in the world of Christian faith and ideas, scarcely a symbol, for which mythical-pagan parallels might not be shown"[14] (*PSF*, II, p. 248/297). As we have already said, religion constitutes itself in the "sublation" of the mythical image world, in its simultaneous destruction and preservation of the image of the idol. "The negation and rejection of certain mythical figures by which consciousness was previously dominated does not mean that they are simply relegated to nothingness" (*PSF*, II, p. 243/291). In their destruction they are taken up by religious consciousness and invested with a new meaning. To express this "fine and fluid transition," religious language draws a distinction that is denied to theoretical cognition. "For the latter there is no middle term between 'reality' ('*Wirklichkeit*') and 'appearance' ('*Schein*'), between 'being' ('*Sein*') and 'nonbeing' ('*Nichtsein*'). Here the alternative of Parmenides applies: *ἔστιν ἤ οὐκ ἔστιν*" (*PSF*, II, p. 243/291). For religion, however, there exists a middle term. Though the image is recognized to be only an "appearance" or "illusion" ("*Schein*"), it is nevertheless said to be an "essential appearance (*Schein*)" (*PSF*, II, p. 244/291). The image does not dissolve into nothing, it is not disregarded as a mere phantasm of the imagination, but rather is taken as an "appearance" of the truth. The truth cannot be represented by just any image, but rather only by a very specific image; namely, the image that has been taken up from the mythical worldview. Even in the most radical denial of the imagery of myth, which "seeks to unmask the lower demonic world as an absolute nothing—a nothingness to which no reality, however mediated—no reality of thought or belief or fear—should be attributed" (*PSF*, II, p. 244/292), even here the images of the mythical fantasy which are negated have their place and function—one need only open the Old Testament and read a few pages to find ample examples of this point. The mystical drive only ends by emphasizing the need for the imagery that it negates. The image, however, is no longer taken in the sense of an idol, as the immediate concrete presence of the truth, but rather in the sense of an icon that is the revelation or an appearance (*Schein*) that "points" to truth but "never wholly exhausts it" (*PSF*, II, p. 239/286).

The "Logic of Absurdity"

And finally it becomes clear why religion must be said to be a "logic of absurdity": for in its concrete manifestation it must take up a twofold and even self-contradictory attitude toward that which is present to consciousness. On the one hand, the mythical image must be recognized as that which "represents the truth" but is not itself the truth. Between the image and the real there exists a fundamental incommensurability that can never be overcome, a primordial difference and heterogeneity between the finitude of the image and the infinitude of the Absolute. The Infinite absolutely transcends the finite, it lies beyond all positive determination and therefore can only be approached through negative predication and silence. In the end, we must resign ourselves to the fact that we know nothing of the Absolute and never will. On the other hand, if no image can express the Absolute, does it then follow that every image equally represents or misrepresents the Absolute? Here we must distinguish between religion as a concrete historical cultural form and the speculative philosophical thought of religion. From the perspective of the latter, the Absolute can only be thought of in terms of the unknowable X that escapes all objective determination, that lies beyond all sensuous or intellectual form, beyond all symbolic representation and all structure. In a word, as that which escapes the binary distinctions of signification.[15] The presence of the Absolute, of the Infinite in the world is reduced to nothing more than the necessary beginning and ground, an *Ur-Sache*, the X that functions as a guarantor of the harmony and homogeneity of existence: the "self-causing cause" (*causa sui*), the "supreme being" (*summum ens*), the "ultimate cause" (*ultima ratio*). However, from the perspective of a concrete historical religion, such an X, such an abstract *causa sui* is nothing but an idol, an illusory concept void of meaning, to which nothing sacred can be attributed. "Man can neither pray nor sacrifice to this god. Before the *causa sui* man can neither fall to his knees in awe nor can he play music and dance before this god."[16] Redemption is not to be achieved through the X, through the *causa sui*. There is only one redeemer, and only one way to the truth. In other words, the infinite is understood to have crossed over into the finite and manifested itself in and through the finite as the truth. The finite image has a religious meaning, only insofar as "it not only represents the truth but *is* the truth itself" (*PK*, p. 295/299; italics my own). Religious consciousness must preserve the mythical belief in the reality that stands before it. It does not, and cannot, see in the image a mere "illusion," but rather an "essential appearance" of the real. Insofar as mythical consciousness takes the *Ur-Bild* for the *Ur-Sache* and thus sees only the concrete presence of the *Ur-Sache*, religious consciousness must see the *Ur-Bild* at once as the *Ur-Sache* and as that which represents the *Ur-Sache*. We might represent this double vision of religion as follows: *Ur-~~Sache~~* or ~~Real~~. The sign ~~Real~~ thus possesses a double sense. It designates the real that lies beyond the symbolic and thus resists signification. And it indicates the fact that it is only through a critique of that which is taken to be the real that we can think this real which lies beyond the symbolic. The cross can be seen as the negation of the real or as the effective presence to consciousness that marks the place from which the ~~Real~~ is perceived as hidden. The ~~Real~~ reveals itself in and through its concealment in the alterity of its difference to itself—in other words, the real (~~Real~~) is other than itself.

The Defining Character of Different Religions

Every religion thus begins from a specific mythical foundation, and it is this different mythical foundation that determines the different natures of the different religions. In each case religious consciousness must struggle to free itself from its own mythical foundations. "But the different religions do not do this in the same way, and it is precisely in this process that each one reveals its historical and spiritual particularity" (*PSF*, II, p. 239/286). However, though the content of each religion differs, according to the nature of its own particular mythical foundation, the structure of its relation to the effective presence of this mythical image world is always the same. Cassirer demonstrates this structure through an examination of four historical examples: Judaism (cf. pp. 240–241); the Persian-Iranian religion (cf. pp. 241–243); the doctrine of the Upanishads and Buddhism (cf. pp. 245–247); and finally

Christianity (cf. pp. 248–250). It is interesting to note that Cassirer gives each example almost precisely the same amount of attention as the others so as not to place one above the others. Thus, if we find a certain predominance is given to Judaism and Christianity in our discussion of religion it is for the simple reason that they provide the traditional framework of images that form the foundation of Western European culture.

The Diachronic Unfolding of Religion

The Antinomy of Religion

As with every symbolic form, religion possesses a fundamental "contradiction" that functions as both its synchronic structure and the catalyst for its diachronic unfolding. Furthermore, in the final stage of this development the binary oppositions of this antimony do not find their resolution, but only their fullest and clearest expression. As we have already said, the opposition between the finite, temporal existence of the individual, on the one hand, and the infinite, eternal existence of the Absolute, on the other, proves to be the basic antinomy of religion. Religion begins and ends in the intuition of the radical opposition between the Absolute and the individual, in the intuition of the alterity of difference of that which stands beyond the effective presence of consciousness to itself: in a word, in the intuition of radical alterity. The mythical world from which religion begins has now been shown to be nothing more than the subjective projection of spirit's own image upon the other—a process by which consciousness turns back to itself. Nature, the world, everything that we see, feel, and think, everything that we take to be real is nothing more than the projection of our own image returning to us as other—the voice returning in the alterity of its difference to its own speaker. Religion seeks to overcome this narcissistic relation of *méconnaissance* of spirit to its own image: for only in this way can consciousness come to recognize that which is truly other, and subsequently truly recognize itself. In the moment of mythical consciousness, spirit has become other, but as yet fails to recognize itself in the alterity of its own difference to itself, in the echo of its own expression returning to itself from the other, it remains therefore alienated from itself. In the moment of religious consciousness, spirit seeks to overcome this alienation. The process of overcoming, however, is not without its difficulties or its dangers. As has already been indicated, the "nameless nothingness" which this overcoming reveals, threatens to destroy consciousness itself. The moment of overcoming must not only be an overcoming *of* consciousness but also an overcoming *for* consciousness. As might be expected, there is no "sudden 'crisis' " that marks, as for Bergson, the clear separation of religion from its mythical foundation. "In the development of human culture we cannot fix a point where myth ends and religions begins" (*Essay*, p. 87). In this section we will follow this diachronic unfolding of religion as it progresses through the same basic three stages that all symbolic forms pass.

Mimetic: "Natural Religion"

As with language there first exists no tension between the "sign" and the "content" that is designated by it. All sensuous existence, insofar as it functions to represent the sacred, is taken as a concrete expression of the *Ur-Sache*. At this level of religious consciousness "the two belong necessarily together.... Here the sign as a fundamental religious form relates everything to itself and transforms everything into itself—but at the same time the sign itself enters into the whole of sensuous-concrete existence and fuses intimately with it" (*PSF*, II, p. 255/305). The effective presence (*Ur-Bild*) to consciousness is taken as the direct and immediate expression of that which is other, such that the *Ur-Sache* of this effective presence is understood in terms of its affect. As with language, the first stage of religious thought, which following Schelling, we may call "natural religion," is indistinguishable from the mythical consciousness in which it is entangled (cf. *PSF*, II, p. 248/297).

Analogical: Revealed Religion

Again as with language, religion possesses a tendency to "surpass the narrow limits of the mere 'mimetic' sign.... In religion the sensuous and the spiritual by no means coincide, but nevertheless they point continuously to one another. They stand to one another in a relationship of analogy, by which they are both interrelated and separated"

(*PSF*, II, p. 256/305). At the level of natural religion the meaning is perceived *in* the sign, *in* the concrete effective presence to consciousness. The meaning therefore is not hidden, but rather immediately apprehended. The effective presence insofar as it functions as a sign possesses a certain transparency. Here meaning is still experienced as objectively real and concretely present. In the analogical stage of religious consciousness, however, the sign begins to be recognized as such, as that which makes manifest the real but which is not itself the real—thus a certain opaqueness begins to make itself felt. Here meaning is perceived *through* the sign, *through* the concrete effective presence to consciousness, the *Ur-Sache* being apprehended through its effects. "Its physical content remains only [a] cloak and mask, behind which its spiritual meaning is hidden" (*PSF*, II, p. 256/306). However, insofar as religious consciousness and mythical consciousness are still fused together, the sign is not so much a "sign" per se, as the historical fact of the world, which, as with all historical facts, remains meaningless without interpretation. (The element of interpretation is already implicit at the mimetic level in the activity of the augur who takes the flight of the birds as a "sign" or omen.) Cassirer illustrates this dimension of religious interpretation of the *text*ure of the real by way of the "fourfold form of exegesis" developed by medieval thought. The interpretation of the objective world must be undertaken according to four categories: historical, allegorical, tropological, and analogical (cf. *PSF*, II, p. 256/306). The first of these determines the historical fact of the event of the world, whereas the latter three aim to disclose the true meaning of this given fact, its ethical and metaphysical significance. Religious consciousness remains immersed in the particular reality of world history, but is not limited to this reality. The world is transformed into a "trope" or "metaphor" that "requires a special art of religious 'hermeneutics' " (*PSF*, II, p. 257/307). *Through* the immanence of the world as the effective presence to consciousness it seeks to understand the transcendence of the *Ur-Sache* that is the ground and cause of this effective presence.

Now, the critique that is often made against this medieval methodology—which is here only taken as an example of the analogical dimension of religious consciousness—is that modern physics teaches us that we cannot move from like effects to like causes, but only from like causes to like effects. There is nothing in the effect itself that can tell us anything about the nature of its cause. It is therefore futile to attempt to understand the ground or cause through an interpretation of an effect, rather we must begin from the knowledge of a specific cause and follow its effects as they unfold from this initial point in a series of ordered events. The critique, however, begins from a basic misunderstanding: for religious consciousness does not in fact move from effects to causes, but rather it begins from the historical presence of the first cause (*Ur-Sache*) from which it then proceeds to order the system of its effects—that which we call the world—accordingly. It begins from a given zero point, which functions as the absolute beginning of the series, its point of origin (ἀρχή), if you will. From it, and it alone, does religious consciousness order the effective presence of the world into a lawful series. This first member of the series possesses, of course, a rather ambiguous status. For although it is evidently a member of the series, as the member whose existence is presupposed by all the members of the series as a whole, it must presuppose its own existence: this self-reflexivity is essential to its proper functioning. This zero point is at once immanent in the ordered series of particular and differentiated effects, and yet prefigures and transcends this order. It is the law that governs the series of events or effects. It is both the origins (ἀρχή) and the principle (ἀρχή) of the series (cf. *PSF*, II, p. 1/3).

> [Thus] there is *one* point at which the world of spiritual, transcendent "meaning" and that of empirical-temporal reality come into contact, despite their inner divergence and antagonism—and at this point they directly permeate each other. All allegorical-tropological interpretation relates to the basic problem of redemption, and thus to the historical reality of the redeemer as its fixed center. All temporal change, all natural events and human action, obtain their light from this center; they become an ordered, meaningful cosmos by appearing as necessary links in the religious "plan of salvation" (*Heilsplan*) by taking a significant place in it. And from this one spiritual center the circle of interpretation gradually broadens. The supreme, the "analogical," sense of a text (*Sinn einer Textstelle*) or event is disclosed when a reference can be found in it to the transcendent or to its immediate historical manifestation, the *Church*. Here even the most far-reaching "spiritual" interpretation, all spiritualization of natural being is bound up with a condition and a contrary motif, [namely, the presupposition] that the Logos itself descended into the sensuous

> world and there was "incarnated" in temporal uniqueness. (*PSF*, II, p. 257/307)

Symbolic: Mysticism

The final stage of religion, exemplified by Cassirer in medieval mysticism—most specifically the mysticism of Eckhart—seeks to overcome the "temporal uniqueness" of the "historical event" of the redeemer by dissolving it into the "eternity" of the Absolute (*PSF*, II, p. 258/308). In the first stage, the divine is thought of in terms of the effective presence that confronts consciousness and awakens it to the presence of.... The returning to itself of consciousness is taken as that which stands over against it, that which is truly other. In the second moment of its development religious consciousness recognizes that the world is only the effective presence of consciousness to itself, that this otherness is only a pseudo-otherness and that the divine lies "beyond" the effective sensuous presence of the world. However, all our knowledge of this *Ur-Sache* can only be achieved through this effective sensuous presence, which we call the world. There exists now a gulf between the infinite Absolute as the ground and cause of the world and the finite individual enclosed in its temporal becoming. The heterogeneity of the Absolute and the finite historical world having been established, a new problem now emerges for religious consciousness, namely the homogeneity of the two. The historical reality of the redeemer provides the schema mediating between the heterogeneity and homogeneity of the Absolute and the finite. In the final stage of religious consciousness all reference to the direct and objective presence of the Absolute *in* the world is suspended. The divine is no longer thought of as a presence in the world (mimetic), nor as present only in the redeemer. The divine is sought neither *in* the effective presence nor *through* it, but rather *in and through* it. The solution of the redeemer—who proves to be a transcendence in immanence and immanence in transcendence, and thus is *the* schema par excellence—is extended to the whole and to each individual being within the whole. The infinite must be seen to dwell in the finite, and the finite in the infinite.

> The process of redemption is restored to the depths of the I, to the abyss of the soul, where it is enacted free from all outside

> mediation in an immediate correlation of I and God, God and I. . . . All sensuous things are and remain signs and metaphors—but the sign no longer has a "wonder" or miracle about it if the character of the wonder is seen in its particularity as an individual revelation of the transcendent. True revelation no longer occurs in any particular but only in the whole: the world as a whole and the entirety of the human soul. (*PSF*, II, p. 258/308)

The effective presence of the world is now understood as the revealing-concealing of the Absolute in and through the finite. Each individual human soul contains within itself the truth of the whole. Each finite being is, as Eckhart says, a "footstep of God." All of creation is nothing other than the "speech of God," a sign, the "continuous speaking of the creator to the creature through the creature" (*PSF*, II, p. 253/302). The effective presence of the world stands before us as a sign that makes possible the presencing of the Divine in and through its absence.

> And thus the "world" is nothing other than the path on which [the] "proximity to God" is gained. . . . The religious word "world" signifies this relation. And if the relation of I and God is eternity, the relation of I and the world is temporality; world, as the dead middle point between God and I, signifies the finding of eternity in temporality, of temporality in eternity. . . . All religion—and in its clearest form . . . the German mysticism of Eckhart—bears witness that the striving for a total sanctification of the world rises from the profoundest source of religious experience.[17]

In the world we stand in the "proximity to God" . . . we dwell in the *temple* that is opened up by the *templum* and as finite historically determined beings contemplate the undetermined infinity of the eternal heavens . . . while the *Ur-Sache*, the God, as that which is nearest to us, remains far. Why does the truth remain hidden? Why does the Absolute withdraw into the alterity of its difference? Because "it is the will of God to conceal himself" (*Essay*, p. 12). Such is the ultimate truth of religion: God remains eternally "a *Deus absconditus*, a hidden God. Hence even his image, man, cannot be other than mysterious. Man also remains a *homo absconditus*" (*Essay*, p. 12). The opposition between the infinite and the finite, between the creator and the creation, between the immanence of the effective presence to consciousness and the transcendence of the real, of the *Ur-Sache* is not resolved. Rather to the contrary: "If this involvement and opposition were ever replaced by a pure and perfect equilibrium, the inner tension of religion, on which rests its significance as a symbolic form, would be negated (*aufgehoben*)" (*PSF*, II, p. 260/311). Thus, the religious intuition oscillates between an intuition of the homogeneity of the Absolute and the finite and an intuition of their heterogeneity. It is only in a philosophy of the Absolute—Hegel's Science of the Absolute—that the unity can be thought in the concept of the symbolic and only in art that a reconciling of the antinomies of religion can be achieved.

The Sacrifice . . .
"From Spell to Prayer"

The Aim of the Cult and the Paradox of the Sacrifice

In the preceding pages we have seen that "to the continuous *building up* (*Aufbau*) of the mythical world there corresponds a continuous drive to *surpass* it, but in such a way that both the position and negation belong to the form of the mythical-religious consciousness itself and in it join to constitute a single indivisible act.[18] The process of destruction proves on closer scrutiny to be a process of self-assertion; conversely, the latter can only be effected on the basis of the former" (*PSF*, II, p. 237/283). It is through this "single indivisible act" that myth and religion not only interpenetrate and form one another, but from which, in fact, each initially arises. This "indivisible act" is understood by Cassirer in terms of the cult devoted to the sacred image (*Ur-Bild*) that constitutes consciousness and represents the nameless presence of the life stream (*Ur-Sache*): "the cult is man's active relation to his gods" (*PSF*, II, p. 219/262)—be it the God of mythical consciousness (*Ur-Sache*) or the God of religious consciousness (*Ur-Sache*).

Now the aim of the cult "consists in overcoming the separation of the I from the Absolute" (*PSF*, II, p. 220/263). In the words of Hegel: "To realize this unity, the reconciliation, restoration of the subject, and his self-consciousness, to bring about a positive feeling of participation in the Absolute and a unity with it—this transcendence of the separation constitutes the sphere of the cult."[19] Thus the cult is, "in general, the eternal process of the subject making itself identical with the essence of its being."[20] In other words, the cult is a process of identification ruled by a logic of negation, insofar as difference is negated in order to establish the homogeneous unity of a real identity between the finite and the Absolute. Now it should already be clear that the process of "overcoming the separation" between the subject and the Absolute not only presupposes the separation that is to be overcome, but in fact, and more importantly, constitutes this separation in and through its overcoming. The fall from the immediate proximity of the Absolute is the condition of possibility of our return, but paradoxically it is our desire to return that brings about our fall.

The history of religion is for Cassirer, as for Hegel, a process in which the essence of the cult unfolds and is made explicit. Now, the more the outward sensuous form of the cult develops, the more determined its form becomes, "the more clearly the *sacrifice* appears at its center [as] the solid core around which the cult action clusters. Here religious 'faith' attains its real *visibility* (*Sichtbarkeit*): here it is transposed directly into action. . . . Fundamentally, every sacrifice implies a negative factor: a limitation of sensory desire, a renunciation which the I imposes on itself. Here lies the essential trait of sacrifice, which raises it from the very outset above the level of the magical world view" (*PSF*, II, p. 221/264). It is thus through the abnegation of desire, or more specifically through the destruction of the sensuous object of desire, that the subject makes itself "identical with the essence of its being" and thus overcomes the separation between itself and the Absolute. However, insofar as it is desire, or the object of desire, which constitutes the subject as such, the destruction of sensuous desire results, or would result if the abnegation were ever absolute, in the subsequent destruction of the subject. In other words, spirit realizes itself and makes itself identical with its own essence only in and through its own self-destruction.

> Spirit *is* only insofar as it turns against itself . . . its own unity is thinkable only in such contrariety. Hence Spirit is not only . . . the ascetic of *Life*, not only that which is able to say "No" *(Neinsagenkönner)* to all organic reality; it is the principle which *within itself* may negate itself. And the paradox of its nature consists precisely in the fact that this negation does not destroy it, but first makes it truly what it is. (" 'Spirit' and 'Life,' " p. 876/54)

Only in the "self-disintegration whereby man turns against himself" does he come to be[21] (" 'Spirit' and 'Life,' " p. 877). Paradoxically, only in the negation of meaning is meaning generated. That which is held to be sacred acquires its meaning as the sacred only in and through its destruction. And in fact etymologically the word "sacrifice" comes from *sacra-facere,* to make sacred. And thus why the sacred, and above all the sacrifice, possesses the paradoxical twofold character of a *mysterium tremendum* and a *mysterium fascinosum* (cf. *PSF*, II, p. 78/99): for we are at once drawn toward the sacrificial altar by an overwhelming fascination and yet at the same time horrified and repelled by it. The sacrifice offers us the passageway to the truth of our being; through it and it alone can we realize the truth of our essence. But the price is high, too high for mere mortals. For redemption from our fallen existence, the overcoming of the barrier that separates us from the Absolute is achieved only by means of the sacrifice, by the destruction of our finite worldly existence: in a word, by way of our death. And thus, for religious consciousness all true religious existence is, as Heidegger has elaborated, a being-toward-death. We can realize the "*essence*" of our existence only by "destroying the *form* of the self" that determines this existence as an existence. "Only pure immersion, which does not so much magnify the I into the godhead as extinguish it in nothingness, brings true redemption" (*PSF*, II, p. 225/269). From one perspective the sacrifice is a process of identification of particular self-consciousness in and with general self-consciousness. What is produced by the sacrifice is meaning, and more specifically that meaning which defines our individuality. At the same time, however, the sacrifice involves the destruction of meaning, and thus a self-destruction of the self: "only if man sacrifices his individuality [can] he break down every barrier that lies between himself and the eternal unity of life" (*MS*, p. 43).

The Unfolding of Sacrifice

The act of sacrifice cannot but appear to us—those not immediately involved in the sacrificial act itself—as a pathological act of madness following an absurd logic. However, if it is an act of madness it is certainly no ordinary madness but rather an "*hieromania,*" a sacred madness in which the subject is freed from its finite existence and enters into a "union with god" (*MS*, p. 43). In the thirteen difficult and often obscure pages devoted to the subject of sacrifice, Cassirer considers the movement by which the religious meaning of the sacrifice becomes explicit from the perspective of a number of characteristic synchronic elements. Given the importance of sacrifice let us consider these pages in greater detail.

The Function of the Sacrifice within Myth

We have said that consciousness is constituted in and through the positing of a "barrier" that separates it from the eternal flow of the life stream. "Only when the barrier is felt and known as such is the road opened by which it can progressively be surmounted; only when man recognizes the divine as a power superior to him . . . does he gradually gain a free feeling of self in confronting it. . . . [T]he growing independence of the gods is the conditions for man's discovery in himself of a fixed center" (*PSF*, II, p. 223/266 f.). In the magical-mythical world, however, there is as yet no experience of such a limit: "For originally there is no such self-limitation in the magical world view, which is based on belief in the omnipotence of human desire (*Wünsche*). . . . Here objects have no independent being . . . no will of their own which man cannot make subservient to himself by the use of the proper magical means" (*PSF*, II, p. 222/265). The ruling ideal of magic is the necessary "compulsion" that the "magical spell" holds over nature and the gods. The "spell" provides a tool with which to order the universe according to our desire. "In its basic form magic is nothing more than a primitive 'technique' of wish fulfillment" (*PSF*, II, p. 222). Certain ascetic measures are necessary in order to concentrate our magical power and focus it upon some specific task: for example, to combat those who possess an evil magic that is against us.[22] At the level of the magical worldview, sacrifice thus serves a "purely egocentric purpose: by submitting to certain physical privations a man aims merely to strengthen his *mana*, his physical-magical power and efficacy" (*PSF*, II, p. 222/266). Nevertheless, the essential point is that already within the magical realm there is found the basic religious "intuition that any extension and intensification of the powers of the I involves a corresponding limitation" (*PSF*, II, p. 222/266).

The "Gift" and the "Economy" of Sacrifice

Within the magical-mythical sphere the sacrifice always takes the form of a speculative sacrifice in the economic sense of the word. The abnegation of the object of desire or value here and now is always undertaken in view of receiving some specific benefit or return in the "future." The greater the sacrifice, the greater the expected return. In the ritual of "gift offering" this economy of the sacrifice is made more explicit: although for this reason it also provides us with a certain distance that allows for a greater degree of freedom vis-à-vis the sacrifice. Again we see that "man withdraws, as it were, from the objects of immediate desire. They cease to be objects of immediate enjoyment and become a kind of religious *means of expression*" (*PSF*, II, p. 223/267). However, once again the abnegation of desire is undertaken in view of a "future" return. Thus there is at first no essential difference between the necessary asceticism undertaken in the magical-mythical realm and this new form of "gift offering": "the magical-sensuous idea of *compulsion* now seems to have been replaced merely by the no less sensuous idea of *exchange*. 'Give me, I give to thee; lay down for me, I lay down for thee. Offer me sacrifice, I offer thee sacrifice.' Thus does the sacrificer speak to the god in a Vedic formula" (*PSF*, II, p. 224/268). In this economy of sacrifice the mechanism of gift exchange now renders each of the partners mutually dependent upon the other, thus leveling the difference between them. In principle each possesses an equal status in a contractual union that is freely undertaken within the marketplace of sacrifice and sacred values.

Up to this point Cassirer's theory differs little from that developed by Hubert and Mauss.[23] As we shall see in a moment, this economy of sacrifice provides the basis upon which a "real identity" between "the individual and the clan and the clan and its gods" is brought about. However, a subtle change in the structure of the gift-giving ritual radically alters its meaning: "This transformation occurs as soon as religious contemplation ceases to limit itself exclusively to the *content of the gift* and concentrates instead on the *form of giving*, in which it sees the heart of sacrifice. Man's thinking now progresses from the mere material performance of the sacrifice to its inner *motive* and determinant. It is only this motive of 'veneration' . . . that can give the sacrifice its meaning and value" (*PSF*, II, p. 224/268). The divine is now "recognized as a power superior [to the giver] which cannot be compelled by magical means but must be propitiated by prayer and sacrifice" (*PSF*, II, p. 223). The focus of that which is sacrificed not only shifts from the exterior to the interior, but the interior "now appears as the only valuable and significant religious gift. The vast sacrifices of horses, goats, cattle, and sheep cannot be fruitful: the *desired sacrifice* . . . is not that in which all sorts of living creatures are destroyed but one which consists in *continuous giving*" (*PSF*, II, p. 224/269; my italics).

Beyond the "Economy of Sacrifice"

A number of points merit close attention here. First and foremost, the sacrifice no longer possesses the structure of an "economy of exchange." There is no longer any talk of receiving some "future" return in exchange for that which has been sacrificed. The sacrifice has become a "continuous giving." It has thus ceased, at least in principle, to be a productive act and has become, in the terminology of Bataille, a pure *dépense*.[24] We find ourselves here at the inverse position from which we began. The sacrifice no longer is a "technique of wish fulfillment," nor is it undertaken within the context of an economy of exchange. The object of desire is sacrificed because it is the "desired sacrifice," because it is desired by the other. The sacrifice of this object, the abnegation of desire, aims only at "propitiating" the Divine Other. In the sacrificial object we search the "will of god," the desire of the Absolute Other and seek to "satisfy" this desire.[25]

Sacrifice as Mediation

Secondly, we see that one of the essential functions of the sacrifice is that it provides a "mediation" between the divine and the human. The sacred object that is "consecrated" in and through its destruction in the sacrifice establishes a "middle link" that "bonds" together the Absolute and finite. Although the sacrifice is "always characterized by the striving for a connection of this sort, the synthesis effected in it is itself capable of the most diverse gradations" (*PSF*, II, p. 226/270). At its most elementary level, the "bond" forged between the finite and the Absolute takes the form of a common "physical identity." "What originally connects man with the god is a physical bond of common blood" (*PSF*,

II, p. 226/271). The earliest expression of this form of "blood relation" is found of course in the example of the totem animal. The eating of the totem animal in the sacral feast provides the means of "confirming and renewing the blood kinship which unites the individual members of the clan with one another and with their totem" (*PSF*, II, p. 227/271). The sacrifice establishes a twofold identification: between particular self-consciousness and general self-consciousness, on the one hand, and between spirit and the life stream, on the other. This basic structure of "communion" is found in Christianity in the Eucharist. In the Eucharist we find perhaps the purest expression of this basic religious intuition that "if there is to be any true unity" between the Absolute and finite then they must "be of the same flesh and blood" (*PSF*, II, p. 228/272).

The Prayer

Prayer too seeks to "bridge the gulf between God and man. But in prayer the means is not merely physical but symbolic and ideal: the power of the word" (*PSF*, II, p. 229/274). Here too there is in the beginning no sharp difference between the sensuous "*existence*" of the word and its pure spiritual "*meaning*." The prayer finds its earliest expression in the magical spell that "not only surpasses the barriers between man and god but actually tears them down" (*PSF*, II, p. 229/274). Even within Christianity the prayer first appears as "the immediate union and fusion of man with god (τὸ ἀνακραθῆναι τῷ πνεύματι [Origen]). But in its later development prayer gradually passes beyond this magical sphere. Taken in its purely religious sense, prayer now rises above mere human desire. It is directed no longer toward relative and particular *goods*, but toward an objective good that is equated with the will of God" (*PSF*, II, p. 229/274). In the higher expressions of prayer and sacrifice it now becomes clear that the religious sacrifice does not function as a mediation between two *already* existing and separated entities or spheres—which is the case in the magical-mythical realm. Rather the separation is constituted in and through the quest to overcome it. In the very gesture of reaching out to the Other, we establish a distance between ourselves and this Other, in the moment transcending the distance we paradoxically constitute it. Religious consciousness thus "*creates* this gulf in order to close it: it progressively intensifies the opposition between God and man in order to find in this opposition the means by which to surpass it" (*PSF*, II, p. 230/275).

The Sacrifice of the God

Up to now we have considered only the "sacrifice *to* the god." However the full signification of the sacrifice does not manifest itself in the "sacrifice *to* the god," but rather in the "sacrifice *of* the god."[26] Now the "sacrifice *of* the god" may be understood to mean either that "*the god himself* is sacrificed" or that "*the god himself* . . . sacrifices himself" (*PSF*, II, p. 230/276). Let us consider both possibilities.

The "God Himself is Sacrificed"

We have already seen that it is only through the communion between the members of the clan that the communion between the clan and the god is achieved. "The true accent of the sacral act is on performance by the community as a *whole*" (*PSF*, II, p. 227/271). Only through the common sharing of the totem animal is the clan's unity with its "totemic ancestor" restored (*PSF*, II, p. 227/271). "Only by being slain and eaten is the sacrificial animal enabled to serve as an intermediary between the individual and his clan and between the clan and its god" (*PSF*, II, p. 228/273). Again we find the same structure in the "mystery of the Eucharist"[27] (*PSF*, II, p. 231/276): for the Eucharist is of course possible only after the crucifixion of Christ. And through the consumption of the bread and wine we partake of His flesh and blood, thus becoming one. There is of course a difference. In the case of the totem animal, closer to the "pure" mythical worldview, that which is consumed is literally the flesh and blood of the totem animal, whereas in the case of the Eucharist what is literally consumed is only some bread and wine, which *are* the flesh and blood of Christ. It is perhaps no accident that it is "bread" and "wine" that are used to celebrate the Eucharist and not, for example, meat and blood (or water). For bread and wine are cultural objects that are clearly distinguishable from "natural substances" that might be confused for the actual "substance" of Christ. Those who are unable to see these cultural substances as the "flesh and blood" of God lack either the cultural background or the imagination necessary to recognize in the finite and ephemeral the presence of the Absolute and Infinite. We see here one of the clearest examples of the contradictory attitude that religious consciousness takes up toward that which is immediately present. The sensuous image "not only represents the truth but *is* the truth itself" (*PK*, p. 295/299; italics my own)—the bread and wine not only represent Christ but they *are* His flesh and blood. Through the sacrifice *of* the god "finite existence ... is raised to the level of the divine" (*PSF*, II, p. 230/276). The bread and wine become the sacred, and through its destruction in the holy communion the separation between the finite and the Absolute is overcome. Again it is not the simple consumption of the bread and wine as such that is important, but rather the partaking of the flesh and blood as a community as a whole. In the final analysis what "distinguishes Christianity from the other religions is not so much the *content* of the motif as the new, purely 'spiritual' meaning that is gained from it" (*PSF*, II, p. 231/276).

The "God Himself . . . Sacrifices Himself"

The second reading of the "sacrifice *of* the god" suggests that the "*god himself*... sacrifices himself." Cassirer does not consider this second possibility in any detail. His only comment seems to be a reference to St. Anselm's "doctrine of satisfaction" in which "man's infinite guilt can be 'satisfied' only by the infinite sacrifice of the God himself" (*PSF*, II, p. 231/276). The idea is of course intriguing: Why would God sacrifice himself? Why does the Absolute negate itself? Certainly this self-negation of the Absolute is a necessary condition of possibility of both our fall into finite existence and eventual redemption from this fallen existence. Only because the Absolute withdraws into the alterity of its own difference is finite existence free to exert itself as an independent and autonomous existence. Only through its turning in on itself—and thus turning away from the Absolute—does finite existence become what it is, namely a determined and limited existence. Without this withdrawal and self-limitation of the Absolute, finite existence would be taken up and absorbed into that of the Absolute. And of course it is necessary that God sacrifices his only son (who is Himself) in order that finite spirit might enter into communion with the Absolute in and through the sacred feast of the Eucharist. This does not, of course, explain why the Absolute negates itself, but rather only the consequence and necessity for our own finite existence. The question remains, however: Why does God sacrifice himself? The question is perhaps ill formed. It assumes that there is a reason or a motive behind this first act of "continuous giving." As the ultimate sacrifice God's self-sacrifice is an act of pure *altruism*—so pure that we—who are always concerned with our own self—are unable to understand that there is nothing in it for the sacrificer, that there is no hidden motive. We find ourselves here at the limits of human understanding. Why does the Absolute withdraw into the alterity of its own difference to open up finite existence? Why is there something rather than nothing? Quite simply, because *"es gibt"* (there is/it gives)!

The Final Conclusion of Sacrifice

At this point, sacrifice arrives at its final stage in the intuition of the mystic. What first appears as a "physical" bond and then as an ideal *"mediation"* now reveals itself to be a "pure *correlation*" (*PSF*, II, p. 231/277).

> For the mystics the question is no longer how the gulf between God and man can be bridged, for they recognize no such gulf; the whole conception is contrary to their fundamental religious attitude. For them man and God are not mere separate entities; they exist together and for each other. (*PSF*, II, p. 231/276 f.)

We see here the purest expression of the religious insight into that "polarity which strives to dissolve into a pure correlation and which must nevertheless be preserved as a polarity" (*PSF*, II, p. 250/298). It is important to keep in mind that there is a difference between the philosophy of religion and religion itself. "The philosophy of religion sees the unity between God and man less as a substantial than as a synthetic unity: a unity of different entities. For it, therefore, differentiation remains a necessary factor, a condition for the achievement of the unity itself" (*PSF*, II, p. 251/299). In the case of religion, however, the difference is understood in terms of our fall from the immediate oneness with the Absolute. "Only when the difference between God and man has vanished, when God has become man and man God, does the goal of redemption seem achieved" (*PSF*, II, p. 251/299). And yet religious consciousness cannot achieve its final goal without either falling back into the image world of myth or extinguishing itself in the "nameless nothingness" of the Absolute.

> Here we find that correlation of "meaning" and "image" and also that conflict between them which are both deeply rooted in the essence of symbolic, of meaning-image expression (*symbolischer, sinnbildlicher Ausdruck*) as such. On the one hand, the very lowest, most primitive mythical configuration proves to be a *vehicle* of meaning, for already it stands in the sign of that primordial division which raises the world of the "holy" from the world of the "profane" and delimits the one from the other. But on the other hand, even the highest religious "truth" remains attached to sensuous existence, to the world of images as well as things. It must continuously immerse and submerge itself in this existence which its "intelligible" purpose strives to cast off and reject—because only in this existence does religious "truth" possess its form of expression and hence its concrete reality and efficacy. (*PSF*, II, p. 260/310)

Religious consciousness, as it realizes itself in the sacrifice, thus encounters its internal limits: For "the spiritualization of the sensuous world through the act of sacrifice results directly in the sensualization of the spiritual world" (*PSF*, II, p. 228/273). In its final stage, the relation between the Absolute and the finite is recognized as a "pure *correlation*," an "immanence in transcendence and transcendence in immanence." However, religion is unable to realize an equilibrium between the two. This final stage of religion brings us to the threshold of speculative thought in which we shall try to think the "harmony" between the two in the concept of the symbolic.

Six

Science: The Writing of a *Lingua Universalis*

Unseen the threads are woven into a whole.
And an infinite combination grows.

—Goethe, *Faust*

At a certain moment in the life of spirit there occurs a radical transformation in its mode of vision. There arises the recognition that within the arbitrariness and heterogeneity of the world of becoming there is to be found the lawful and homogeneous world of Being. This realization awakens in spirit the desire to know and understand the raison d'être of things beyond the mere appearance of things. There is perhaps no activity more essential to, or more characteristic of, human existence than this eternal quest for knowledge and truth. A qualitatively different dimension of meaning begins to open itself up here. Through the negation of its embodiment in the concrete reality of existence, thought liberates itself from its active and concrete entanglement with being and turns toward the contemplation of ideal and "pure signification." It is this general dimension of meaning or attitude of the mind that Cassirer understands by science, and to which we now turn.

A Definition of Science *Grosso Modo*

It is perhaps important to emphasize here that when Cassirer speaks of science he is not speaking specifically about the sciences of nature. In English the term science is often employed in a restrictive and limited sense as referring to the exact natural sciences. In German, however, the term *Wissenschaft* has a much more general meaning, referring to any theoretical and systematic body of knowledge. In a word, science is a process of "interpretation." Scientific knowledge represents a method of translating our "observations" of the world into a "system" of "well-ordered symbols" so as to render them "interpretable in terms of scientific concepts" (*Essay*, p. 217). Insofar as the "sign" determines, as we have seen time and again, all our thoughts, perceptions, and intuitions of the world and ourselves, "the true universality of thought issues from the universality of the sign" (*PSF*, III, p. 401/270). Likewise, the systematicity and logical coherence that characterizes scientific thought issues from the coherence and systematicity of the system of signs that determines it. Although every mode of understanding the world or cosmos is for Cassirer essentially an awareness of lawful order, scientific thought distinguishes itself from other modes of knowledge insofar as it is an "explicit" and "systematic" understanding of the "law" of lawful order—whether this law represent the structuring principle of nature or spirit. Such is, *grosso modo*, the nature of science as a symbolic form.

The Relation between Language and Science

For science, as for religion, "everything objective" comes to be seen as "mere 'phenomenon' " or as "mere 'appearance' " (*PSF*, III, p. 173/207). Insofar as science and religion are both orientated toward knowing the "truth" of the things beyond their simply "appearances," it is not surprising to discover that "the relation between linguistics and scientific concept formation presents the same dialectic we have encountered . . . in the advance from the mythical to the religious consciousness" (*PSF*, III, p. 329/384). Insofar as it is language that constitutes our intuition of the world, the movement from perception to scientific thought represents the movement from the "verbal signs" and "word-concepts" of language to the "pure relational and ordinal signs" and concepts of science. Science thus constitutes itself in and through the "sublation" of the linguistic signifier. However, it is no more able to dispense with language than religion was able to dispense with myth. Although science constitutes a new dimension of pure signification above and beyond the dimension of linguistic representation and intuition, it nevertheless remains bound to language and is forced to return to it as its sole means of expression. As in the case of religion, science does not represent "a simple *reversal* of the spiritual process on which the formation of language rests, but . . . a continuation and ideal *heightening* of that process" (*PSF*, III, p. 330/385). As in the case of myth, language transforms itself from within in the course of its own development, thus preparing the way for its own overcoming. In its final stage language comes to its internal limits and breaks through its own circle of formation to transform itself into a new dimension of meaning. The final stage of the linguistic process represents—as in the case of myth—the first stage of science (cf. *PSF*, III, p. 330 n3/386 n1).

> All strict science demands that thought free itself from the constraint of the word, that it become independent of it. But once again this act of liberation cannot be performed by a mere turning-away from the world of language. The road begun in language cannot be abandoned but must be followed to its end and continued beyond this end. Thought presses beyond the sphere of language; but precisely in so doing it takes up a tendency which is originally contained in language and which from the very outset was active as a living factor in its own development. . . . The indispensable act of detachment from language proves to be conditioned and mediated by language. (*PSF*, III, p. 329 f./384)

The Difference between Perception and Scientific Thought

"In a changing universe scientific thought fixes the points of rest, the unmovable poles. . . . The scientific process leads to a stable equilibrium, to a stabilization and consolidation of the world of our perceptions and thoughts" (*Essay*, p. 207). Science gives, as Kant says, a "stable" form or structure to the mere "rhapsody of perception" (*PSF*, III, p. 407/475). However, the contents of perception and thought are always already formed, ordered, and unified into a single enduring manifold. We have already seen that "not only [can] the structureless not be thought, it [can] not be perceived or become objectively intuited" (*Logic*, p. 18). Even at its most elementary level perception (*Wahrnehmung*) represents a "taking-for-true" (*Für-Wahr-nehmen*) and thus as such constitutes a process of "selection" (*Ausleseproseß*) by which the "real" and the invariant are distinguished from the "apparent" and variable. "The tendency toward this 'consolidation' already belongs to perception itself—and without it, it could never become the perception of 'things.' . . . For even here the process of selection realizes itself by virtue of which we distinguish the "real" color of an object from its apparent color and its true size from its apparent size" (*Logic*, p. 74). Wherein lies the difference, then, between linguistic and scientific determination? "Science is distinguished here from perception—in a highly significant way, to be sure—only by the fact that it requires a strict *determination*, whereas perception contents itself with a mere *estimate*" (*Logic*, p. 75).

Lived Perception and the Function of Lived Language

In order better to understand the task and nature of the linguistic concept and how the scientific concept differs from it we must first briefly consider why our lived perception must "content itself with a mere *estimate*." Each "individual perception aspires to be something more than a mere position in a series" (*PSF*, II, p. 407/476). Lived perception is characterized by its *particularity*: a particular "object" is perceived by a particular "subject," from a particular perspective at a particular moment: "its meaning resides precisely in this particularity. . . . Each perception is given only to one observer, under his special spatio-temporal character" (*PSF*, III, p. 407 f./476). For this reason perception is always "incomplete" and "fragmentary." For in any one perception, for example, I can only see one side of the object given to me in perception. Certainly I can turn the object around so as to see its other side, but then I will no longer be able to see the side that was present to me only a moment ago. Although I can change the perspective from which I see an object, I can never perceive it from more than one perspective at a time because as a perceiver embodied in space I can never be in two places at the same time. Certainly I can envision the unity of all the possible perceptions of this object, but I can do so only in "thought" and not in "perception": for I can grasp the unity of all the possible perceptions only by going beyond the real content of any one particular perception to the virtual reality of the idea of the whole of the object. Of course, each particular perception of the object always already implicitly presupposes such an awareness of the ideal unity of the object of which it is a particular and partial representation: for it is only in the context of the ideal unity of the whole that each particular perception derives its meaning, a meaning that must be understood as the meaning of a "position." "Each individual phenomenon 'represents' the thing but as a particular can never truly *coincide* with it. In this, 'critical' idealism . . . holds that the mere 'phenomenon' necessarily points beyond itself, that it is an 'appearance of something' " (*PSF*, III, p. 327/381). Each perception leads to another, and to a series of others, and it is the unity of this series that constitutes the meaning of each. As far as the temporal dimension of our perception of the world is concerned, here too all perception is determined by its particularity. All lived perception is always a perception that occurs *in* the present—though it need not necessarily be a perception *of* the present. Each particular perception distinguishes itself as belonging to one unique moment. As such, no two perceptions are ever the same as no two perceptions can ever occur in one and the same moment of time. By changing my perspective vis-à-vis an object of perception I can now perceive one side, now another. At any time I can return to a previous perspective from which my perception of the object will be the same as it was a moment ago. Evidently, as the number of possible perspectives of any object is infinite, it is, practically speaking, impossible to ever take up precisely the same spatial perspective. But even if we were to return to precisely the same spatial perspective of the object, the perception itself would be radically unique from the first insofar as it would occur at another moment in time. In my lived perception of the world I can never return to a moment that has past, nor enter into another that has not yet come to be. In the very moment of my perceiving I am eternally situated in the eternal moment of the "now"; and it is this awareness of the radical uniqueness of the now that characterizes any perception as being lived.

> Strictly speaking, we cannot say that three times [past, present, future] "are"; rather, we should say that the present time comprises three different relations and through them three different aspects and determinations. There is a present of the past, a present (*Gegenwart*) of the present (*des Gegenwärtigen*) and a present of the future. "The present of the past is called memory, the present of the present is called intuition, that of the future is called expectation." Thus we may not think of time as an absolute *thing*, divided into three absolute *parts*: rather, the unitary *consciousness* of the now encompasses three different basic directions and is first constituted in this triality. (*PSF*, III, p. 167/195)

The perception of a unique moment manifest itself in a perception of the duration of that moment, each instance implies another instance, and a series of instances. Once again, we see that the content of perception implicitly contains the consciousness of the ideal and virtual unity that goes beyond it. The perception of the unique moment refers beyond itself to the ideal and virtual unity of the temporal horizon that provides it with its meaning, a meaning that must be understood as a value of position.

However, if the content of lived perception gains its meaning through its position in the whole, this meaning nevertheless always remains a position fused together with its content, and thus never rises up to the status of a pure abstract position. As a result, lived perception is characterized and distinguished by a certain spatial and temporal "heterogeneity."

> *Without* this inherent heterogeneity, perception would not seem to be perception, for then it would lose the qualitative particularity pertaining to its very essence; and *with* this heterogeneity it seems never genuinely to fit into the form of the system, which is an indispensable condition of the possibility of *knowledge* and theoretical *understanding* as such. (*PSF*, III, p. 408/476)

Of course this "heterogeneity" is a relative heterogeneity, for as we have said, we are never confronted by the pure heterogeneity of the Heraclitean flux of becoming. Each perception is itself already a differentiated unity, though the nature of this manifold is always "accidental" and "incomplete." Thus it forms more of an "aggregate of elements" than a "true synthetic" unity of a homogeneous whole. "In its continuous flow, actual perception as a *process* knows nothing of such a unity. Every content that emerges in it is immediately replaced by another content, every form that it seems to mould is caught up in the vortex of the process and carried away with it" (*PSF*, III, p. 322/375).

It is only "from the standpoint of . . . representation that one may first speak of the unity of a 'thing' " (*PSF*, III, p. 322/375). As we saw in chapter 3, it is the function of language to provide perception with the relative unity and relative stability necessary for it to act as a "representation" of something, while at the same time preserving the unique particularity and heterogeneity that characterizes it as the lived perception of a particular subject. This is why there remains a certain "ambiguity" inherent in all linguistic concepts: for linguistic meaning can never be absolutely fixed or absolutely determined. It must remain open such that each word is able to adapt itself to the particularity of lived perception and the context of speech. Linguistics meaning thus "subsists only by re-establishing and asserting itself in the movement of speech, in its surge and flow" (*PSF*, III, p. 336/393). Depending upon the context, the same object can be perceived by different people, or even by the same person, to be both hot and cold. The water can be at once too hot for a bath and yet too cold to cook with. If you place one hand in a sink of hot water and the other on a large block of ice, then, after a few minutes, place both hands on the same surface, you will perceive that the surface is in fact at once cool and warm. That something is said to be hot or cold thus says less about the object than it does about the context of speech or the speaker's subjective state.

Of course "the spoken word itself should never be thought of as a mere product of intuition" as it "contains within it an act of 'reflection' " (*PSF*, III, p. 335/391). Language already marks a negation of the "immediate" presence of reality, but its product returns as that which is given in perception. The scientific "concept must . . . unlike direct perception, move its object off into a kind of ideal distance, in order to bring it within it horizon. The concept must annul 'presence' in order to arrive at 'representation.' . . . The function of the concept does not create a break in the whole of knowledge—it continues a basic trend which already proved to be at work in the first stages of sensory knowledge, perceptual effective *knowledge*" (*PSF*, p. 307/359).

> The positive reality of the empirical object is constituted through a double negation: through its differentiation from the "absolute" on the one hand and from sensory appearance on the other. This object appears "phenomenal" but it is not "illusory," since it is *grounded* (*gegründet*) in necessary laws of knowledge, since it is a *phaenomenon bene fundatum*. (*PSF*, II, p. 34/45)

Language is able to bring about only the first step in this process as it is itself never able to break completely away from the intuitive givenness of perception: for that which the linguistic sign designates is always to be found in the context of the intuitive world of its speaker, and this intuitive context is always in the process of changing.

> Language can never definitively leave and break through this sphere: for even where as *discourse* (*Rede*), as objective "logos," it is directed towards something absolutely non-sensuous, it can only designate this non-sensuous something from the standpoint of the *speaker* (*Redender*). It is never pure statement, for it always contains a mode, an individual form of saying, in which the speaking subject expresses *himself*. All living speech contains within it this dichotomy, this polarity of subject and object. It not only embraces a reference to certain relationships, but also expresses the position of the subject toward them. This inward participation of the ego in the content of what is said is expressed in innumerable subtle shadings, in changes of dynamic accents, in changes of tempo, rhythm, and "melody." To divest speech of this "feeling tone" would be to destroy its heartbeat and breath. (*PSF*, III, p. 339/395)

The Problem of the Truth

Because perception is always relative to the perceiver, the judgments that we make based upon it are not so much wrong as they are relative and limited. For the most part our perceptions of the world are trustworthy. If I sense that the stove is hot, then I do not touch it. When someone extends their hand, I do not ask myself whether or not this figure before me is an illusion or a holographic image, but rather extend my hand in an act of mutual recognition. However, "this absolute trust in the reality of things begins to be shaken as soon as the problem of *truth* enters upon the scene. The moment man ceases merely to *live* in and with *reality* and demands a *knowledge* of this reality, he moves into a new and fundamentally different relation to it" (*PSF*, III, p. 282/330). To inquire into the truth of things is to have already thrown into doubt the immediate reality of lived perception, to have transformed the affective texture of perception into an appearance that represents within consciousness something that is other than itself and that requires further explanation. It is to have recognized that our perceptions of things are but the surface of a more profound reality. Beyond our subjective and partial impressions there is now seen the independent existence of a thoroughgoing unity of lawful order: the "hidden harmony that is better than the visible harmony" as Heraclitus taught. "At first, to be sure, the question of truth seems to apply only to particular *parts* and not to the whole of reality. Within this whole, different 'strata' of validity begin to be marked off, 'reality' seems to separate sharply from 'appearance.' But it lies in the very nature of the problem of truth that once it arises it never comes to rest. The concept of truth contains an immanent dialectic that drives it inexorably forward, forever extending its limits" (*PSF*, III, p. 282/330). To broach the question of the "truth" is to inquire ultimately into the "whole," for "the truth is the whole." However "this whole cannot be presented all at once but must be unfolded progressively by thought [and] it is this unfolding which constitutes the essence of science" (*PSF*, III, p. xiii/vi).

The Negation of *La Parole* and the Anchoring of the Signifier

How does thought bring about this transformation in its view of the world? We have already seen that in the natural world attitude perception is conditioned by language, and that both represent the object only from the individual "standpoint" of the speaker. This "standpoint" represents *la parole* of the perceiving subject, an "individual form of saying, in which the speaking subject expresses *himself*." To do away with it would amount to the destruction of the vital force of the living individual subject. "And yet there is a stage in the development of spirit, at which this very sacrifice is demanded of it. The spirit must progress to a pure *apprehension* of the world, in which all particularities resulting from consideration of the *apprehending* subject are effaced. . . . And it is this transition that opens up the realm of genuine, rigorous 'science.' In *its* symbolic signs and concepts everything which possessed any sort of mere expressive value is extinguished. Here it is no longer any individual subject, but only the thing itself that 'speaks' " (*PSF*, III, p. 339/396). However it is not enough to negate the viewpoint of the individual speaker, for every particular language also possesses its own "subjective world view" (*PSF*, III, p. 341/398), which must therefore also be negated and overcome. To illustrate the arbitrariness of the historical contingent system of linguistic designation, Cassirer cites the example of a language in which a butterfly is classified as a bird because it flies (cf. *PSF*, III, p. 312/364). Such a system of classification is based upon "intuitive factors" and not upon a rule or logical "criteria." As such, language, as a system of classification and designation, suffers from the same shortcomings as does perception. It forms an aggregate rather than a systematic whole ruled by a governing rule; its classifications are incomplete and ambiguous, and thus its form of designation is accidental and arbitrary.

A *Lingua Universalis*

To establish the universality of thought, science must construct a new universal language. In "this universality the national differences as well as individual differences are annulled. The plural concept of 'languages' loses its justification: it is thrust aside and replaced by the idea of a *characteristica universalis,* which enters the scene in the form of a '*lingua universalis*' " (*PSF,* III, p. 339/396). To achieve this universal language scientific thought must bring to an end the continuous "surge and flow" of language.

> Dialectic is the art of determining and fixing the fluctuating meaning of words. Speech is moving—and in this movement all our words and terms undergo an incessant change. But it is for philosophy [i.e., science], for dialectic, to bring this change to a standstill, to transmute the mobile and uncertain shape of words into steadfast and constant concepts. ("Influence," p. 311)

The Two Postulates of a Scientific Language

The construction of a *lingua universalis* proceeds according to two basic principles of construction. The first of these is the "postulate of *identity;* the 'same' sign must always be chosen for the 'same' content, the 'free play' of signification that is essential for language and that makes possible its movement, the power of a word to be taken sometimes in one and sometimes in another 'sense,' must now be deliberately abolished. The concept strives for a strict, unambiguous correlation between 'sign' and 'signification' " (*PSF,* III, p. 337/393). In other words, the incessant sliding of the signifier over the signified that gives language the suppleness necessary to at once determine perception while at the same time preserving its particularity is brought to an end by fixing the meaning of each signifier *a priori* to its use. The meaning of a term no longer depends upon the context in which it is used, nor does it depend upon the subjective state of the speaker, but rather it is determined beforehand by the "exactness" of its "definition." Hence, the second principle, which states that each concept must derive its meaning exclusively from its *place* in the system of concepts to which it belongs, and that this system of concepts must be ordered according a general ruling principle.

> Every new concept that is set up in scientific thought is related from the outset to the whole of this thought, to the totality of *possible* concept formations. What it signifies and is depends on its validity in this whole. All "truth" that can be attributed to it is bound to this continual and thoroughgoing verification with respect to the whole range of the contents and propositions of thought. From this it follows that concept *signs* must form a self-contained *system*. It does not suffice that certain signs be correlated with certain thought contents; in addition, all must stand in a fixed order, so that the totality of the signs is articulated in accordance with a set rule. Just as one thought content is conditioned by and "grounded" in another, so one sign must also be grounded in another—that is to say, it must be possible to *derive* one sign from another in accordance with a determined *structural law* (*Gesetz des Aufbaus*). (*PSF*, III, p. 337/393)

Perhaps Cassirer's clearest example of the ideal structure of the scientific concept is to be found in chemistry. As one knows, each element is defined by its *place* in the periodic table, which is itself governed by the periodic law. The elements are organized according to the increasing order of their atomic number. The number represents the positive charge or the number of protons in the nucleus of the atom of the element in question. Anything that possesses the same atomic weight is essentially the same element. From this perspective the meaning of any element is only the "pure value of position." Whatever its name, its religious and economic value, its aesthetic appearance, as an element, gold is nothing more than that substance that has the atomic weight 196.9665 and that occupies the 79th place in the periodic table of elements. To express this in mathematical terms: the element is thus the infinitesimal part of any magnitude or differential. We have already seen that the model of the concept for Cassirer is found in the differential equation: $\varphi(x)$.

Our scientific understanding of reality comes about by way of a twofold movement of an analytical deconstruction of the object of inquiry into its basic elements and a systematic reconstruction into a synthetic unity. "That 'the' object (*Gegenstand*) is thought of as *one* does not prevent this unity itself, as a *functional* unity, from being progressively constructed. It must run through a series of determinations, and it is exhausted in no member of the series, not even in the final, concluding member, for the object is the all-embracing principle of the series, according to which the progression from member to member is determined" (*PSF*, III, p. 322/375). To see the world scientifically, is to recognize in the content of perception the expression of a law that can be thought and represented by a system of pure conceptual signs. Even in the most chaotic of phenomena there is to be found the rule of progression, a lawful structure that remains fixed and inviolable throughout.

The Relativity, Validity, and Dialectic of Scientific Truth

Unlike the "living representations" of the linguistic concept, the conceptual signs of science possess no correlate in the intuitive world of perception. "The concept no longer remains attached to the 'reality' of things but rises to the free construction of the 'possible' " (*PSF*, III, p. 319/372). Scientific thought does, however, "set up a rule of determination which must be confirmed in the intuitive sphere" (*PSF*, III, p. 282/330). This "rule of determination," which organizes and structures the internal unity of thought is meant to represent the "law," which animates the presence of being. It is for this reason that all theoretical knowledge is never anything more than an *interpretation* of being.

> Every theory... may be called an interpretation of the facts to which it refers. If, for instance, in optics I adopt the Newtonian theory of light, if I think that light is produced by the emission of imponderable particles from luminous bodies, then I am interpreting light in terms of mechanics; if I adopt the theory of Maxwell I am interpreting the same phenomenon in terms of electrodynamics. (*SMC*, p. 135)

It is through an interpretation of the heterogeneous elements of phenomena that scientific thought establishes their intellectual and theoretical unity. However, are all interpretations equally valid? A scientific interpretation of events and phenomena is said to be valid when it is *internally* and *externally* coherent and systematic—that is to say, insofar as there are no contradictions within the structure of the theory; and insofar as there are no contradictions between this theoretical explanation and that which is present to thought through the "resistance presented by the datum" (*PSF*, III, p. 408/476). Reality itself possesses a certain autonomy from, and resistance to, thought. As Lawrence Cahoone writes: Cassirer "preserves the independent Being—for Levinas, the Otherness or alterity—of entities, of nature, and thus preserves the distinction of the Being of the objects of knowledge and the Being of the knower."[1] "This antinomy [between the theoretical structure of explanation and the 'resistance presented by the datum'] contains the dialectical germ of all scientific concept formation" (*PSF*, III, p. 408/476). From a certain perspective the internal and external coherence amount to the same thing. For the facts are nothing outside of the theoretical structure of their interpretation. They are seen by the scientist as nothing more than the material expression of a scientific hypothesis itself. Insofar as a "fact" does not follow the law of the theory there is a problem. However, that the facts do not correspond to the theory does not necessarily disprove the theory. It is possible that the theory is valid, but only within a certain range of phenomena. In which case what is called for is a more general theory to account for a more general range of phenomena.

As such, there always exists the possibility of a new and more comprehensive interpretation of being: "since both the simplicity and the systematic completeness are always relative, there is always a possibility that we may arrive at another and more satisfactory result through a suitable variation of the original assumption" (*PSF*, III, p. 421/492). The relative nature of scientific thought does not, however, deprive it of its value: for the interpretation does not derive its meaning from some "transcendent object" that exists in itself and which thought attempts to copy, but rather from the specific form of objectivization that is achieved in and through it.

> Even though this function may never achieve its end, may never arrive at a *non plus ultra*, its *direction* is established. The endlessness

> of the road does not negate the determinacy of the direction: for it is precisely through their relation to "infinitely distant" points that the directions are defined. (*PSF*, III, p. 421/492)

The Relation between Thought and Being

Thought now thinks being through a sign—or better, thought now thinks being explicitly through a sign, as all thought is always already mediated by the symbolic force of the sign. "For what distinguishes science from the other stages of cultural life is not that it requires no mediation of signs and symbols and confronts the unveiled truth of 'things in-themselves,' but that, differently and more profoundly than is possible in the other forms, it knows that the symbols it employs are *symbols* and comprehends them as such" (*PSF*, II, p. 26/34). Through the fabrication of symbols thought is able to transcend being while nevertheless remaining immanent within it: a transcendence in meaning and not, of course, in being. It is able to achieve this paradoxical state because the nature of its being is structured and governed according to the law of determination that also structures and governs being. Science is phenomenological in the sense that it seeks the logic or λόγος of the phenomena. Beyond the phenomena of our immediate perceptions there is nothing. The world, as such, is not that which is perceived but the horizon and structure of perceiving, the projected horizon in which and through which being is made present to thought. Insofar as number—or the propositional function $\varphi(x)$—represents the prototype and purest expression of the pure theoretical sign and the purest expression of the symbolic structure of reality, it is at once immanent in the phenomenon of being before perception and yet transcends it in thought. As for Heidegger, there is nothing, no being other than the phenomena that are present to our perception of the world. What is, is and becomes what it is, only in and through the invariant horizon of the world of symbolic forms.[2] The problem of how thought and being are related to each other is of course not new to our age, it is perhaps the problem of philosophy.

> Already in the Pythagorean doctrine, we find a characteristic vacillation in the expression of the central idea. Side by side with the fundamental formula, according to which all being *is* essen-

> tially number, stand other formulations to the effect that all being "imitates" number and participates in it through this imitation. In the fragments of Philolaus it is said not only that things *are* numbers but also that everything knowable, whatever its nature, *has* its number. At first sight this "having" of number strikes one as a strangely contradictory and baffling relationship. For it embraces unity and otherness, identity and difference—it *differentiates* (*auseinander*) "being" and "number," but at the same time measures *one by the other* (*aneinander*) and links them indissolubly together (*miteinander*). (*PSF*, III, p. 354/414)

Being and thought are related through the identity of symbolic form. Being remains distinct from thought, as thought remains distinct from Being. Nevertheless, thought, in returning to itself, constitutes itself against the alterity of its own difference to itself, that is to say, against the alterity of Being. Being, too, comes to "be" only in and through its own difference to itself, through the alterity of thought. Thought thinks being in and through the world, and so thought is. Being is thought in and through the world, and so Being "is." The symbolic represents the "in between," the structure in and through which Being and thought not only take on form, but in and through which they are simultaneously united and differentiated. *The symbolic is the mirror in which Being is reflected in its image of thought, as thought is reflected in the image of Being.* Only in this way is the whole in the part, and the part in the whole—and infinitely so.

The Difference between the Sciences of Nature and the Sciences of Culture

In his treatment of the natural sciences Cassirer's position does not substantially go beyond the classical position of the Marburg school. In three now classic studies Cassirer establishes the structure and conditions of possibility of concept formation in the natural sciences. In his first systematic work, *Substance and Function,* Cassirer sought to determine the structure of the concept found in mathematics and classical Newtonian physics. In his 1921 work, *Einstein's Theory of Relativity,* and his 1936 work, *Determinism and Indeterminsim in Morder Physics,* Cassirer set out to establish the validity of his 1910 thesis in light of the theory of relativity, on the one hand, and Heisenberg's principle of uncertainty and the tenets of quantum mechanics, on the other. As these two revolutions in our conception of the nature and the physical universe brought into question the presuppositions of Newtonian physics upon which neo-Kantian thought had been constructed, they were viewed by many as marking the final death blow to neo-Kantian philosophy. It was thus imperative, from the perspective of neo-Kantianism, to account for these two shifts in paradigm. Certainly in his defense of the neo-Kantian perspective, Cassirer was forced to adapt and modify certain doctrinal elements of the classical argument as it had been developed by Cohen and Natorp. Cassirer himself writes, in *Determinism and Indeterminism*:

> [T]he bond which links me with the founders of the Marburg school is not loosened, and my debt of thanks with regard to them is not diminished, if it follows from the following investigations that . . . I have arrived at substantially different results than those that have been established in the work of Cohen, *Logik der reinen Erkenninis* (1902), or in that of Natorp, *Die logischen Grundlagen der exakten Wissenschaften* (1910). (*DI*, pp. 132 f.)

However, despite Cassirer's claim to have arrived at "substantially different results" there is no shortage of literature demonstrating the continuity and compatibility of his general conception of the structure of mathematical natural science with that found in the work of Cohen, and especially that of Natorp.[3] Where Cassirer's conception of the structure of the *Naturwissenschaften* is concerned, at least in the three works mentioned above, there would seem to be some agreement—as William Werkmeister concludes his comparison of Cassirer and Natorp—that in this respect "Cassirer has advanced beyond orthodox neo-Kanianism only in a very restricted sense."[4]

However, when Cassirer turned his attention from the natural sciences to the structure of the "cultural sciences" (*Geisteswissenschaften*), it quickly became clear to him that the "general epistemology, with its traditional form and limitations," could not provide an adequate "methodological basis for the *cultural sciences*" (*PSF*, I, p. 69/v). What was needed, esteemed the author of the *Philosophy of Symbolic Forms*, was a "broadened" epistemology that would account for all the "various fundamental forms of man's 'understanding' of the world. Only when such a 'morphology of spirit' (*'Formenlehre' des Geistes*) [had been] established, at least in general outline, could we hope to arrive at a clear and more reliable methodological approach to the individual disciplines of the cultural sciences (*Geisteswissenschaften*)" (*PSF*, I, p. 69/v). With this, Werkmeister writes, Cassirer "departs radically from the position of orthodox neo-Kantianism: for Natorp is committed to the idea that the prototype of all knowledge is found in the mathematical sciences. The cultural sciences find no consideration in the *Logiche Grundlagen* or in Natorp's other epistemological writings."[5]

This notwithstanding, the model of the mathematical sciences seems to have nevertheless continued to act for Cassirer as the model of all scientific knowledge worthy of the title. When we consider, for example, the basic structure of the third volume, which was to deal with scientific knowledge, we find that Cassirer only treats the "foundations of the natural sciences" and not those of the "cultural sciences." Cassirer himself seems to have recognized this shortcoming, for in the next systematic work explicitly devoted to the philosophy of symbolic forms, *Zur Logik der Kulturwissenschaften* published in 1942 almost thirteen years after the third volume of his *magnum opus*, the question as to the difference and the unity of the *Naturwissenschaften* and the *Kutlurwissenschaften* is explicitly addressed.[6]

What both, the natural sciences and the cultural sciences, have in common is their logic of "subsumption" (*Subsumtion*) (*Logic*, p. 70), or concept-formation, which we have considered in detail above. Thus "we understand a science in its logical structure only once we have clarified the manner in which it achieves the *subsumption of the particular and the universal*" (*Logic*, p. 69). As we have seen, scientific thought, whatever its object, "subsumes" the particular x under a universal ϕ, which thereby becomes an expression or instance of the more general law. Now, the natural sciences perform this "subsumption" in such a way as to leave no distance between the particular and the universal; "gold," to return to Cassirer's own example, is nothing for the scientist but an element characterized by a "certain specific weight (itself strictly determinate quantitatively), a specific electrical conductivity, a specific coefficient of expansion, etc." (*Logic*, p. 71). In short, the unity conferred upon the particulars of natural science is a "unity of being" (*Einheit des Seins*) (*Logic*, p. 73). In contrast, the sciences of culture, in their subsumption of the particular under the general rule, can never exhaust the particular; the particular never absolutely corresponds to the universal. What is established here is rather a general "unity of direction" (*Einheit der Richtung*) and not a unity of being. They "*coordinate*" (*einordnen*) the phenomena without "*subordinating*" (*unterordnen*) them to a general law (*Logic*, p. 72). Here again, an example will prove illuminating. An historian of the Renaissance will try to describe the "ideal" Renaissance man, by incorporating all the essential traits of that epoch. However, it is not possible to point out a concrete, historical example of someone who completely coincides with this token. There will always remain an irreducible finite difference between the universal ideal form and the particular instantiation. This is why the work of the historian does not consist simply in collecting facts, but rather in providing an "interpretation" of these facts that goes beyond their mere facticity in order to establish the unity that defines them as not only belonging to a given historical period, but that determines its specific characteristic. Such an account cannot reduce the difference of the particulars to an overriding identity, as is the case in the natural sciences, but rather must show how even totally opposed characters are, each in its own way, "typical" of the spirit of their times:

> What we assert of them is just this, that, this opposition notwithstanding, and indeed perhaps just through it, they stand in a certain ideal connection to one another; that each in his own way cooperates in the construction of what we call the "spirit" of the Renaissance or the culture of the Renaissance. It is a unity of *direction*, not a unity of *being* which is expressed in this way. The particular individuals belong together—not because they are alike or resemble each other, but because they cooperate in a common *task*, which, in contrast to the Middle Ages, we sense to be new and to be the distinctive "meaning" of the Renaissance. All genuine concepts of style in the sciences of culture reduce, when analyzed more precisely, to such concepts of meaning. (*Logic*, pp. 72 f.)

Now, insofar as the science establishes a critique of perception, Cassirer traces the differences between the natural sciences and the cultural sciences to the structure of perception itself. The natural sciences are concerned primarily with things and causal analysis, whereas the cultural sciences are concerned primarily with meaning and form analysis.

> The difference between the concepts of form and style, on the one hand, and the concepts of things, on the other hand, expresses in purely logical terms the same difference which we encountered earlier on in the structure of perception. It is, as it were, the logical translation of a definite opposition of direction, which as such does not appear solely in the domain of concepts, but whose roots descend deep into the soil of perception. Here the concept expresses "discursively" what perception contains in the form of a purely "intuitive" knowledge. (*Logic*, p. 73)

The reference to "what we encountered earlier" calls for a brief explanation. Within the presence of this alterity to consciousness, we can, according to Cassirer, distinguish between the presence of an "it" (*Es*) and the presence of a "thou" (*Du*). "In both cases the alterity persists; but in this very alterity a characteristic difference reveals itself. The 'it' is quite simply an other, an *aliud*; the 'thou' is an *alter ego*" (*Logic*, p. 39). In the one case, the objective presence before us is perceived as a "thing-world," as a physical world composed of objects existing in space and time. In the other, the objective presence is perceived as "something like ourselves."

From an historical perspective, the separation of the two types of approach can be observed from the very beginnings of our philosophical tradition. As Cassirer points out, the struggle between the philosophers of "being" and the philosophers of "becoming" began with the Presocratics and "fills the entire history of Greek philosophy" (*Logic*, p. 88). It found its first and, for many centuries, decisive reconciliation in the thought of Aristotle, who managed to think the formal (εἶδος) and the efficient cause (αἰτία) together by uniting them with the telic principle (*τέλος*). The form of an object becomes cause precisely because it pursues the end of maintaining its own identity outside itself: thus, the form is at once the principle and the end of the causal process. As Aristotle often says, "a man begets a man" (ἄνθρωπος ἄνθρωπον γεννᾷ): the form of man perpetuates itself in becoming the cause of another man possessing the same form, which is the end, or goal, of the generative process.[7] The later Middle Ages and the advent of modern science bring a gradual devaluation of explanations in terms of form, a devaluation finding its first culmination in the science of Galileo:

> The dynamics of Galileo, in its mathematical form, opened up the realm of becoming and made it accessible to strict conceptual

> knowledge. Accordingly, all claims of the Aristotelian concept of form-cause are denounced as worthless. Only the mathematical cause is a *causa vera*. . . . However, with this elimination of the concept of form the gulf between the science of nature and the science of culture had to become evident once again. (*Logic*, pp. 89 f.)

However, in the contemporary development of the natural sciences, Cassirer observes a certain renaissance of the concept of form, though stripped of the teleological dimension that it used to have in Aristotle. He illustrates this transformation in paradigm through a brief study of the physics, psychology, and biology of his time. In each of these, he finds a renewed importance, and indeed centrality, accorded to the ideas of the "whole," "system," and "structure." In the physics of Cassirer's time, we witness a transition from the classical "substance theory" to the modern "field theory" of Faraday and Maxwell. "The field is not a thing-concept but a relation-concept; it is not composed of pieces, but is a system, a totality of lines of force" (*Logic*, p. 92). Similarly, the psychology of elements has become Gestalt psychology, which accords a primacy to structure and the whole over the elements making up this whole. Finally, modern biology has given up the "machine-theory of life" (*Logic*, p. 93), embracing instead a more organic view. These developments undo the unjustified separation between the methods of the *Naturwissenschaften* and the *Geisteswissenschaften*, showing that, despite their clear distinction, they remain complementary and interpenetrate each other:

> The recognition of the concept of wholeness and of the concept of structure has by no means effaced or eliminated the difference between the sciences of nature and the sciences of culture. But it has eliminated a separating barrier which, until now, has stood between them. The science of culture can immerse itself in the study of *its* own forms, *its* own structures and formations with greater freedom and ease than before as the other fields of knowledge have become more attentive to their own particular problems of form. The logic of research is now able to attribute each one of these problems its rightful place. Form-analyses and causal analyses now appear as orientations which do not conflict with each other, but rather complement each other, and which must interrelate in all knowledge. (*Logic*, p. 96)

Le style, c'est l'homme lui-même

The sciences of culture can now study cultural phenomena either through form analysis or causal analysis, or by both. And inversely the natural sciences can also employ form or causal analysis in their investigation into natural phenomena. We find in the new theory of chaos, which is essentially a theory of "morphology," an excellent example of this. We must ask ourselves, however, if the methods of the two sciences are the same, if both can equally employ formal or causal analysis, where precisely the difference is between the nature and spirit. We saw that in the case of nature, there is no divergence between the particular and the universal. The particular represents a concrete and full expression of the universal law that determines it. Thus from the point of view of nature each particular, insofar as it fills the general scientific definition, is identical to every other particular. One piece of gold is identical to every other, insofar as it is a sample of gold. In the case of spirit, however, we said that the particular never corresponds absolutely to the universal, there always remains a difference. To characterize this difference, Cassirer seems to have introduced the concept of "style." Although the form of culture is universal to every culture, no single culture provides a pure expression of this universal form. What distinguishes one culture from other is its style, its specific manner of actualizing the universal form of spirit. We can define style as the historical expression of the universal form of spirit. The sciences of culture must extract this universal form from its historical and particular expression in the different cultures, and in so doing negate the individual style that determines their particular identity. Although this scientific knowledge provides us with the universal form of our existence, it tells us nothing about ourselves. If we are to know anything of ourselves, we must inquire into the historical expression of this universal form, into this living form that constitutes our personal style. For, as Lacan says, "le style, c'est l'homme lui même."[8] To render visible our living form requires another mode of understanding than the one we find in science. It is rather the work of art that reveals to us the living form of our nature.

Seven

Art: The "Eye of Spirit" and the "Cloak of Reality"

Ce que j'essaie de vous traduire est plus mystérieux, s'enchevêtre aux racines même de l'être, à la source impalpable des sensations.

—J. Gasquet, *Cézanne*

From the very beginning we have created beautiful images and adorned ourselves and our world with them. The art of fabricating images is without doubt the quintessence of being human: for wherever we find human existence, we find that being who not only *contemplates* itself and its world in and through aesthetic images, but who creates itself in light of its image and ends by transforming itself into its own image of itself. The symbolic form of art occupies a crucial and twofold place in the thought of Cassirer, and thus within the system of symbolic forms. However, for one reason or another, Cassirer never wrote the volume on art that he had long planned for the *Philosophy of Symbolic Forms*.[1] In writing *An Essay on Man* Cassirer took advantage of the opportunity to develop his theory of aesthetics. In a letter addressed to the Paul Arthur Schilpp, Cassirer writes: "With regard to content it [*An Essay on Man*] would be new, as it would give here for the first time a thorough presentation of my theory of aesthetics."[2] However, this chapter appears, in a way that is difficult to explain, as if it were only a first draft, and as such incomplete.[3] The precise nature of art as a symbolic form and its function within culture were thus never rendered entirely clear by Cassirer. As in the case of religion, we must work from the fragments of what Cassirer says about art and reconstruct his theory of aesthetics. Our observations here remain preliminary; they seek only to prepare the way for further investigation by determining the structure and function of art as a symbolic form within the philosophy of Cassirer.

The Twofold Place of Art in the System of Symbolic Forms

We have already seen that each symbolic form derives its meaning from the place it occupies within the system of forms and in relation to the other spiritual energies of spirit. What then is the place of art within the system of cultural forms? "Art is closely connected to all of them," writes Cassirer, "in regard to both its basic meaning and its development" (*ECN*, I, p. 80/78). The symbolic form of art always seems, as if by its very nature, to be in the service of other symbolic forms. We have already seen that the sphere of spirit is internally divided into two fundamental and mutually exclusive dimensions: namely, the concrete life world of mythical "expression" on the one hand, and the world of "pure signification" on the other. Art is located, as we shall see, at once at the heart of the lived world of expression, and at the center of hermeneutic turn that liberates spirit from its immediate and concrete engagement with its life world, orientating it toward the constitution of the sphere of pure signification.

The "Cloak of Reality"

As we have seen, the concrete life world of spirit is composed of three initial forms: language, myth, and art (cf. *LM*, p. 156). Like language, art appears from "its earliest beings . . . to belong completely to the mythic sphere; the images it creates do not exist for their own sake but are interwoven with certain magical purposes. . . . Word magic and picture magic stand in the center of the magical worldview" (*ECN*, I, p. 80/78; cf. also *PSF*, II, p. 25/34). Language and art are understood by Cassirer to be the "basic ways of objectification, of raising consciousness to the level of seeing objects. This raising is in the end possible only when 'discursive' thinking in language and the 'intuitive' activity of artistic seeing and creating interact so as together to weave the cloak (*Kleid*) of 'reality' " (*ECN*, I, p. 83 f./81); that is to say, the sensible texture of consciousness that mythical intuition takes for the real. We have already examined how language differentiates and structures the flux of content of perception through an act of phonic designation that creates the diverse centers of signification while at the same time weaving the different contents of perception into a system of relations. However, these various "centers" and "relations" require a certain sensible "presence" in order to be "seen." For example, even though language has named the mana, thus providing it with a relative stable signification, without a face, without a sensuous Gestalt to lend this objective reality its objective presence, this absolute force of life would remain invisible to the human eye: to forge the sensible figure of reality and in this way render it visible, such is the essential and original function of art as a symbolic form. "The 'visibility of nature' is the actual, even the only goal of artistic activity" writes Cassirer (*ECN*, I, p. 84/81). It is through its aesthetic figure that nature, life, and especially spirit, acquire the form of their "visibility," if not their "reality."

> This "visibility" (*Sichtbarkeit*), we must recognize, is neither a predicate attributed to things as such, as absolute things, nor does it consist in the simple passive possession of certain sense-data, certain optical sensations or perception. It requires an act of spirit, an act of spontaneity. "Things" attain a "look" (*Gesicht*) because spirit lends it to them through a particular kind or direction of activity. This activity is none other than that of artistic production. It does not imitate what has been seen; rather, its basic significance and true achievement consist in transforming the merely sensed or dully felt into something seen. (*ECN*, I, p. 83/80)

Thus, from a certain perspective mythical consciousness has no other content than that which has been provided by the spiritual activities of language and art. This explains why when we observe a culture other than our own—or our own from a certain critical distance—all that we sees are the aesthetic form of the linguistic activity that makes up the concrete life world of that culture. It is enough to travel abroad, or to observe a group of foreigners to discover a multitude of examples that illustrate this point. Each culture gives itself form and a sensuous presence through its aesthetic comportment toward the world. Not only architecture, language, dress, gestures, and mannerism, but also the body and the face are formed and sculpted according to a common aesthetic norm that defines the identity of a culture and its time. This cultural aesthetic appears in the sensuous presence of reality itself. It is the sensuous embodiment of cultural meaning and cultural identity that is found in tastes, smells, sounds, tactical impressions, and visual gestalts.

Even within the limits of a single culture, or the limits of a single region or metropolis, one can find clear examples of a common aesthetic norm that distinguish one group from another; a Gestalt that belongs to the living heritage and identity of this group and that, in the final analysis, cannot be separated from it. In the chapter on myth we saw that mythical consciousness assumes the image of its god as its mask, and then becomes this mask in and through its ritual life around this holy figure. The mask provides, in other words, the gestalt of our lived existence. Strip away this aesthetic form and what remains is indistinguishable *Dasein*. The Cartesian ego knows only that it is, "I think, therefore I am." *Dasein* knows that it "is," it is aware and preoccupied with its own being, but it cannot tell you "who" it is without referring to culture and, in the end, to the aesthetic form of culture that gives its existence its visibility, and thus its objective presence and reality.

The Emancipation of Spirit and the Contemplation of the Truth

As we have seen, at a certain moment spirit takes up a new attitude toward its own life world, toward its own objective expression. This new attitude of critique, which is brought about by a hermeneutical turn within spirit, manifest itself through the presence of two new cultural forms: namely, religion and science. The work of art is instrumental in bringing about this hermenutical turn:

> Here for the first time the image world, which spirit opposes to the mere world of things and objects, acquires a purely *immanent* validity and truth. It does not aim at something else or refer to something else; it simply "is" and consists in itself. Beyond the sphere of *efficacy*, to which the mythical consciousness clings, and the sphere of *signification* in which the linguistic sign perseveres, we are transposed into a sphere where, as it were, only the pure "being," only the intrinsic and inherent essence, of the image is apprehended as such. Thus for the first time the world of the image becomes a self-contained cosmos with its own center of gravity. And only now can the spirit enter into a truly free relation with it. Measured by the empirical, "realistic" view, the aesthetic world becomes a world of "appearance"; but insofar as

> it severs its bond with immediate reality, with the world of existence and efficacy that constitutes the magical-mythical intuition, it embodies a new step toward the "truth." (*PSF*, II, p. 25 f./34)

It is only once the image is no longer mistaken for a fragment of substantial reality, that is to say, only once it has been recognized as being the expression of the creative energy of spirit, that spirit can freely take up this new critical attitude toward the truth of being—whether this "truth" is understood from the perspective of religious or from the perspective of scientific consciousness. Art denounces itself as an "illusion," as an "appearance" (*Schein*) and introduces the distinction between the image and reality that is foreign to the natural worldview of mythical consciousness, and in this way opens up the space in which spirit can "contemplate" itself and the reality beyond the words of language and the images of art (cf. *PSF*, II, p. 261/311).

> This liberation is achieved not because spirit throws aside the sensuous forms of word and image, but in that it uses them both as *organs* of its own, and thereby recognizes them for what they really are: forms of its own self-revelation. (*LM*, p. 99/158)

However, the "emancipation from this circle takes place only gradually and step by step" (*ECN*, I, p. 80/78). This is why religion and science remain, in their historical development, closely linked to art. "Religion and art are so close to one another in their purely historical development, and so permeate one another, that sometimes the two seem indistinguishable in content and in their inner formative principle. It has been said that the gods of Greece owed their origins to Homer and Hesiod. But as it progressed, the religious thought of the Greeks moved farther and farther away from its aesthetic beginning and sources. After Xenophanes, it rebelled more and more resolutely against the mythical-poetic and the sensuous-plastic concepts of the gods, which it rejected as anthropomorphic" (*PSF*, I, p. 82/13). However, as we saw in our investigation of religion, religious consciousness is never able to entirely escape its relation to the aesthetic image. The movement from idol to icon requires the work of the aesthetic imagination. Thus, the same sense of rebellion against the "mythical-poetic and the sensuous-plastic" figures of God is found throughout the history of the Judeo-Christian and Islamic traditions. This dialectic is so prominent to the history of religious thought that it hardly seems necessary to illustrate it with examples.

As for the importance of beauty to the birth of science and philosophy, there hardly seems any need to remind the reader of the importance of beauty to the founders of our philosophical tradition. "To the Greek mind beauty always had an entirely objective meaning. Beauty is truth; it is a fundamental character of reality. If the beauty which we feel in the harmony of sounds is reducible to a simple numerical ratio it is number that reveals to us the fundamental structure of the cosmic order" (*Essay*, p. 211).

The Cut of the Cloak of Reality

Although it is religion and science that seek—each according to its specific orientation—to determine the logos (λόγος) that orders the cosmos (κόσμος), it is the force of the aesthetic imagination that gives this logos its sensuous presence and thus renders the cosmos visible as such. Not only is the aesthetic image therefore a symbol, it is *the* symbol par excellence. As one knows, etymologically the term κόσμος signified for the Greeks to arrange or order. However, it also meant *ornament* or *to adorn*.

> *Kosmos* can also be read as adornment, especially feminine, for indeed "cosmetic" comes from *kosmos*. *Chrōs* (skin or color) is the Homeric word for the living body, which was understood as a surface and the bearer of visibility, visibility being the guarantor of existence or being. For the Greeks appearing was surface, with *epiphaneia* a word used for both. For them, when a woman *kosmēse* (adorned) herself, she wrapped her *chrōs* in a second skin or body, in order to bring the living surface-body so clothed to light; to make it appear. If women, in ancient Greece, were essentially invisible, cosmetic *kosmos* made them visible.[4]

As we have already said: "The 'visibility of nature' is the actual, even the only goal of artistic activity" (*ECN*, I, p. 84/81). The aesthetic image "weaves the cloak (*Kleid*) of 'reality' " (*ECN*, I, p. 83 f./81), that is to say, the texture that at once gives a sensuous presence or appearance to the real, and confers upon this presence an internal order, a structure, or simply a form. We must understand the term aesthetics here, not in its modern and restricted sense, but rather in the original sense of *aisthetikos* indicating presence or that which is sensuous. We can represent this by the crossed-out life: ~~life~~. The aesthetic image of the cross (><) represents, as we have already seen, the *templum* that functions as the primordial image (*Ur-Bild*) that provides the original archetype of the cosmos, the *Gestalt* that forms and structures the opening of being. The cross of the templum cloaks the real, it reveals the real by hiding it, and thus the aesthetic image of this templum provides the form of the cloak and thus the form of the sensuous appearance of the real.

Mythical consciousness sees in the templum the concrete presence of the mana and the pure form of reality as such. The auger sees in the templum a sign whose meaning must be interpreted and deciphered, through which the truth of reality is to be understood. The aesthetic consciousness leaves this problem behind it: "from the outset it gives itself to pure 'contemplation,' developing the form of vision in contrast to all forms of action, the images fashioned in this frame of consciousness gain for the first time a truly immanent significance" (*PSF*, II, p. 261/311). In other words, whereas science and religion focus their attention on the "invisible harmony that is better than the visible harmony," the aesthetic imagination limits itself to the "pure 'contemplation' " of the "visible harmony" of the templum. And in fact the word "contemplation" comes from the Latin *contemplatus*, the past participle of *contemplari*, which means to gaze attentively or observe and which originally indicated the process of marking out a space for the observation of the augur. The goal of aesthetic imagination, therefore, is to create the templum, the pure signifier par excellence, the sensuous presence that all the other dimensions of consciousness will interpret according to their specific modes of vision.

The real subject of art is thus "to be sought in certain fundamental structural elements of our sense experience itself—in lines, design, in architectural, musical forms. These elements are, so to speak, omnipresent. Free of all mystery, they are patent and unconcealed; they are visible, audible, tangible. In this sense Goethe did not hesitate to say that art does not pretend to show the metaphysical depth of things, it merely sticks to the surface of natural phenomena" (*Essay*, p. 157 f.). The artist "is absorbed in the pure form of things; he intuits their immediate appearance" (*SMC*, p. 159). However, this "surface," or what we have called the texture of consciousness, is not immediately given, and in fact "we do not know it before we discover it in the works of the great artists" (*Essay*, p. 158). Once again we see that the primary objective of the work of art is the "visibility of nature" and it accomplishes this task by "weaving the clock of reality."

Art as the Perfect Harmony of Spirit

The work of art is thus situated at the threshold between the mythical world of expression, on the one side, and the religious and scientific knowledge of pure signification on the other, and as such functions as a sort of passage way between the two mutually exclusive realms of meaning: a passage way that both separates and joins the two domains. "If one can mark the world of *expression* and the world of pure *signification* as the two extremes, between which all cultural development moves, then to some extent the ideal equilibrium between these two extremes is reached in art" ("Form und Technik," p. 87). "It is the merger of the one in the other, the ideal equilibrium which presents itself between them that constitutes the aesthetic stance as well as the aesthetic object" ("The Problem of the Symbol . . . ," p. 424). In the last two chapters we have seen how religion and science constitute themselves through the transformation of the texture of consciousness into the *text*ure of the real that demands interpretation. Religion attempts to return to the pure expression of the pure life stream (*einheitlicher Lebensstrom*) through the *Aufhebung* of the mythical image. Science, on the other hand, seeks to establish a system of pure signification through the *Aufhebung* of the linguistic image. The religious attitude desires to establish a pure subjectivity unaffected by the objectifying and differentiating tendencies of language, and this is done by negating all representation in order to arrive at a voice that speaks without a language. This absolute subjectivity, however, lies beyond the life world of human experience, and can be achieved only through our worldly demise. On the other hand, the scientific attitude endeavors to negate the subjectivity of the knower in order to establish a pure system of differentiated signifiers, a *lingua universalis* without a voice. In the end the empty abstractions of the scientific formulae prove to be meaningless to the speaking subject as an existential being. Both religion and science must therefore reinscribe into their centers that which they have negated and relegated to the margins. The mystic must speak the language of the world, must return to the sphere of representation, and with this to the dimension of myth. The scientist too must return to the sphere of perception, to language, and thus to the subjective point of view of the speaker. As in Plato's famous analogy of the cave, in seeking the truth, spirit must first leave the world of shadows. However, the absolute truth proves, in the final analysis, to be unattainable to living spirit because it is unable to live beyond the limits of its world and is thus forced to return to its shadowy existence. The opposition and dialectical tension between the mythical image world and religious consciousness, on the one hand, and between linguistic perception and scientific consciousness, on the other, can never be resolved: for it is precisely in the dialectical tension between one pole and the other of their respective oppositions that each constitutes itself.

In the concrete life world of spirit the different tendencies of spirit are in a constant struggle to overcome each other. "The particular cultural trends do not move peacefully side by side, seeking to complement one another; each becomes what it is only by demonstrating its own peculiar power against the others and in battle with the others" (*PSF*, I, p. 82/13). At times it seems that expression has won the "battle," but in the end it can never completely do away with the dimension of representation without at the same time destroying itself. At other times it would seem as if representation, "reason and logic" have "triumphed" over mythical expression. But here too the expressive dimension of myth can never be totally extinguished. The same dynamic is seen between the forces of mythical imagination and those of religious vision, and between the linguistic force of representation and the conceptual force of scientific thought. Strife seems to be, as Heraclitus taught, at the origins of all things.

> But in art the combat seems to be reconciled, and this reconciliation is one of its essential privileges and one of its deepest charms. Here we feel no longer the conflict between opposed tendencies. All our different powers and all our different needs seem to be melted into a perfect harmony. ("Language and Art II," p. 191)

We have seen that linguistic representation is a centrifugal force that moves toward a separation and differentiation of being, whereas mythical expression is a centripetal force that draws everything into its center so as to establish the unity and identity of being. The work of art is both centrifugal and centripetal. It "aims at pure representation in the power of pure expression and vice-versa" ("The Problem of the Symbol," p. 424). It is in and through this "perfect harmony" between centrifugal and centripetal force, between expression and representation, subject and object, that the aesthetic imagination renders reality visible. Without the productive power of the aesthetic imagination nothing that can be rigorously called a presence could ever come about. For every presence presupposes the differentiation between that which is present, the object, and the subject for whom this presence is. However, there is also a certain unity between the two, for they are united in and through the event of presence itself. In this way it is clear that for Cassirer the subject and object are only the two ideal poles of one and the same reality. The objective pole of this presence can be understood as the presence of a god, an object, another subject, a word, and so forth. But whatever the mode of vision by which the subject sees this presence before him, that which is seen, the formed sensuous presence before the subject is the product of the aesthetic imagination.

The Eye of Spirit

For Cassirer the work of art is of course never a copy of an already existing objective reality, nor is it a simple expression of some subjective state. Cassirer never tires of critiquing any theory that see in the work of art nothing more than a "simple mechanical reproduction of reality" (*Essay*, p. 138) or an "overflow of emotions and passions" (*Essay*, p. 140). Neither the "onomatopoetic theory of art" nor the "interjectional theory" are able to render justice to the aesthetic activity of the artist, for in accounting for the presence of the work of art they overlook the creative dimension of the aesthetic process itself. The work of art "is neither an imitation of physical things nor a mere overflow of powerful feelings. It is an interpretation of reality—not by concepts but by intuitions; not through the medium of thought but through the sensuous forms" (*Essay*, p. 146).

Now, on the one hand, this interpretation is never for Cassirer a simple "frenzy of the individual artist. . . . The imagination of the artist does not arbitrarily invent the forms of things. It shows us these forms in their true shape, making them visible and recognizable" (*Essay*, p. 145). What the work of art discloses is the "living forms" of reality. On the other hand, Cassirer insists that this disclosure of the living forms of reality nevertheless depends upon the particular "temperament" of the artist (ibid.): "these essential forms *stand* before us in reality only because the eye of the artist has *released* them there" (*ECN*, I, p. 79/77). In other words, the aesthetic imagination must discover the pure forms of things, create the vision that renders these forms visible, and express this vision in an objective representation that renders it accessible and comprehensible to the world. Evidently all these elements are complimentary. For to discover the pure forms of things, it is necessary to see them, and in order to see them it is first necessary to discover them.

> [What is more,] artistic activity, above all, shows how impossible it is to draw a line between "inner" vision and "outward" formation; it shows that here vision *is* already formation, just as formation *remains* pure vision. The "expression" is never something subsequent and relatively accidental that follows a finished and given inner prototype (*Vorbild*): rather, the inner image acquires its content only by composing itself into a work and so manifesting itself through the work. (*PSF*, III, p. 39 f./47)

The artistic imagination is the vision of a "genius," a creative force par excellence. For Cassirer, as for Kant before him, only the greatest of artists can be called "geniuses" in the strict sense of the word. Only their work "brings about the perfect harmony and equipoise of all the different faculties of spirit" ("Language and Art II," p. 191). Mythical thought, linguistic expression, religion and scientific thought all remain "one-sided," insofar as they negate or repress the other powers of spirit (cf. ibid.). It is the vision of the great artists, by their "divine inspiration" (θεία μανία), that the act of seeing comes about, that realty becomes visible. To see, is thus always, as Goethe puts it, to "*Sehen mit Geistes Augen*" (to "see with the eyes of spirit") (*ECN*, I, p. 81/78).

> The artist chooses a certain aspect of reality, but this process of selection is at the same time a process of objectification. Once we have entered into his perspective we are forced to look on the world with his eyes. It would seem as if we have never before seen

> the world in this peculiar light. . . . By virtue of the world of art [this light] has become durable and permanent. Once reality has been disclosed to us in this particular way, we continue to see it in this shape. (*Essay*, p. 146)

The Role of the Spectator

The aesthetic process does not, however, come to an end with the production of the work of art by the artist. There is a certain tendency today to understand the work of art as a simple thing and not as an activity or process. From this perspective, the true aesthetic activity is limited to that of the artist, and the spectator is relegated to an essentially passive role. However, the meaning of the work of art is closed to the passive spectator. The beauty of the work is found in our "susceptibility to the dynamic life of forms, and this life cannot be apprehended except by a corresponding dynamic process in ourselves" (*Essay*, p. 151). The work of art is not a thing, but a way of seeing. The word "spectator," as well as the word "spectacle," come from the Latin *spectare*, which means "to see" or "to behold." The spectator must enter into the spectacle of the artist, into the artist's way of seeing or beholding the world. "Even the spectator of the work of art is not restricted to a mere passive role. In order to contemplate and to enjoy the work of art he has to create it in his measure. We cannot understand or feel a great work of art without, to a certain degree, repeating and reconstructing the creative process by which it has come into being" (*SMC*, p. 212). The *work* of art is thus not the simple *object* of art. Rather the *work* of art is the aesthetic process of the productive imagination.

The Three-Dimensions of the Work of Art

Cassirer distinguishes between three dimensions of the work of art which determine its internal structure.[5]

> These three dimensions—the dimension of the physical existence, of the objectively represented (*Gegenständlich-Dargestelltes*), and of the personal expression (*Persönlich-Ausgedrückten*)—are determining and indispensable for everything that is a "work" (*Werk*) and not merely an "effect" (*Wirkung*). (*Logic*, p. 43)

In the work of art these three dimensions are reciprocally determined and form a single organic reality. They are three ways of understanding one and the same reality, rather than three independent autonomous elements. Every work of art possesses a certain "physical existence." Cassirer does not seem to understand by this the raw material used to create the work of art. Rather the basic stuff of which the work of art is made is a material that has always already been formed by the aesthetic imagination into the lines, shadows, spots of color, rhythms, and so on that make up the work of art (cf. *Essay*, p. 154). The artist sees in the raw material an already formed reality that is used as a means of expression. And what is expressed is precisely the form that transforms the raw material into the physical existence of the work of art. "These formal elements [the melody, rhythm, etc.] are not merely external or technical means to reproduce a given intuition; they are part and parcel of the artistic intuition itself" (*Essay*, p. 155). The intuition of the artist cannot be separated from the medium of the intuition.

> In truth . . . the particular mode of expression does not only belong to the *technique* of the formation of the work, but is already part of the *conception* of the work of art itself. Beethoven's intuition is musical, Phidias' intuition is plastic, Milton's intuition is epic, Goethe's intuition is lyric. All this concerns not only the outer shell but also the very kernel of their creations. . . . Here both factors are so completely taken up into each other that, although they can of course be separated in reflection, they constitute an inseparable whole for the aesthetic intuition and aesthetic feeling. . . . But from this it follows that aesthetic intuition is born as musical, plastic, lyric, or dramatic, and that these differences expressed here are, therefore, not mere verbal notations or labels which we attach to individual works of art, but that genuine differences of style, divergent directions of artistic intention, correspond to them. (*Logic*, p. 120)

Every work of art is unique and different, and what renders it unique is the personal expression of the artist. The disclosure of the living forms of reality depend, as we have already said, on the particular "temperament" of the artist (cf. *Essay*, p. 145). "In this respect, Goethe was right in saying that *style* rests in the deepest foundations of knowledge, in the very essence of things, insofar as we are permitted to have knowledge of it through visible and tangible forms" (*Logic*, p. 31). When we enter into the perspective of the work of art, we begin to see the world according to the eyes of the artist and thus begin to take up his or her way of seeing things. What is seen is determined by the way of seeing, and visa versa.

The *work* of the artist thus accomplishes simultaneously three tasks. To begin with, it must transform the raw material of mere sensation into the formed sensuous material with which the work of art is composed. Next, it must weave this formed material into a differentiated but organic whole that represents the sensuous living form of nature or spirit. It is important to emphasis the fact that the work of art possesses "a definite teleological structure." Each line, each shadow, each blotch of color, each rhythm, but also each word, each gesture, and so on is situated in the whole of the work, and derives its aesthetic meaning from it is place within this whole. Finally, through this work of formation, the artist renders visible a way of seeing the living forms of nature or spirit. But, of course, this vision is discoverable only in and through the work of art, and is only created in and through the process of formation itself.

> Subjective and objective, feeling and form must merge into one another and must be completely absorbed in one another if a great work of art is to be created. However, it follows from this that, and why, the work of art can never be a mere reproduction of the subjective or of the objective, of the spiritual or of the objective world, but that a genuine discovery of both. . . . (*Logic*, p. 31)

That which transforms the mere sensuous material into the formed sensuous presence, that which weaves this formed material into teleological whole, that which renders visible the living form of reality, is the individual style of the artist. Style is, as it were, the universal form of a particular form of spirit. The style of the individual artist is, of course, an expression of the style of the times, which is itself the historical expression of the style of a particular culture, a style that is itself a unique expression of the form of humanity itself. Every work of art brings together and expresses each of these different levels, though according to the degree of sensibility of the artists or spectator. It is the "degree of intensification and illumination that is the measure of the excellence of art" (*Essay*, p. 148). The greater the intensity, the greater the illumination. In every work of art it is the individual style of the artist that is expressed. In most works of art, it is the style of a particular historical epoch and culture that is expressed. But only in the very greatest of works do we find a pure expression of the universal form of humanity itself.

The "Catharsis" of the Soul

The aesthetic imagination introduces an opening in which the cosmos comes to be seen. As for the being of the artist and spectator, the work of art functions as a "catharsis" of the soul. In and through the work of art, spirit frees itself from the tyranny of effective and emotive reality that forms the concrete texture of consciousness, without completely breaking from this concrete presence. The work of art functions as a mirror that reflects the sensuous forms of life, nature, and spirit. "The imitation of nature and expression of feelings are the two basic elements of art. They are, as it were, the stuff of which the cloak of art is woven" (*SMC*, p. 211). However, the mirror is also a light. As we have already seen, art is never a simple copy of a pregiven reality. When we contemplate the forms of our passions in the work of art, they have already been transformed and charged with a new meaning. Certainly the aesthetic image is "filled with the liveliest energies of passion, but passion itself is here transformed both in its nature and in its meaning. Wordsworth defines poetry as 'emotion recollected in tranquillity' " (*Essay*, p. 147). In the mirror of the aesthetic image, we find ourselves before our concrete reality, or more precisely its ideal form, and with this distance we no longer feel the force of this reality as it is lived in our everyday lives.

> [T]he image of a passion is not the passion itself. The poet who represents a passion does not infect us with this passion. At a Shakespeare play we are not infected with the ambition of Macbeth, with the cruelty of Richard III, or with the jealousy of Othello. We are not at the mercy of these emotions; we look through them; we seem to penetrate into their very nature and essence. (*Essay*, p. 147)

Cassirer characterizes this aesthetic contemplation by means of Aristotle's theory of "catharsis." The catharsis of the soul is neither a "purification" nor a "purgative" of emotions. Rather here "our emotions themselves become a part of our active life, not of our passive life. They are elevated to a new state" (*SMC*, p. 211). Through their expression in the work of art, we are able to adopted a new attitude toward our intimate emotional life, toward our mythical existence. Certainly, we still experience these various emotions, but we are no longer dominated by them. We find here the harmony between the concrete and immediate sphere of mythical expression, on the one hand, and the sphere of pure representation, on the other.

> By tragic poetry the soul acquires a new attitude towards its emotions. The soul experiences the emotions of pity and fear, but instead of being disturbed and disquieted by them it is brought to a state of rest and peace. . . . For what Aristotle looks upon as the effect of tragedy is a synthesis of two moments which in real life, in our practical existence, exclude each other. The highest intensification of our emotional life is thought of as at the same time giving us a sense of repose. We live through all our passions feeling their full range and highest tension. But what we leave behind when passing the threshold of art is the hard pressure, the compulsion of our emotions. (*Essay*, p. 148)

However this "aesthetic freedom" is not to be confused with "Stoic apathy." It is an active acceptance or recognition of our emotional life and its sensuous form, and not a passive indifference to it. Through the work of art we come to see things from a certain distance, and we cannot help but remark at the absurdity of our existence. We see that we are only an image of ourselves, a simple marionette controlled by our internal emotions and the image of ourselves that we have fabricated. We play our role on what Shakespeare has rightly called the stage of life. However, as Cassirer points out, there is only one step from the tragic to the comic (cf. *Essay*, 149). The tragedy of our existence is that there is nothing we can do about it, it just is, a small joke of nature.

> We are perhaps never nearer to our human world than in the works of a great comic writer—in Cervantes' *Don Quixote*, Sterne's *Tristram Shandy*, or in Dickens' *Pickwick Papers*. We become obser-

> vant of the minutest details; we see this world in all its narrowness, its pettiness, and silliness. We live in this restricted world, but we are no longer imprisoned by it. Such is the peculiar character of the comic catharsis. Things and events begin to lose their material weight; scorn is dissolved into laughter and laughter is liberation. (*Essay*, p. 150)

What is surprising is to see to what point Cassirer insists that we must maintain this sense of humor.

> The form of humor that dominates here must maintain itself in the immediate presence of suffering and even death. (*Die Platonische Renaissance in England und die Schule von Cambridge*, p. 124)

Conclusion

Cassirer's Metaphysics of the Symbolic Forms

A Unity in the Symbolic Forms?

> When, at the end of the long road which our considerations have traveled, we look back in order to compare and unite the manifold aspects which have presented themselves to us in the different phases of our journey, even the attempt of such a unification meets with a difficulty which is due to the problematic and the method of our investigation itself.[1]

Such is the first sentence of Cassirer's notes for the planned, though never finished fourth volume of the *Philosophy of Symbolic Forms* that have only recently been published. The quotation suggests not only the reasons why this final part of Cassirer's magnum opus was undertaken, but perhaps also why it was never to appear during the author's lifetime: "even the *attempt*" to think the unity of the system of symbolic forms encounters a structural difficulty. Is not the project of the *Philosophy of Symbolic Forms* an investigation into the irreducible multidimensionality of human rationality? And, if so, would the tentative to reduce this multiplicity to an overriding unity not contradict the very spirit of Cassirer's entire project?

A lot is at stake in these questions. The answers that they receive will be decisive for our evaluation of the merits and demerits, the success or failure, of Cassirer's "repetition" of modernity. Does Cassirer, at the end of the *Philosophy of Symbolic Forms*, yield to the temptation to reduce the multiplicity of forms of rationality that he has discovered in human culture to a self-identical systematic unity? Or will the whole edifice of the symbolic forms disintegrate into a chaos of unrelated, heterogeneous elements? Or is there another possibility, one permitting us to think a new kind of nontotalizing systematicity?

A Brief Retrospective

In the present conclusion, I shall endeavor to answer these questions, thus returning to the problematic, set out in chapter 1, that was to guide our reading of the philosophy of symbolic forms. The notion of the symbolic was presented as the key element in Cassirer's thought enabling him to transform the modern project of rationality from within. As an answer to the loss of unity in man's knowledge of himself, or the fact that modern man has become lost in a "labyrinth" of heterogeneous cultural discourses (cf. *Essay*, p. 22), Cassirer proposes a widening of the Kantian project of a critique of reason, which he transforms into a critique of culture, that is to say, a critique of the symbolic. As an answer to the basic crux of Western metaphysics, based as it is upon the "myth of the given," thus essentially being a metaphysics of presence, Cassirer proposes a philosophy of representation that, through the concept of the symbolic, understands everything "given" to man as always already mediated by a sign. As an answer to the logocentrism of a metaphysical tradition culminating in the Hegelian phenomenology of spirit, that is, a system closed upon itself in which nature is reduced to the idea, Cassirer proposes a phenomenology of culture, in which life and spirit are co-constitutional elements fused and separated by the symbolic. Having shown the centrality of the concept of the symbolic to Cassirer's transformation of modern rationality, we turned to a consideration of the symbolic as "dialectical structure," and then deduced, as it were, the multiplicity of symbolic forms from the different logical possibilities existing in the relationship between the signifier and the signified. Subsequently, in chapters 2 through 7, we analyzed each of the symbolic forms thus unfolded in and for itself. Now is the moment to synthesize, to explore the problem of the unity and systematicity of the different cultural forms.

An Ethical Unity of Function

From Substance to Function

As we already know, Cassirer's philosophy defines itself from the very start as a philosophy of function as opposed to traditional substantialist metaphysics. We have seen that Cassirer extended the neo-Kantian turn from substance to function to the whole domain of human culture. This primacy of function over substance now becomes the mechanism by which he attempts to explain the unity of the symbolic forms as a system. For, as Cassirer argues, the difference between the various cultural forms turns into an antinomy and, indeed, an irreconcilable contradiction if it is understood in the context of the old metaphysics that sees each of them as expressions of a static "being." Therefore, rather than look at them "objectively," we need to consider the cultural forms from a "subjective" point of view, one that understands them as *diverse* expressions of the *one* spiritual energy of the human spirit:

> The older metaphysics, as well as psychological positivism, which started from an unequivocal "being" (that of the "world" or of the simple "sensations"), again and again entangled itself in unresolvable contradictions and antinomies in the *interpretation* of this supposedly one being. The different world views (e.g., that of "knowledge" and that of faith, of "religion" and of science, of experience and of metaphysics, etc.) contradicted themselves, were irreconcilable. And yet each of them claimed to give and represent the One true being (*das Eine, wahre Sein*)!
>
> These contradictions cannot be resolved as long as one holds on to being as an *unequivocally* certain *starting point (Sein als eindeutig gewisser Ausgangspunkt)*. . . .
>
> But here there has to be the turn: "subjective instead of objective." What is required is not the unity of "the" thing, the absolute object—rather unity of *spirit*, of the spiritual *energy* as such in all the diversity of the "symbolic forms." (*ECN*, I, p. 262)

From Function to Freedom

"This is what the philosophy of the symbolic can give and accomplish!" Cassirer concludes. Cassirer's "symbolic idealism" is not simply the reversal of "realistic metaphysics" in that it "*does not start from the simplicity of the thing (of the substance), but from the unity of the function,*" thus replacing one "common origin" (*gemeinsamer Ursprung*) of human meaning with another (*ECN*, I, p. 263). The Cassirerian "turn," or

Wendung, is much more radical, insofar as, for Cassirer, spirit cannot grasp its identity *as* its origin, *as* its ἀρχή, but only as its future goal, its τέλος. The quest for the (metaphysical) unity and the origins of spirit thus turns into an (ethical) task. Metaphysics, for Cassirer, is transformed into ethics. Like Socrates, he asks

> not (metaphysically) *whence* (*woher*) all this—
> but he asks (ethically) for the *"towards what end"* (*"Wozu"*),
> for the εἶδος as τέλος. (*ECN*, I, p. 127)

Thus, the multiplicity of the different cultural forms is no longer conceived of *negatively* as a "falling away" from the unity of the origin, but rather as a means enabling spirit to constitute its identity as it moves ahead into its future.[2] Furthermore, the ideal is not to overcome the multiplicity of cultural forms sometime in the future in order to reconstitute a simplicity, or stale unity; rather, spirit's identity *is* nothing but the consciousness of its multiplicity as it differentiates itself in action:

> In relation to the unity of *action* thus understood the multiplicity of possible symbolic views is not opposed and hostile: but it rather constitutes for it the necessary *correlate*. It is only in the manifoldness of symbolic directions that the unity (*Einheit*) of spirit—not as substantial simplicity (*substantielle Einfachheit*), but as functional manifoldness (*funktionale Mannigfaltigkeit*)—represents itself. The spirit is one (*eins*), in that in the multiplicity of manifold directions of action it becomes conscious of its *identity* (as action in general). (*ECN*, I, p. 263)

There is no "unity" and "identity" for spirit—except an imaginary one—in which the multiplicity of cultural forms could be undone, reduced to simplicity, or absolutely transcended. Identity is the awareness of irreducible difference; transcendence, the realization that spirit is inextricably immanent in the multiplicity of the cultural forms. As Cassirer says in the *Logic of the Cultural Sciences*, "here the Hegelian statement holds good, that he who *knows* a limit (*Schranke*) is already beyond it. This becoming aware is the beginning and end, the alpha and omega, of the freedom that is granted to man; to know and to acknowledge necessity is the genuine process of liberation which 'spirit,' in contradistinction to 'nature,' has to accomplish" (*Logic*, p. 25). Thus, the entire process of the differentiation of spirit and its subsequent self-consciousness *as* differentiated, can be interpreted as the self-liberation of spirit. In other words, the "*Wozu*," the τέλος that constitutes the unity of the system of symbolic forms, is freedom: "Human culture taken as a whole may be described as the process of man's progressive self-liberation" (*Essay*, p. 228). Or, in the words of a text from the unfinished fourth volume:

> The proper and highest accomplishment (*Leistung*) of each "symbolic form" consists in this, that, with its own means and according to the peculiar direction appropriate to it, it contributes to this goal: the transition from the realm of "nature" to that of "freedom." (*ECN*, I, p. 109)

An Internally Differentiated and Dynamic Unity

The Dialectics of Life and Spirit

The unity of the symbolic forms is, as we have seen in the preceding section, not a "simple" unity (*Einfachheit*); it is no substantial unity, but a functional one; a unity not of origin, but rather of end: of τέλος and "*Wozu*"; it is, finally, a unity not in the sense of traditional metaphysics, but rather one conceived in terms of an ethical task. To use the neo-Kantian terminology Cassirer employs elsewhere in his oeuvre, it is not something just *gegeben*, but an *Aufgabe* (cf., e.g., *Logic*, p. 30). Let us now consider more closely the nature of this functional, teleological, and ethical unity of the symbolic forms.

We have already discovered that the symbolic forms have their unity only in their function to mediate the movement from "nature" to "freedom." In other words, explaining the unity of the symbolic forms requires an investigation into what Cassirer calls the problem of "spirit and life." This problem is, of course, the basic question addressed in Hegel's philosophy of spirit, which describes the movement from "substance" to "subject." According to Cassirer, the relationship between life and spirit is also at the heart of the philosophical discussions of his time, which he reads as a struggle between philosophers of "life" and philosophers of "spirit."[3] Cassirer's project must therefore be understood in the context of his attitude both toward Hegel and toward the philosophical movement in the first decades of this century.

It is interesting that Cassirer's attempts to think the unity of the symbolic forms in the unfinished fourth volume of the *Philosophy of Symbolic Forms* coincide with a heightened awareness concerning the problematic of "life." As a matter of fact, the first three volumes do not explicitly address the dialectic of life and spirit. It is, therefore, reasonable to suggest that it is only in rethinking the project of the philosophy of symbolic forms more profoundly in the light of this dialectic that Cassirer could move toward a unification of the system of symbolic forms.

Cassirer Between Hegel and Heidegger

Cassirer's recurring criticism both of Hegel and of contemporary thinkers such as Bergson, Scheler, and Heidegger is that they have, in thinking about life and spirit, tended to privilege one of the two poles. Hegel's metaphysics had to "collapse" (*ECN*, I, p. 159) because, in the final analysis, nature comes to be absorbed into idea[4] (cf. *Logic*, p. 35); but somebody like Heidegger commits the opposite mistake, by suggesting that, as *Dasein* moves away from the "immediacy" of life, it falls away from authenticity into the inauthenticity of the One (*Man*) (cf. *ECN*, I, p. 219 f.). The question for Cassirer will be how the "*transcendence* of the *Idea* [can] be reconciled with the *immanence* of *Life*" (" 'Spirit' and 'Life'," p. 866/42), without, as in the case of Hegel, reducing life to spirit, or, as in the case of Bergson, Heidegger and others, negating the intrinsic value of spirit. True to his usual approach, Cassirer thus does not totally reject either the Hegelian philosophy of spirit or the Heideggerian philosophy of life.

The *"Zug zur Idee"*

In his own mind, life is not merely the "other" of spirit, but it carries spirit within itself—such that the negation of life in spirit, or in the "idea," is a negation within life itself:

> How is it to be explained that life follows the pattern (*Vorbild*) set before it by the idea—if there is not contained in life itself an immanent "trend toward the idea" ("*Zug zur Idee*") . . . ? May not life, after all, be something other and something more than mere impulse, more than a drive into the indeterminate and the aimless—does there not exist originally within life itself the will to attain its own self-representation (*Selbstdarstellung*), its own self-objectification, its own "visibility"? (" 'Spirit' and 'Life,' " p. 866/43 f.)

As Cassirer explains in the third volume of the *Philosophy of Symbolic Forms*, "life cannot *apprehend* itself (*Selbsterfassung*) by *remaining* absolutely within itself. It must give itself form (*Form*); for it is precisely by this 'otherness' ('*Andersheit*') of form that it gains its 'visibility' ('*Sichtigkeit*'), if not its reality (*Wirklichkeit*)" (*PSF*, III, p. 39/46). Now life, by moving out of itself, toward its "other," in a way *does* remain in itself, insofar as it contains within itself the "*Zug zur Idee.*" Similarly, spirit is not simply the negation of life, but possesses an intrinsic tendency to turn against itself in a movement toward life. It is in this sense that Cassirer writes in his essay on " 'Spirit' and 'Life,' " that, because life "has no other language than that which spirit lends it . . . wherever it is summoned against the spirit, the latter in truth is always both assailant and defendant, plaintiff and judge in one. The real drama takes place not between life and spirit, but in the midst of the spirit's own realm, indeed at its very focus" (" 'Spirit' and 'Life,' " p. 876/54). These movements—the movement from life to spirit, which is the movement from life into its own truth, and the movement from spirit to life, which is a process of spirit's coming to itself[5]—are mediated by the symbolic forms. Indeed, the symbolic forms are nothing but the "in-between" (*Zwischenreich*) binding these two poles together (cf. " 'Spirit' and 'Life,' " p. 874/51). But they are also what constitutes these two poles in the first place, creating them, as life and spirit move toward their interior "other" splitting within themselves and thereby separating from one another. That spirit and life are, as other, *the interiority of each other*, cannot but appear paradoxical, if not contradictory. However, it is ineluctable that an attempt to articulate the way in which the symbolic forms "create" the binary opposites of life and spirit—while themselves being nothing but the relation "between" them—should run into antinomies. For the attempt to articulate in terms of binary opposites and spatial metaphors (such metaphors constitute the nature of our language [cf. p. 78], the "origins" of these binary opposites) is only possible, if at all, through a subversive turning against itself of language. As Cassirer himself writes:

> Thus, that great "crisis," that *process* of separation through which the world of spirit comes originally into existence, cannot be elucidated by any spatial comparison, by any "here" or "there," any "inside" or "outside." The image-language of space entangles us here inevitably in aporias and antinomies: each formulation which we try within it turns immediately into its opposite. The world of spirit is no more "immanent" to the world of life than it is "transcendent" to it—it remains no more caught up "in" it than it rises "above" it. For this doubleness (*Doppelheit*) of "inside" and "outside," of "above" and "below" is not one that exists in itself, that is merely given, but it is one of spiritual standpoint (*geistiger Aspekt*): it exists only for the "viewpoint" (*"Blickpunkt"*) of spirit. Because this point is not established in itself, because each direction of vision contains the possibility of its own reversal, the possibility of "reflection"—[that is why] for us, as spiritual subjects, this twofoldness (*Zwiespaltigkeit*) can arise and exist. The apparent dualism, the split in "being" (*Riss im "Dasein"*) is in truth nothing but the consequence of this necessary duality of "sight" (*Sicht*). It means that life, without having fallen from itself, without simply having come "out of itself," has become transparent to itself, has become *objectified* (*gegenständlich*) to itself. In this turn from the mere being-in-itself (*An-Sich-Sein*) to the being-for-itself (*Für-Sich-Sein*) each single symbolic form collaborates in its way and with its means, and through it that new way, that peculiar mode of *consciousness* (*Bewusstheit*) which represents itself in man is now attained, together with the objective formations of culture. (*ECN*, I, p. 59 f.)

If the symbolic forms are the means of the transformation, *within* life, of life into spirit—the means, that is, of the "original cleavage of being within itself" (*ursprüngliche Entzweiung des Seins in sich selbst*) (" 'Spirit' and 'Life,' " p. 860/35) by which the binary opposition of spirit and life existing undifferentiatedly within life itself is unfolded and differentiated without simply negating the unity of life, then the unity of the multiplicity of symbolic forms is nothing other than the differentiated/undifferentiated unity of life and spirit themselves.

Life, Spirit, and the Symbolic Forms: a Metaphor

Let us try to formulate this difficult relationship of identity and difference between life, spirit, and the symbolic forms in another way, drawing upon a very old metaphysical metaphor.[6] Imagine a beam of light illuminating a spiral of smoke. Without the opacity of the smoke the beam of light would remain invisible; but without the illumination of the light, so would the smoke. For it is only in and through the smoke that the light is given form and through this form gains its "visibility, if not its reality." On the other hand, the smoke itself, which gives form to light, would equally lack presence without the illumination of the light. Now neither the smoke nor the light is the luminous presence itself; the luminous presence as the interplay of the smoke and of the light possesses a reality that neither the light nor the smoke can claim. Nevertheless, it is of course nothing "apart from" or "beyond" the smoke and the light. Now if we understand the light to be life, the smoke to be the symbolic forms and the luminous presence to be spirit, we see that life comes to visibility in and through the symbolic forms, which give it shape and presence, but that the presence of life itself is spirit. Throughout our reading of Cassirer's philosophy we have seen that the unity of the multiplicity of symbolic forms is nothing but the differentiated/undifferentiated unity of life and spirit themselves. In terms of our new metaphor, the smoke unites and differentiates light and its luminous presence: it unites them insofar as it is only in and through the smoke that the light gains its visible existence, but it is also in and through the smoke that the possibility arises to distinguish the light "in itself" from this visible existence. Finally, the symbolic forms are of course fundamentally different from the smoke of our metaphor in one way: they possess no substantial existence independently of the interplay of life and spirit. This complicates matters such that they can no longer be expressed conceptually, but only contemplated. Is it perhaps for this reason that, in the fourth volume of the *Philosophy of Symbolic Forms,* Cassirer experimented with a second model to account for the relationship between life and the symbolic forms?

The Dialectic of the *Urphänomene*

Urphänomene: The "Focal Point" of Cassirer's Philosophy?

Our consideration of the question of the unity of the symbolic forms thus leads us to an analysis of Cassirer's reception of Goethe's reflections on the "basic phenomena," the *Urphänomene*. The *Urphänomene* and the important role that they seem to play in the thought of the later Cassirer have attracted considerable attention in the recent critical literature: the editor of the fourth volume of the *Philosophy of Symbolic Forms*, John Michael Krois, has even voiced the opinion that it is the doctrine of the *Urphänomene* that constitutes the most important discovery in Cassirer's unpublished manuscripts on the planned fourth volume. According to Krois, the philosophy of symbolic forms finds its "focal point" in this doctrine![7] Nevertheless, the question as to how precisely the *Urphänomene* bring together the whole of Cassirer's thought, and resolve the complex issue of the unity of the symbolic forms, is difficult to answer. Irene Kajon, in an article on "The Problem of the Unity of Consciousness in the Thought of Ernst Cassirer," writes that "the theme of the relationship between I and Thou in the medium of language and other cultural forms, a theme that Cassirer developed in the last phase of his thought in the course of his polemics against *Lebensphilosophie*, has never been clearly linked up by him with his concept of the unity of consciousness."[8] Now the "relationship between I and Thou in the medium of language and other cultural forms" is precisely what is thematised in the doctrine of the *Urphänomene*. In spite of the difficulties in determining the status and function of this doctrine in the whole of Cassirer's thought, we will attempt to show how the unity of the symbolic forms can be seen in the interplay of the three "basic phenomena" of I, Thou, and It.

I, Thou, It

The first of the three basic phenomena that Cassirer distinguishes following Goethe is "life," or the "I." This "stream of consciousness" with its "centripetal" movement is a "monad" that embraces the totality of present, past, and future (cf. *ECN*, I, p. 123 f. and 133 f.). However, "the 'monad' as *isolated* individual is an abstraction" (*ECN*, I, p. 134). It has to "turn to the 'outside' " (*ECN*, I, p. 124). In this decentering movement of "action" (*Tun*) and "love" (*ECN*, I, p. 124), the I discovers the *"resistance"* (*Widerstand*) (*ECN*, I, p. 134) of the outside world, and in this consciousness of resistance the consciousness of the "object" as *Gegen-Stand* is born (*ECN*, I, p. 134)—*Gegen-Stand* in the etymological sense of something "standing over against" the monadic I. Now this *Gegen-Stand* is originally experienced as a "Thou" (*Du*), not as an "It" (*Es*) (*ECN*, I, p. 135). This is why the second *Urphänomen* can simply be called the "Thou" (*ECN*, I, p. 137). Now, however, arises the question as to "how we become recognizable to *others*" (*Wie werden wir andern kenntlich?*) (*ECN*, I, p. 125). Not, Cassirer replies, "through *ourselves*, not through what we live or are, but through the *objectivization*, through the 'work' ('*Werk*') that we create" (*ECN*, I, p. 125). Through this work, the I enters a new "order" obeying "objective criteria" (*ECN*, I, p. 125). This order of objective culture can be experienced by the I as a "restraint" (*ECN*, I, p. 125) of its unformed stream of consciousness, indeed as a factor of "alienation" (*Ent-Fremdung*) (*ECN*, I, p. 136). Its work, moreover, somehow transcends the I and escapes its control. What its work means and "is," is now no longer the private affair of the I, but becomes something "extending over the centuries—it becomes clear only in its total effect (*Wirkung*) and interpretation (*Auslegung*)" (*ECN*, I, p. 125 f.). As Cassirer writes, citing Heine: *"was er webt, das weiß kein Weber"*—"what he weaves, no weaver knows" (*ECN*, I, p. 125). Yet it would be completely mistaken to interpret this sphere of the "work," which can also be termed the "It" (*Es*) or the "world" (*Welt*) (*ECN*, I, p. 137), as a mere "degradation" (*ECN*, I, p. 137). Rather, it constitutes a "genuine consciousness of *reality*" (*eigentliches Wirklichkeitsbewusstsein*) (*ECN*, I, p. 136).

Cassirer stresses that it would be to misunderstand the three *Urphänomene* if they were to be conceived of as simple "beings": such as an I standing over against a Thou, the two of them being put into some relationship by the It. The basic phenomena have no "absolute being," they are nothing that we come to know through some kind of mediation, but rather they are the mediation itself. In his notes on the basic phenomena for the fourth volume of the *Philosophy of Symbolic Forms*, Cassirer puts it like this:

> We can describe them correctly, not as a something that "*is*," that is at hand (*vorhanden*) in the sense of *absolute* being, neither [as something] whose being, understood in this sense, can be inferred, whose absolute being can be logically *deduced*— . . . In all the real basic phenomena it is not a question of *such* a being—they are not that which is somehow mediated to us, but they are the ways, the *modes of mediation* itself.
>
> *Figuratively* speaking: they are not something that is in itself *at hand* (*an sich Vorhandenes*), which somehow comes into us *through* the windows of our consciousness . . . —but they are themselves the windows of knowledge of reality—that by means of which we open ourselves up to reality. (*ECN*, I, p. 132)

A Hypothesis: The *Urphänomene* as the Symbolic Function

The *Urphänomene* are, Cassirer continues in rather poetic language, our "view" (*Blick*) of the world, the "eye" that we open (*das Auge, das wir aufschlagen*) (*ECN*, I, p. 132). Let us now try to interpret this difficult concept of the *Urphänomene* and its place in the overall structure of the philosophy of symbolic forms. The hypothesis guiding us in this interpretation is that the *Urphänomene* constitute the unity of the symbolic forms that Cassirer himself refers to as the "symbolic function"—the "factor which reoccurs in each basic cultural form but in no two of them takes exactly the same shape" (*PSF*, I, p. 84/16). All the symbolic forms will turn out to be different moments in the dynamic process of the presence of meaning to spirit, a process that will be shown to be describable in terms of the three basic phenomena.

We have seen in our brief summary of Cassirer's notes on the *Urphänomene* that the I and the Thou are not recognizable to each other immediately, or "through themselves," but rather only through the sphere of the works that they create. The "resistance" of the Thou is thus never experienced directly, but rather in a mediate fashion in and through the presence of the work which somehow "restrains" the I's unformed stream of consciousness. In other words, the I encounters the Thou through the objective order of signifiers, which announce within the consciousness of the I the presence of an existence fundamentally other than it. The "it" is in fact ambiguous, referring at once to the "I" of consciousness and to the signifier. I have previously called this presence of the objective order of signifiers to consciousness, the "texture" of the real. This texture, although a moment of "alienation" in the life of consciousness, brings it to a "genuine consciousness of reality," and through this consciousness of reality to a consciousness of itself. The different symbolic forms represent the different modes of the presence of the Thou to the consciousness of the I through the order of signification, that is to say, through the texture of the real as the sphere of works. The symbolic function could thus be summarized in the following algorithm in figure C.1.

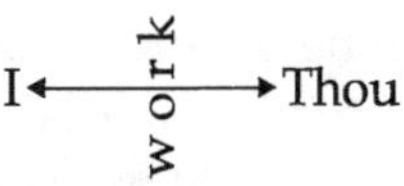

Figure C.1

In the language of structuralism introduced in chapter 2, the Thou is the ultimate signified of all human signification, of the whole order of signifiers. It is the τέλος toward which all signification moves. The world of human culture has no other function than to announce to the I the presence of a Thou, which will, in a sense, never be attained. Insofar as the work can be seen as the order of signifiers, and the Thou as the ultimate signified of this order, the symbolic function can be represented as in figure C.2.

Figure C.2

Urphänomene and the Problem of Reflexivity

With regard to the *Urphänomene,* Goethe insisted that nothing "behind" them should be sought; "for here is the limit," as he said in a conversation with Eckermann quoted by Cassirer in the *Logic of the Cultural Sciences* (*Logic,* p. 99). The *Urphänomene* just "*appear*" (*erscheinen*), to see in them anything but "surface" (*Oberfläche*) is to introduce a " 'metaphysical' depth" (*'metaphysische' Tiefe*) into the only perspective—the artist's contemplation—which is appropriate to them (*ECN,* I, p. 126). Cassirer nuances this Goethean point of view, without, however, questioning its basic validity. He asks whether "an attitude such as Goethe calls for here as artist and [such as he] practices, is *possible* in the *whole* of spiritual life" (*ECN*, I, p. 127). And his answer is negative; for there is no such *"unbroken* unity" (*ungebrochene Einheit*) in spirit, to whose "original and essential functions" it belongs to *question*. The *Brechung*, the "rupture," which spirit thus introduces into its own realm is, in fact, an "immanent ('dialectical') necessity" (*immanente ('dialektische') Notwendigkeit*) (*ECN*, I, p. 127). Hence the problem that Cassirer proposes to address in his notes on the basic phenomena:

> Can the *awe* (*Ehrfurcht*) before the *Urphaenomene* be maintained—without acting against the 'spirit' of critique—without becoming guilty of *committing a sin* against this spirit—which consists in that we deny it its original right, its *autonomy*—that we treat it like a foreigner and intruder (*L'intruse*).
> That is the question which we want to pose ourselves in what follows (ECN, I, p. 131).

Alas, the reader will read on in vain if he or she expects a response to this question in the fourth volume. Before we turn to an attempt to answer it for Cassirer, by using elements from his own thought, it is interesting to point out that Heidegger finds himself confronted with a similar question in his famous essay on "The End of Philosophy and the Task of Thinking." There, like Cassirer, he uses the Goethian term of *Urphänomen* to characterize the *Lichtung*, the opening in which the event differentiates Being and beings, thus constituting the world. Heidegger also quotes Goethe as saying that one should not look for anything behind this *Ur*-phenomenon.[9] And yet, it is precisely the *Lichtung* that presents the philosopher with the "task of thinking" alluded to in the title of Heidegger's essay...

Reflection as an Immanent and Dialectical Necessity

Presence and Representation

The relationship between mediacy and immediacy has already been touched upon a number of times in the preceding chapters. In chapter

3, after discussing the paradoxes of a philosophy of language, I ventured the hypothesis that "speaking about language, the very tentative to bring language to language as language through language, is not only the condition of possibility of the *presence* of language, but of language as such: language is language only in its self-showing" (cf. p. 62). In the terms of modern linguistics, metalanguage is not just a contingent appendix to object-language, but language cannot exist as language without the metalinguistic function. Or, more generally, reflection is a necessary element in the constitution of nonreflexive reality. This claim could not yet be substantiated in the chapter on language, though the problematic that it embodies recurred in the chapter on myth. There, we saw not only that λόγος constitutes itself upon the basis of μῦθος, by distinguishing itself from it, but that μῦθος, as the "immediate" presence of the real itself is always already mediated by the λόγος of language, and thereby transformed into *mythos*. Μῦθος, as presence, is present only in the mode of its absence as *mythos*.

In truth, we are led back here to one of the fundamental principles of Cassirer's philosophy, namely, his critique of the "myth of the given." All *Präsenz*, for Cassirer, is made possible only through *Repräsentation* (cf. *PSF*, I, p. 98 f./32 f.). But it would be wrong to conceive of the presence of representation as though it were the mere negation of some "original" presence that must, for us humans, unfortunately become mediated in order to become real. Rather, the representation of a content of consciousness positively constitutes the presence of that content. Presence, therefore, *is* only as the "other" of representation, and is nothing "outside" or "before" the dialectics of presence and representation. "Must all form as such necessarily signify concealment (*Verhüllung*) rather than manifestation and revelation (*Manifestation und Offenbarung*)?" (*PSF*, III, p. 39/47). No, for the concealment of ~~presence~~ (the nonexistent, imaginary, "original" presence) *is* its revelation as presence. The λήθη *is* the ἀλήθεια.

For the question raised at the end of the preceding section—can the *awe* before the *Urphänomene* be maintained without acting against the spirit of critique?—the differentiated/undifferentiated unity of presence and representation[10] means that the "awe" before the basic phenomena does not whatsoever contradict their representation in thinking. Indeed, it presupposes thinking. For the *Urphänomene* are nothing outside their represented presence to thinking.

Presence and Representation in the Relationship between the Symbolic Forms

The unity of presence and representation can be further elucidated by a consideration of the dialectical interrelation between the different symbolic forms. Myth, as the identification of the signifier and the signified, presupposes the differentiating movement of religion as already existing within it. We have seen the mythical thought contains within it the immanent conditions that will lead it to its own transformation into religious consciousness. If there existed no implicit distinction in mythical consciousness between the presence of the mythical image and that which it represents—even if this distinction is always already negated—then the mythical state would basically be tantamount to the animal state: it would be without any transcendence. Mythical man would, like the animals, be absorbed by the sheer immediacy of the real, if this "real" were not mediated by an image. Now, in the same way that myth contains within itself the germs of religion, so language's relation to science is not a merely extrinsic one. The function of language is to show, to designate something that is other than itself. Now insofar as the sign, the word, represents, says, shows, and indicates something, it must be distinguished from that which it represents. If this were not the case, if the sign were taken to be the thing, we would have an example of mythical consciousness. Linguistic consciousness, which sees in the sensuous image a sign that says and shows, which represents something that is not immediately present, necessarily assumes that the sign itself announces to consciousness that it is not the thing, but the means of representing the thing. Language, therefore, cannot function as language, it cannot show something by representing it, unless consciousness is aware that the sign is a sign of language. Language must therefore show itself, or better "denounce" itself as language, it must turn on itself and bring itself to language. In short, the presence of language as a means of re-representing non-linguistic reality, presupposes the re-presentation of language itself.

If, more generally, the realm of myth and language constitute the sphere of *Zuhandenheit*, whereas religion and science constitute the sphere of *Vorhandenheit*, then *Zuhandenheit* is not possible without *Vorhandenheit*, which, in turn, is founded in *Zuhandenheit*. Or, again in different words, the texture of the real as "that elusive quality of resistance or effective presence which announces to consciousness from within it the presence of an existence that is other than itself and thus transcends it," requires the "text" in order to be texture.[11]

The Necessity and Nature of Thinking

The Creativity of Thinking

We can take our reflections a step further. If all presence requires representation, and, in fact, is nothing other than representation, then there can be no presence, no "world," without reflexive activity. This reflexive activity is accomplished by the symbolic forms, but is also, as we have seen, a necessary element in the relationship between the various symbolic forms (myth—religion, language—science). For, metaphysically speaking, the world of human meaning, the world of spirit, has its "origins" in a *turn of life upon itself*—which is a *turn of spirit upon itself*, at least insofar as life and spirit are only differentiated in the turn upon itself of life/spirit in their differentiated/undifferentiated co-"existence." Inasmuch as *all* the different symbolic forms are forms of reflection, they constitute together the realm of what, in the *Logic of the Cultural Sciences*, Cassirer calls "thinking" as a "productive" function creating human meaning (cf. *Logic*, p. 53). "Thinking" is not to be misunderstood here as the activity of a cultural élite of particularly well-educated people in the age of modern science . . .

> For, diverse as they are from one another, all cultural forms are *active expression-forms*. They are not mere reactions—like blushing, frowning, or doubling of the fist—but genuine actions. They are not simple events which play themselves out within and upon us, but are, as it were, specific *energies*. It is through the exercise of these energies that the world of culture takes form. (*Logic*, p. 51)

As we have already discovered above, thinking is the act of questioning that instills us with, and arises from, an "awe" in the face of the fundamental structure of reality. Again, it would be wrong to imagine that true thinking could take place only in institutionalized "philosophy"—indeed, Cassirer has some scathing remarks about any education that was to exhaust itself in an empty "parroting" of "information":

> We are to suppose that in examining his students a teacher sets down a certain problem in arithmetic, for instance, a problem taken from the multiplication tables. From one student he will receive a "correct" answer and from the other a "false" answer. But does this "correct" answer prove anything more than that a mere word-formula has imprinted itself upon the memory of the student and that he is able to repeat it? (*Logic*, p. 52)

This does not exclude that philosophy, at its best, *can* become an act of true thinking. Here, Cassirer cites the example of the Platonic dialogues in which there is no mere repetition of already known facts, but rather an opening-up of a new world shared between the two partners of the dialogue, as well as, co-constitutively, the constitution of a new "I" and a new "Thou" (*Logic*, p. 53 f.).

Cassirer would not be himself if, in his exultation of active speech, he were to forget the important role played by its opposed other, "passive speech" (*passive Rede*) (*Logic*, p. 52). Although passive speech, with its "language habits," is of the kind that only repeats, that is handed down from generation to generation without creating true insights, it is the necessary counterpoise of active speech. Active speech cannot create a new world, a new vision of reality, as it were *ex nihilo*, but only as a productive transformation, an active repetition of the transmitted culture. There is no direct access to a presence unmediated by cultural representation:

> The creative process must always satisfy two different conditions: on the one side, it must tie itself to something existing and enduring, and, on the other, it must be receptive to a new use and application which alter what remains the same. (*Logic*, p. 116)

Thinking between μῦθος and λόγος

For the project of philosophy, this means that true philosophical thinking can realize itself only through a constant return to, and repetition of, the tradition. Of course, the tradition should not be approached as if it dispensed us from thinking ourselves! The task is to uncover, in the great thinkers of the past, the original insights into the world that have come to be obliterated in the "traditional" transformation of what was intended to be a "monstration" of reality through productive speech into passive speech and the mere transmission of facts through "propositional phrases." We shall discuss Cassirer's strategy in "using" the history of philosophy for the constitution of his own "system" in a moment.

In relation to philosophical thinking, tradition serves the same function as μῦθος in relation to λόγος. It has been pointed out in chapter 4 that the sublation of myth in the "higher" cultural forms of religion and science does not at all imply a total annihilation, a total destruction of its spiritual energy. We saw that μῦθος, as that which is other, is therefore always present in the interior of self-conscious λόγος (cf. p. 86). What does this mean for philosophical thinking? It means that it must resist the temptation to repress and deny the presence of "mythical" elements within it. A rationalist philosophy pretending that absolute transparency is possible in the reflexive turn of reason upon itself, is guilty of a profound *méconnaissance*. Every theory contains, at its heart, an opaque "other": not only as an element subverting it from within and thus containing the germs of its future dissolution, but also as its condition of possibility. Cassirer's own "system" is no exception to this rule. Despite the fact that, in the fourth volume of the *Philosophy of Symbolic Forms*, we are warned against any attempt to search for the unity of the system of symbolic forms in an origin, in an ἀρχή—for the unity is, as we know, a matter of function and τέλος—Cassirer himself presents the birth of man in the transition from life to spirit, from sheer presence to representation, in a "structural myth," namely, that of the "radical metaphor":

> In its most charged state, the I (*Ich*) turns towards [the] *One* (*Einen*), lives in it and forgets (*vergißt*) itself in it. Thus, we find here, instead of a widening of intuition (*Anschauung*) its most extreme narrowing; instead of an expansion which gradually leads it through ever new spheres of being, an drive (*Trieb*) towards concentration; instead of an extensive diffusion an intensive compression. This focusing of all forces upon a *single* point is the prerequisite for all mythical thought and all mythical formation.

> When the I (*Ich*) is, on the one hand, completely given up to a momentary impression and "possessed" by it and, on the other hand, there is the utmost tension between [the I] and the outside world, when the external reality (*Sein*) is not simply contemplated and perceived, but suddenly overcomes man in its sheer immediacy, with the affect of fear or hope, terror or wish fulfillment, then, as it were, the spark jumps across, the tension finds a release, in that the subjective excitement objectifies itself, and presents itself to man as a god or demon. Here we stand before [the] mythico-religious *Urphänomen*. (*LM*, p. 33/103)

Upon rereading this quotation, is the incoherence of its argument not obvious? How can an "I" turn toward a "One" before the existence of the symbolic, given that, as Cassirer emphasizes time and again, it is only in and through the symbolic that the I and its other are constituted as different? How can there be a "tension" between the "sheer immediacy" of external reality and its "contemplation" by man—a tension thought to result in the "creation" of the first sign—if it is only through signs that man overcomes the immediacy of the animal world? The whole idea of the "creation" of a "first" sign is quite untenable. And yet, the "myth of the given" proves to be ultimately ineluctable, as the vertiginous dialectics between different poles that are, all of them, poles of representation, becomes impossible to think.

Philosophical thinking necessarily oscillates between the "principle of sufficient reason"—the drive toward an all-encompassing explanation leaving no room for opacity—and what Cassirer terms the "rightful claim" of skepticism. Indeed,

> it is better to renounce knowledge than to be blind to a problem because we have contented ourselves with a pseudosolution. All genuine skepticism is relative skepticism. It declares certain questions as unsolvable, in order to draw our attention all the more effectively to the sphere of solvable questions and to get a surer grip on them. (*Logic*, p. 100)

The enigma thus plays an essential role in the process of thinking, constituting at once its internal limit and the force driving it forward—a truly Cassirerian dialectic.

Le style, c'est l'homme lui-même

That Cassirer took the exigencies of "thinking" seriously can be seen in the very style of his philosophy. For, as in Heraclitus' case, the form of Cassirer's writing reflects his fundamental philosophical tenets: "Thus, on the basis of Heraclitus' general view of the world, we can understand the fundamental form of his *style,* whose reputed 'obscurity' is not accidental and arbitrary, but the adequate and necessary expression of his thought. Heraclitus' linguistic style and his style of thought condition one another: the two represent in different aspects the same basic principle of his philosophy, the principle of the ἐν διαφερόμενον ἑαυτῷ" (*PSF*, I, p. 120/59). Of course, for a philosophy according to which there is no presence without representation, no content without form, and that thinks the relationship between the two as a complex dialectics of identity and difference, the importance of the *style* of representation is obvious.

Every reader of Cassirer is struck by his apparent doctrinal indecisiveness: in the mass of historical material presented to the reader, Cassirer's own "point of view" seems to remain strangely absent. In other words, in the representation of the tradition of philosophy one asks about the presence of Cassirer himself. The author continuously floats from the explanation and interpretation of one doctrine to that of another, opposed one, pointing out merits and demerits, following one position to its logical conclusion where it paradoxically transforms itself into its opposite, which he then follows to its logical conclusion, and so on. This puzzling strategy often leaves the reader at a loss as to the point of this historical game. And, indeed, a game it seems to be, as a recent commentator on Cassirer's style has pointed out, who even wanted to see the meaning of the philosophy of symbolic forms in a kind of game theory: "And while he plays with games, he himself—in the vivid dynamic execution—forms a kind of system of these games as game."[12] Cassirer "plays," moreover, not merely with philosophical doctrines, but also with ideas that come from an analysis of literature, science, the fine arts, religion, myths, and history. Each time, these ideas are much more than illustrations of an already present "doctrine"; rather, their representation is *the only way* of making the doctrine "present." In this way, Cassirer's philosophy wins its unity only by running through the multiplicity of different elements constituting it. It is, therefore, a philosophy that cannot be broken down into a simple series of propositional phrases, but has to be read and understood in the *movement* of its "monstration" (*Zeigen*). In this respect, too, Cassirer's thinking is close to the spirit of Heidegger, who urges his readers at the beginning of his essay "Time and Being": "What counts is not to listen to a series of propositional phrases, but to follow the movement of the showing."[13] Finally, due to the thorough co-constitutionality of Cassirer's "thinking" and the "elements" constituting it, his philosophical thought cannot unambiguously be characterized either as science, religion, art, language, or myth. It is, in a way, all of these—and yet none of them.

Notes

Introduction

1. Cf. *Sein und Zeit* (1979[15]), p. 51 and the review of *Das mythische Denken*, in *Deutsche Literaturzeitung* 21 (1928): 1000–1012.

2. Cf. *Phenomenology of Perception*, trans. Colin Smith (London: Routledge and Kegan Paul, 1981), pp. 36, 65, 80, 336, 337. On the influence of Cassirer on Merleau-Ponty, cf. R. Bernet, *La vie du sujet: Études sur Husserl et la phénoménologie* (Épiméthée) (Paris: Presses Universitaires de France, 1994), p. 181 f.

3. Cf. M. Foucault, "Une histoire restée muette," *La quinzaine littéraire* 8 (1966): 3–5. Indeed, as David Macey points out in his new biography on Foucault, some have described Foucault as "a disciple of . . . Cassirer" (David Macey, *The Lives of Michel Foucault* [London: Hutchinson, 1993], p. 215).

4. Cf. G. Bataille, *L'érotisme* (Arguments) (Paris, Éditions de Minuit, 1957), p. 51.

5. Cf. C. Lévi-Strauss, *Les structures élémentaires de la parenté* (Paris: Presses Universitaires de France, 1949), p. 613. For an interesting comparison between Cassirer and Lévi-Strauss, cf. Roger Silverstone, "Ernst Cassirer and Claude Lévi-Strauss: Two Approaches to the Study of Myth," *Archives de sciences sociales des religions* 41 (1976): 25–36.

6. Cf. Hans Blumenberg, *Work on Myth*, trans. Robert M. Wallace, Studies in Contemporary German Social Thought (Cambridge: MIT Press, 1985), pp. 50, 51, 64, 117, 128, 160–61, 167–68. Cf. also Hans Blumenberg, "Ernst Cassirers gedenkend: Bei Entgegennahme des Kuno-Fischer-Preises der Universität Heidelberg im Juli 1974," *Revue internationale de philosophie* 85 (1974): 457–63.

7. Author unknown, "La raison avant Freud: Compte rendu de la *Philosophie des formes symboliques* de Cassirer," *Scilicet* 6/7 (1976): 295–325. Cf.

my article "L'ordre symbolique de Jacques Lacan à la lumière du symbolique d'Ernst Cassirer," in S. G. Lofts/P. Moyaert (eds.), *La pensée de Jacques Lacan: Questions historiques—Problèmes théoriques,* Bibliothèque philosophique de Louvain, 39 (Louvain-la-Neuve: Éditions de l'Institut supérieur de philosophie; Louvain/Paris: Peeters, 1994), pp. 83–105.

Besides the above-mentioned authors, there are other notable examples of important figures in whose texts one finds references to Cassirer's work and for which there is some evidence that they have taken Cassirer seriously: Erwin Panofsky (cf. *La perspective comme forme symbolique et autres essais,* trans. under the direction of Guy Gallangé (Le sens commun) (Paris: Les Éditions de Minuit, 1975), pp. 4, 43, 78, 92, 158); U. Eco (cf. "On Symbols," *Semiotic Inquiry* 1/2 (1982): 15–44); Charles Hartshorne (cf. "Freedom Requires Indeterminism and Universal Causality," *The Journal of Philosophy* 55 [1958]: 793–810).

8. Cf. Fredric Jameson, "Postmodernism and the Consumer Society," in Hal Foster (ed.), *The Anti-Aesthetic: Essays on Postmodern Culture* (Port Townsend, Wash.: Bay Press, 1983), p. 111.

9. Félix Guattari, "The Postmodern Dead End," *Flash Art* 128 (1986): 40.

10. *CPR,* p. 370; cited in *Essay,* p. 180.

11. Jacques Derrida, *Phèdre, suivi de La pharmacie de Platon* (Paris: Flammarion, 1989), p. 257: "Un texte n'est un texte que s'il cache au premier regard, au premier venu, la loi de sa composition et la règle de son jeu. Un texte reste d'ailleurs toujours imperceptible. La loi et la règle ne s'abritent pas dans l'inaccessible d'un secret, simplement elles ne se livrent jamais, au *présent,* à rien qu'on puisse rigoureusement nommer une perception."

12. "If writing is a rewriting that is, in effect, reading, then every work is a patchwork of passages that are drawn directly and indirectly from other works. . . . The (inevitable) theft entailed in writing establishes an ineradicable secondariness that robs the writer of all originality." Mark C. Taylor, *ERRING: A Postmodern A/theology* (Chicago: University of Chicago Press, 1984), p. 180 f.

13. "[O]rigin always comes to meet us from the future." Heidegger, "A Dialogue on Language," in *On the Way to Language,* trans. Peter D. Hertz (New York: Harper & Row, 1971), p. 10.

14. Jorge Luis Borges, *Labyrinths: Selected Stories & Other Writings,* ed. Donald A. Yates and James E. Irby, trans. James E. Irbry (New York: New Directions Books, 1964), p. 43.

15. For a more thorough discussion of the structure of science and the problem of truth, see chapter 6.

16. J. Ralph Lindgren, "Cassirer's Theory of Concept Formation," *The New Scholasticism* 42 (1968): 91.

17. John M. Krois, *Cassirer: Symbolic Forms and History* (New Haven: Yale University Press, 1987), p. 10 (referred to from here on as J. M. Krois, *Cassirer*).

18. For a more detailed discussion of Krois' work, see my critical notice "Une nouvelle approche de la philosophie d'Ernst Cassirer," *Revue philosophique de Louvain* 90 (1992): 523–38.

19. There are three other new full-length publications on Cassirer: Andreas Graeser, *Ernst Cassirer* (Denker). (Munich: Beck, 1994); Heinz Paetzold, *Ernst Cassirer zur Einführung* (Hamburg: Junius, 1993); *idem, Ernst Cassirer: Von Marburg nach New York: Eine philosophische Biographie* (Darmstadt: Wissenschaftliche Buchgesellschaft, 1995). The first two are basic introductions to Cassirer and his philosophy. The third provides us with an intellectual biography of Cassirer.

20. Fabien Capeillères, "L'édition française de Cassirer," *Revue de métaphysique et de morale* 4 (1992): 550; my translation. Capeillères goes on to suggest a solution to the problem of the unity of Cassirer's theory of culture. Despite the many differences in our respective approaches, there is nonetheless a certain fundamental affinity.

21. Iredell Jenkins, "Review of *The Philosophy of Ernst Cassirer*, ed. Paul Arthur Schilpp," *The Journal of Philosophy* 47 (1950): 47.

22. D. P. Verene, "Kant, Hegel, and Cassirer: The Origins of the Philosophy of Symbolic Forms," *Journal of the History of Ideas* 30 (1969): 33.

23. J. M. Krois, *Cassirer*, p. ix.

24. Cf. also Reto Luzius Fetz, "Ernst Cassirer und der strukturgenetische Ansatz," in H.-J. Braun, H. Holzhey, and E. W. Orth (eds.), *Über Ernst Cassirers Philosophie der symbolischen Formen* (Frankfurt am Main: Suhrkamp, 1988), p. 156; P. Causst, "Entre Humboldt et le structuralisme," in Jean Seidengart (ed.), *Ernst Cassirer de Marbourg à New-York* (L'intinéraire philosophique) (Paris: Les Éditions du Cerf, 1990), pp. 233–48.

25. M. Heidegger, "Zeit und Sein," in *Zur Sache des Denkens*, p. 2.

Chapter One

1. For a more detailed comparative study on the similarities and dissimilarities of Husserl's, Heidegger's, and Cassirer's respective positions concerning the "crisis," cf. my study "Husserl, Heidegger, Cassirer—trois philosophies de 'crise,' " *Revue philosophique de Louvain* 92 (1994): 570–84. Cf. also Lawrence E. Cahoone, "The Interpretation of Galilean Science: Cassirer Contrasted with Husserl and Heidegger," *Studies in History and Philosophy of Science* 17 (1986): 1–21.

2. Cf. Philip Buckley, *Husserl, Heidegger and the Crisis of Philosophical Responsibility*, Phaenomenologica, 125. (Dordrecht, The Netherlands: Kluwer Academic Publishers, 1992), p. 129: "Husserl, of course, can never . . . speak of necessary moments of irrationality within rationality itself."

3. Cassirer begins his *The Logic of the Cultural Sciences* by establishing the place of the philosophy of symbolic forms in the tradition of philosophy as a "renaissance" of the Greek ideal of logos and knowledge (cf. the first study: "The Science of Culture"). The term "renaissance" comes form the final study of this work in which Cassirer establishes the dialectical structure between the tradition and novelty. For a more detailed consideration cf. translator's introduction to *The Logic of the Cultural Sciences.*

4. Cassirer also critiques, as did Husserl, the dominance of historicism, psychologism, and naturalism as limited reestablishments of the Greek ideal of knowledge. Cf. *Logic,* p. 57 ff.

5. Cf. also Ernst Cassirer, "The Concept of Philosophy," in Donald Phillip Verene (ed.), *Symbol, Myth, and Culture* (New Haven: Yale University Press, 1979), p. 60. In his inaugural address to the University of Göteborg Cassirer speaks about the problem of the "unity of knowledge" and of the "failure" of philosophy to achieve its ethical vocation. The fourth volume of *The Problem of Knowledge* (*Philosophy and Science of Recent Times: From Hegel's Death up to the Present*) is also concern primarily with the loss of unity in science and the role of philosophy in this crisis. (Cf. translator's introduction to *The Logic of the Cultural Sciences* for more detail.)

6. R. Bernet, *La vie du sujet,* p. 151.

7. R. Bernet too has recognized the similarity between Cassirer's and Derrida's critiques of Husserl. "Parmi les nombreuses définitions [de représentation] et descriptions qu'en donne *La philosophie des formes symboliques,* le lecteur familier de Husserl, de Heidegger, et surtout de Derrida, est peut-être le plus sensible à la suivante." (For the definition referred to here by Bernet see p. 49 of this work.) Bernet concludes that: "Cette fonction de la représentation qui est commune à la perception, à la conscience d'image, et à la manière dont le signe renvoie à la signification efface donc l'opposition entre 'présentation' (*Gegenwärtigung*) et 're-présentation' (*Vergegenwärtigung*) sur laquelle reposait toute la théorie de la perception chez Husserl" (R. Bernet, *La vie du sujet,* p. 149 f.).

8. For a discussion of the genesis of the term "*symbolische Prägnanz*" in Cassirer's thought, cf. J. M. Krois, *Cassirer,* p. 52 ff.; cf. also Philipp Dubach, " 'Symbolische Prägnanz'—Schlüsselbegriff in Ernst Cassirers Philosophie der symbolischen Formen?," in E. Rudolph and B.-O. Küppers (eds.), *Kulturkritik nach Ernst Cassirer,* Cassirer-Forschungen, 1 (Hamburg: Meiner, 1995), pp. 47–84; and for a comparison with Husserlian intentionality and phenomenology, cf. Christian Möckel, "Symbolische Prägnanz—ein phänomenologischer Begriff? Zum Verhältnis von Ernst Cassirers Philosophie der symbolischen Formen und Edmund Husserls Phänomenologie," *Deutsche Zeitschrift für Philosophie* 40 (1992): 1050–63.

9. Cassirer's attitude toward Hegel is difficult to define. On the one hand, there are numerous critical remarks, such as the ones cited, on the short-

comings of the Hegelian metaphysics of spirit and the injustices it does to life. On the other hand, not only does the *Philosophy of Symbolic Forms* seem to be modeled after the Hegelian project of a phenomenology of spirit, but, more specifically and paradoxically, Cassirer has positive references to the very dialectics of life and spirit in Hegel that he criticizes in other places. Was Cassirer rereading the Hegel of the *Phenomenology of Spirit* in the light of the young Hegel, the logocentrism of spirit in the light of a philosophy of life? The question must remain open at least until the publication of volume 18 of *Ernst Cassirer. Nachgelassene Manuskripte und Texte*.

Chapter Two

1. To my knowledge this is the first textual reference to the philosophy of symbolic forms to be found in Cassirer's writings. Cf. J. M. Krois, *Cassirer*, p. 23.

2. *Struktur*: *Logic*, p. 10: *PSF*, I, p. 102/37: *PSF*, III, pp. 49/58, 333/389. *Aufbau*: *PSF*, III, p. 79/93. Cassirer also uses a number of other Germanic synonyms for "structure" besides *Struktur* and *Aufbau*, for example, *Gebilde*: *Logic*, p. 26; *LM*, p. 87/148; 34/104: *PSF*, III, p. 333/389; *Gliederung*: *PSF*, II, p. 71/91. These terms are, however, less common.

3. Cf., for example, *Essay*, p. 122 ff.

4. The parallelism between the structure of organic forms and cultural forms is also developed by Cassirer in *The Logic of the Cultural Sciences* where he uses the vitalism of J. von Uexküll to establish the difference between the world of nature and the world of culture, but subsequently also their similarity. For Uexküll "every organism presents a self-enclosed world in which everything 'weaves itself into the whole.' The organism is no aggregate of parts, but a system of functions which condition each other. In the 'blueprint' [*Bauplan* or quite literally the structural plan] of every animal we are able to read off immediately the nature of this interconnection" (*Logic*, p. 23). Cassirer will never say anything else about the organic structure of spirit.

5. In a lecture given at Yale in 1942 Cassirer explicitly associates de Saussure theory of linguistic structuralism developed in *Cours de linguistique générale* and Humboldt's theory of language (cf. "Language and Art II," in *Symbols, Myth and Culture*, p. 189). In the same lecture, having just quoted de Saussure, Cassirer says that he "by no means wishes to contradict this statement that is in perfect accordance with my own position" (cf. *ibid.*, p. 183). What Cassirer objects to is that for de Saussure language is the *only* way of structuring the world, whereas for him language is "only one approach to reality" (*ibid.*).

6. G. Deleuze, "À quoi reconnaît-on le structuralisme?" in F. Chatelet (ed.), *Histoire de la philosophie: Idées, doctrines: Le XXe siècle* (Paris: Hachette

Littérature, 1973), p. 306. (Cited hereafter as: G. Deleuze. The translations are mine.)

7. G. Deleuze, p. 301.

8. A. Lemaire, *Jacques Lacan*, trans. David Macey (London and New York: Routledge & Kegan Paul), 1977, p. 67.

9. G. Deleuze, p. 304.

10. *PSF*, I, p. 102/37.

11. G. Deleuze, p. 308 f.

12. G. Deleuze, p. 312 f.

13. In this passage, note the play on words, typical of Cassirer's language: Cassirer distinguishes the fact that the difference between the materiality of the sign and its meaning is always already *angelegt* in the symbolic, that is to say, implicit in its structure, from the fact that it is not necessarily always *ausgelegt*, that is to say, explicitated.

14. G. Deleuze, p. 318 f.

15. G. Deleuze, p. 321 f.

16. "Extimity" is a term used by Lacan to designate the paradoxical structure of the "zero point of desire" (J. Lacan, *Écrits* [Le champ freudien] [Paris: Éditions du Seuil, 1966], p. 46), which Lacan calls the "object a"—that is to say, the element of the structure of the unconscious that functions as the condition of possibility of the establishment of meaning. This "zero point of desire" is the element that determines all unconscious meaning structures, as it is the principle in light of which all connections between signifiers are accomplished.

17. G. Deleuze, p. 324 f.

18. G. Deleuze, p. 331.

19. *ECN*, I, p. 30/29: "The image always refers us, by its constitutive meaning, to the 'imagination,' and if we trace this back to its roots, it proves to be never a reproductive, but a productive function. We do not need to establish this here or go through it all in detail. It is this very achievement of the 'productive imagination' that we meet with everywhere in the construction of the particular worlds of form and which is the unifying ideal thread that ties them all together."

20. Cassirer employs the German term *Moment* throughout his work. The term appears to be rather innocent, but it contains a double meaning that is difficult to translate. It can be translated as either moment or element. Cassirer clearly seems to be playing on this double meaning. The symbolic forms are the elements of a structure but also the moments in a process. The term almost certainly comes from Hegel as the following quote shows.

21. Hegel, *Vorlesungen über die Philosophie der Geschichte, Sämmtliche Werke* (Leipzig, 1949), IX, p. 98; emphasis my own. (Cited by Cassirer: *PSF*, III, p. 78/92.)

Chapter Three

1. Cf. *Logic*, p. 42: "Without reservation or epistemological dogma, we must attempt to understand each sort of language—the language of science, the language of art, of religion, etc.—in its particularity."

2. R. Sheldrake, *The Presence of the Past: Morphic Resonance and the Habits of Nature* (New York: Times Books, 1988), p. xvii.

3. This is, of course, the thesis worked out by Hegel in the *Phenomenology of Spirit*. The reader familiar with Hegel will no doubt have recognised that my exposé on the structure of animal desire follows Alexandre Kojève's reading of Hegel: cf. A. Kojève, *Introduction to the Reading of Hegel*, trans. James H. Nichols Jr. (Ithaca and London: Cornell University Press, 1969^2).

4. Or what Hans Blumenberg calls the "absolutism of reality." Hans Blumenberg, *Work on Myth*, trans. Robert M. Wallace (Cambridge: MIT Press, 1985), p. 3.

5. "Sobald einmal der Funke übergesprungen ist, sobald die Spannung und der Affekt des Augenblicks sich im Wort order im mythischen Bilde entladen hat, setzt gewissermaßen eine Peripetie des Geistes ein. Die Erregung als bloß subjektiver Zustand ist erloschen, ist in dem Gebilde des Mythos oder im Gebilde der Sprache aufgegangen."

6. J. Lacan, *Écrits* (Le champ freudien) (Paris: Éd. du Seuil, 1966), p. 504.

7. W. von Humboldt, "Über die Verschiedenheit des menschlichen Sprachbaues und ihren Einfluß auf die geistige Entwicklung des Menschengeschlechts," (Introduction to *Zawi-Werk*), *Werke* (Akad.-Ausg.) VII, T1. 1. S. 55. (Cited in Cassirer, *Aufbau*, p. 135.)

8. W. von Humboldt, *Linguistic Variability and Intellectual Development*, trans. C. Buck and Frithjof A. Raven, Miami Linguistic Series No. 9 (Miami: The University of Miami Press, 1970), p. 40.

Chapter Four

1. This is certainly the interpretation and critique of Cassirer's theory of myth given by Hans Blumenberg: cf. *Work on Myth*, trans. Robert M. Wallace (Cambridge: MIT Press, 1985), p. 51; cf. also H. Blumenberg, "Ernst Cassirers gedenkend: Bei Entgegennahme des Kuno-FischerPreises der Universität Heidelberg im Juli 1974," *Revue internationale de philosophie* 85 (1974): 458 ff.

2. Heidegger, "Review of Mythic Thought," trans. James G. Hart and John G. Maraldo, in *The Piety of Thinking: Essays by Martin Heidegger* (Bloomington: Indiana University Press, 1976), p. 45.

3. Cited from G. S. Kirk, J. E. Raven, and M. Schofield, *The Presocratic Philosophers: A Critical History with a Selection of Texts* (Cambridge: Cambridge University Press, 1983), p. 245.

4. The precise quote reads: "For Usener mythology is nothing more than the theory (λόγος) of myth" (*PSF*, II, p. 22/29). As will become clear for Cassirer myth as a "narrative" of μῦθος contains a theoretical element to it. Thus, I feel justified in attributing Usener's position to Cassirer.

5. As far as I know, Cassirer does not employ the term *Gegenwärtigung*. It comes from Husserl, where it plays an important role in his philosophy of perception. However, it would seem clear that when Cassirer speaks of something that is *gegenwärtig*, he is speaking about the process that Husserl called *Gegenwärtigung*. Thus, as R. Bernet has pointed out, Cassirer's conception of representation throws into question the clear distinction that Husserl makes between representation and "presentation": "Cette fonction de la représentation qui est commune à la preception, à la conscience de l'image, et à la manière dont le signe renvoie à la signification efface donc l'opposition entre 'présentation' (*Gegenwärtigung*) et 're-présentation' (*Vergegenwartigung*) sur laquelle reposait toute la théorie de la perception chez Husserl" (R. Bernet, *La vie du sujet: Études sur Husserl et la phénoménologie* (Épiméthée) (Paris: Presses universitaires de France, 1994), p. 150).

6. Cited by Cassirer, *PSF*, II, p. 107/132: Usener, *Götternamen*, p. 193.

7. "The most proper and the best feature of the homeland (*Heimat*) consists in its being in the nearness to the Origin (*Ursprung*)—and nothing but this." M. Heidegger, *Erläuterungen zu Hölderlins Dichtung*, Gesamtausgabe, Abt. I, vol. 4, (Frankfurt am Main: Vittorio Klostermann, 1981), p. 23.

8. It is interesting to note that, in fact, the primary meaning of μῦθος is defined as, "*tale, story, narrative. . . . fiction* (opp. λόγος, *historic truth*)." (cf. *Oxford Greek-English Lexicon*, s.v. μῦθος). Μῦθος is therefore like λόγος but "without the distinction of true and false." It is, we read on, "μῦθος, *word, speech*." But if we continue and consider the root of μῦ-θος we find, according to Hjalmar Frisk, that μῦ-θος is derived from μῦ, which represents "*a muttering sound* made with the lips," and imitates "the sound of *sobbing*"(cf. *Oxford Greek-English Lexicon*, s.v. μῦ). Μῦ is also the root word for μύζω, which means "to make the sound μὺ μῦ, mutter, moan . . . hence to denote displeasure, *murmur, growl*"—again, we find the idea of an utterance, an expression of strong emotion, perhaps a feeling of protest or grieving. Μῦθος therefore has its roots in the expression of protest and emotion. Μῦ is also the root for μυχός, which refers to the "*innermost part of the house* [or a] *creek* running far inland." In the context of the mythical image as the sacred, the metaphor of something hidden in the interior which leads inward into the interior of the unknown is striking.

9. This figure, "*Sierpinski's carpet*," has been taken from Laurence Bouquiaux, *L'harmonie et le chaos: Le rationalisme leibnizien et la "nouvelle science,"* Bibiliothèque Philosophique de Louvain, 38 (Louvain-la-Neuve: Éditions de l'Institut supérieur de philosophie; Louvain-Paris: Éditions Peeters, 1994), p. 23, where it is used as a means of graphically representing the mathematical theory of chaos and fractal structures.

10. This image was created by L. Lapré and can be found on his web site: www.xs4all.nl/~ljlapre/gal.htm. On the same site you will find the program that generates this image and others like it.

11. It is interesting to note that etymologically the terms "story" and "history" come from the same root. In French the word "histoire" is still used to express both meanings.

12. Jean-François Mattéi has also noted the similarity between Cassirer's conception of the fourfold structure of the mythical world and the fourfold (*Geviert*) of Heidegger. Cf. Jean-François Mattéi, "Les modes de pensée philosophique," in *Histoire des mœurs*, vol. 2 (La Pléiade) (Paris: Gallimard, 1990), p. 1514 ff. Also cf. Dominique Janicaud and Jean-François Mattéi, *Heidegger from Metaphysics to Thought*, trans. Michael Gendre, SUNY Series in Contemporary Continental Philosophy (Albany: State University of New York Press, 1995), chapter 3: "The Heideggerian Chiasmus of the *Setting Apart* of Philosophy," p. 39 ff. Cf. also O. Pöggeler, *Der Denkweg Martin Heideggers* (Pfullingen: Neske, 1983[2]), p. 248.

13. M. Heidegger, *Poetry, Language, Thought*, trans. Albert Hofstadter (New York: Harper & Row, 1975), p. 179.

14. This diagram is based upon one found in Johnson J. Puthenpurackal, *Heidegger through Authentic Totality to Total Authenticity: A Unitary Approach to his Thought in its Two Phases*, Louvain Philosophical Studies 2 (Leuven: Leuven University Press, 1987), p. 190.

15. Cassirer cites as an authority Sir Baldwin Spencer and F. J. Gillen, *The Native Tribes of Central Australia* (London and New York: Macmillan, 1899, reprinted 1938), p. 419.

16. Thus, Cassirer would agree fully with Heidegger when he writes in 1940: "The German *Bildung*, although not an exact equivalent, most closely approximates παιδεία . . . '*Bildung*' means two things: first, a forming (*Bilden*), in the sense of an explicating imprinting. At the same time, however, this 'forming' 'forms' (imprints) by the anticipatory fitting to a determining view, which is called the model (*Vorbild*). '*Bildung*' is guidance and, especially, imprinting by an image (*Bild*)." Heidegger, "Platons Lehre von der Wahrheit," in *Wegmarken* (Frankfurt am Main: Vittorio Klostermann, 1976), p. 230 f.

17. A direct comparison between Freud and Cassirer, as interesting as it might be, would constitute a considerable detour from the subject matter at hand. I thus have elected to leave Freud in the margins, as it were. For a brief

discussion of Freud and Cassirer, see: Alfred Lorenzer, *Kritik des psychoanalytischen Symbolbegriffs* (Frankfurt am Main: Suhrkamp-Verlag, 1970), esp. p. 276 f.; cf. also S. Langer, "De Profundis," *Revue internationale de philosophie* 110 (1974): 450 f.

18. Those familiar with Lacan will no doubt also recognize "between the lines" something of Lacan's reading of Freud as my interpretation of Cassirer is here, more than anywhere else, influenced by my understanding of Lacan. However, if I have not rendered the presence of Lacan more explicit, it is because it would only complicate things. For, despite the many similarities, there remain many important differences.

19. Henri Focillon, *The Life of Forms in Art*, trans. Charles Beecher Hogan and George Kubler (Zone Books) (Cambridge: MIT Press, 1989), p. 119 f.

20. The drama of the *dance* is no imitative theatre, but rather the event itself. In an interesting footnote Cassirer maintains that "there is no consecration without dancing" (*PSF*, II, p. 39 n7/52 n2). "Dance" seems to be instrumental, and not accidental, to the process of establishing identity. That the impulse to dance is present from birth, and in fact precedes the acquisition of language, is easily witnessed in any newborn child. One needs only put on a little music. There is no society in which one does not find dance. And the more fundamental the society (I use the word "fundamental" so as to avoid the term "primitive," which suggests a degree of inferiority that I, and I think Cassirer also, do not want to attribute to it) the more important dance is. The more complex a society is, the more dance becomes an expression of its rebellious youth. Even within the animal realm the ritual of dance is easily recognized—especially where mating and territory rituals are concerned. In and through the rhythmic movement of the body, time and space dissolve into each other and become one. The dancers "are fused with each other and fused with all things in nature. They are not isolated; their joy is felt by the whole of nature and shared by their ancestors. Space and time have vanished; the past has become the present" (*Essay*, p. 95). The impulse to dance, therefore, represents a primordial expression of that "becoming aware" (*Gewahrwerden*) and "listening" ("*Horchen*") which brings about a new form of "obedience" (*Gehorsam*) (*Aufbau*, p. 136). (Cf. above, p. 81) It is a primordiąl exteriorization whose purpose is to establish a fusion with life that constitutes a determined and existing life.

21. "[I]n Plato's *Menexenos*, we still find it said that it is not the earth which imitates women in conceiving and giving birth but women who imitate the earth" (*PSF*, II, p. 190/228).

22. It should be remembered that we are speaking here of the realm of meaning. "Here . . . causality is replaced with real identity" (*MS*, p. 39). The "mother" is not necessarily the real biological mother, but rather the "symbolic" mother—rather the biological mother represents the symbolic mother. Thus, the father is not the biological father, but rather the "symbolic" father. In the construction (*Aufbau*) of patriarchal society the biological father has been taken as the "symbolic" father. The present deconstruction (*Abbau*) of patriarchal

society involves the reestablishing of the difference between the two. The problem is that the framework of meaning structures, and the imagery and language in which these structures are embodied, make it difficult to speak about the "symbolic" mother and father in any other terms without drifting off into empty abstractions. We cannot just throw away the language of the tradition, which is essentially what the position of politically correct language does, without at the same time suffering a loss of meaning. Rather it is necessary to transform language and thought by taking it up and investing it with a new meaning, through its "repetition."

23. Hegel, *Vorlesungen über die Philosophie der Religion, Werke*, 15, p. 67. (Cited in Cassirer: *PSF*, II, p. 220/263.)

24. One sees this also in Shakespeare's tragedies, above all in *King Lear*. Lear abdicates his position as king to two of his three daughters—sending the third into exile for speaking the truth. In the moment that Lear abdicates his power all of nature is thrown into turmoil, the order of things has been destroyed and chaos reigns. Of course, the same scenario takes place in the story of Oedipus. Having become king through the killing of his father and marrying of his mother the order of the world begins to disintegrate. Order is restored only after Lear and Oedipus have plucked out their eyes.

Chapter Five

1. J. Lacan, *Television: A Challenge to the Psychoanalytic Establishment*, trans. Jeffrey Mehlman (New York: W.W. Norton, 1990), p. 1. Lacan is not speaking here specifically of religion. Thus, in a certain sense the quote has been taken out of its context. However, there exists a certain parallel between the structure of Lacan's psychoanalytic theory and negative theology, which as we shall see represents for Cassirer the highest expression of religion. On this see Steve G. Lofts and Philipp W. Rosemann, " 'Ai-je besoin ici d'évoquer les néoplatoniciens?,' " in *La Pensée de Jacques Lacan: Questions historiques—Problèmes théoriques* ed. Steve G. Lofts and Paul Moyaert, Bibliothèque Philosophique de Louvain, 39 (Louvain-la-Neuve: Éditions de l'Institut supérieur de philosophie; Louvain-Paris: Éditions Peeters, 1994), pp. 107–24.) The reader need only reread this quote as though it were from the pen of a religious thinker such as St. Anselm for whom God was knowable only through His unknowability to appreciate its relevance in the present context.

2. Thus, the fact that Cassirer himself was of Jewish heritage and faith should not lead us to assume that his philosophy of religion is, explicitly or implicitly, a Jewish philosophy of religion—as opposed, for example, to a Christian philosophy of religion. Certainly one finds that references to the Jewish Prophets are abundant, but no less abundant than are the references to Christian metaphysics. And if the two religions figure more prominently in Cassirer's analysis, and my own, it is for the simple reason that these two

religions constitute the central intellectual and moral force of modern European culture. For one of the rare considerations of the importance of Cassirer's Jewish heritage to his life and work, see Heinz Paetzold, *Ernst Cassirer: Von Marburg nach New York: Eine philosophische Biographie* (Darmstadt: Wissenschaftliche Buchgesellschaft, 1995), pp. 127–47.

3. In *The Philosophy of the Enlightenment* (cf. pp. 134–96) and *The Problem of Knowledge: Philosophy, Science, and History since Hegel* (cf. pp. 294–326) there are found two chapters devoted to religion. However, these chapter do not deal with religion in terms of its function as a symbolic form. Their treatment here is primarily historical, rather than systematic. As J. M. Krois has argued, however, Cassirer's "systematic works abound with historical discussions while his historical worlds are interwoven with philosophical arguments and often develop systematic theses" (J. M. Krois, *Cassirer*, p. 3). Although I agree with Krois on this point, in the end—practically speaking—it is "easier" to abstract the historical from the systematic works, than to abstract the systematic from the historical works. In fact, the former already proves to be a considerable challenge, and thus the latter must await until Cassirer scholarship has progressed.

4. This characterization in Heideggerian terms is taken from Cassirer's own account of Heidegger's thought, which he recognises as essentially religious in its orientation (cf. *ECN*, I, pp. 219–229).

5. Summarizing the position of Pascal, Cassirer writes: "For wherever we encounter man, we find him not as a complete and harmonious being but as a being divided against himself and burdened with the most profound contradictions. These contradictions are the stigma of human nature. As soon as he attempts to understand his position in the cosmos, man finds himself caught between the infinite and nothingness; in the presence of both, he is incapable of belonging to either one of them alone" (*The Philosophy of the Enlightenment*, p. 143).

6. That the "fall" of man must be understood as a myth and not as an actual historical event is not completely without support within the tradition of Christian thought. Cf. Steve G. Lofts and Philipp W. Rosemann, " 'Ai-je besoin ici d'évoquer les néo-platoniciens?'," in S. G. Lofts and P. Moyaert (eds.), *La pensée de Jacques Lacan: Questions historiques—Problèmes théoriques*, Bibliothèque Philosophique de Louvain, 39 (Louvain-la-Neuve: Éditions de l'Institut supérieur de philosophie; Louvain and Paris: Éditions Peeters, 1994), p. 118 f.

7. "Wie für Eckharts mystische Grundanschauung alle Kreaturen nichts anderes als ein 'Sprechen Gottes' sind, so wird hier die gesamte Schöpfung, so wird alles natürliche, wie alles geistig-geschichtliche Geschehen zu einer fortlaufenden Rede des Schöpfers an die Kreatur durch die Kreatur."

8. That the mythical image must be seen as a "hieroglyphic" that religious consciousness must interpret comes from Cassirer himself when, in the

context of a discussion of Giambattista Vico's work on myth and religion, he writes: "He [Vico] made the first attempts to decipher this language [the language of myth], gaining a method by which to interpret the 'sacred pictures,' the hieroglyphics, of myth" (*PK*, p. 296).

9. Cf. *Dictionaire de théologie catholique*, vol. 13, 1937, p. 2182 f. The connection between *religio* and *relectio* is quite commonly made by Scholastic authors; cf., for example, Thomas Aquinas, *Summa theologiae*, II[a] II[ae], qu. 81, art. 1, c: "*religion* seems to be derived from the rereading of those things which pertain to the divine worship"—*religio videtur dicta a relegendo ea quae sunt divini cultus*. This etymology stems from Cicero.

10. "[E]very new means here changes the conception of the goal that stands at its end, since for the religious consciousness it is always the means which determines and forms man's view of the end" (*PSF*, II, p. 226/271).

11. In the end of *An Essay on Man* Cassirer clearly equates myth with "traditional thought": "Mythical thought is, by its origin and by its principle, traditional thought" (*Essay*, p. 224).

12. This is essentially the meaning of St. Anselm's so-called "ontological proof for the existence of God."

13. In fact, Cassirer is not at all clear in his intentions. The reader must constantly pay close attention to the context in which "magic," "myth," "mythical-religious," "primitive religion," and "religion" are used.

14. Research into the roots of Christian symbolism, liturgy, morals, and dogma in the pagan culture of antiquity is a comparatively recent phenomenon. The project of a systematic and comprehensive comparison between Christianity and the life and ideas of antiquity was first conceived by F. J. Dölger (1879–1940), a Catholic priest who, like Cassirer, was connected with the circle of Aby Warburg.

15. Thomas Aquinas, *Summa theologiae*, I[a], qu. 3, prologus: "We cannot know about what God is but only what he is not"—*de Deo scire non possumus quid sit, sed quid non sit*.

16. Heidegger, *Identity and Difference*, trans. Joan Stambaugh (Harper Torchbooks, 1947) (New York: Harper & Row, 1974), p. 72.

17. Albert Görland, *Religionsphilosophie als Wissenschaft aus dem Systemgeiste des kritischen Idealismus* (Berlin and Leipzig: W. de Gruyter, 1922), p. 263 f. Cited by Cassirer in *PSF*, II, p. 258.

18. The title of this section is taken from one of the chapters in Marett's work *The Threshold of Religion*, which is frequently cited by Cassirer.

19. Hegel, *Vorlesungen über die Philosophie der Religion*, *Werke*, vol. 15, p. 67. Cited by Cassirer in *PSF*, II, p. 220.

20. *Ibid*.

21. "Die Negation des Geistes ist also nicht ein Akt des Lebens—sie hat Sinn nur als Akt des Geistes selbst—daher ist eben diese Negation nicht Rückkehr zum Leben sondern sie ist stärkste Selbstbejahung des Geistes" (*ECN*, I, p. 258).

22. We do not find in magical consciousness the same conviction as we do in religious faith that good will in the end be victorious over evil. In all the early myths we see that the war between the two forces is eternal. The struggle against black magic is a perpetual one, indisssociable from life itself.

23. Cf. H. Hubert and M. Mauss, "Essai sur la nature et la fonction du sacrifice," in M. Mauss, *Œuvres*, vol. 1 (Paris: Éditions de Minuit, 1968).

24. The idea that is implicit in Cassirer's argument here has been explicitly developed by G. Bataille in his theory of "general economy" and religion. "Le sacrifice est l'antithèse de la production faite en vue de l'avenir, c'est la consommation qui n'a d'intérêt que pour l'instant même. C'est en ce sens qu'il est don et abandon; mais ce qui est donné ne peut être un objet de conservation pour le donataire." *Théorie de la religion* (Tel) (Paris: Éditions N.R.F., 1973), p. 66 f.

25. My interpretation of Cassirer here has been inspired by the following quotation from Lacan: "le sacrifice signifie que, dans l'objet de nos désirs, nous essayons de trouver le témoignage de la présence du désir de cet Autre que j'appelle ici *Le Dieu obscur*." *Le Séminaire*, XI: *Les quatre concepts fondamentaux de la psychanalyse* (Le champ freudien) (Paris: Éditions du Seuil, 1973), p. 246 f.

26. H. Hubert and M. Mauss, *Essai sur la nature et la fonction du sacrifice*, in M. Mauss, *Œuvres*, vol. 1 (Paris: Éditions de Minuit, 1968), p. 305.

27. "Le cœur de ce mystère [l'Eucharistie], c'est que la communion avec Dieu passe par la communion des hommes entre eux. C'est pour cela que le signe de la communion avec Dieu est le partage entre les hommes. Il ne faut pas oublier que l'Eucharistie, c'est avant tout un repas dont le partage est le signe de la communion de ceux qui y participent. Et la communion de ceux qui la partagent est à son tour le signe de la communion avec Dieu." B. Besret, *De commencement en commencement. Itinéraire d'une déviance* (Paris: Seuil, 1976), pp. 176 and 179.

Chapter Six

1. Lawrence E. Cahoone, "The Interpretation of Galilean Science: Cassirer Contrasted with Husserl and Heidegger," *Studies in History and Philosophy of Science* 17 (1986): 21.

2. Ontology is thus phenomenology. Cf. "Language and Art II," in *SMC*, p. 167 f.

3. Cf., for example, William H. Werkmeister, "Cassirer's Advance beyond Neo-Kantianism," in Paul Schilpp (ed.), *The Philosophy of Ernst Cassirer*, pp. 759–98; Jean Seidengart, "Une interprétation néo-kantienne de la théorie des quanta est-elle possible?," *Revue de synthèse* 120 (1985): 395–418; Fabien Capeillères, "Sur le néo-kantisme de E. Cassirer," *Revue de métaphysique et de morale* 3 (1992): 517–46.

4. Werkmeister, "Cassirer's Advance beyond Neo-Kantianism," p. 792.

5. *Ibid.*, p. 793.

6. The reader will note that in the preface to the 1923 volume of the *Philosophy of Symbolic Forms* Cassirer speaks about the *Geisteswissenschaften*, whereas in 1942 he employs the term *Kulturwissenscaften*. According to J. M. Krois it would seem that "Cassirer uses the terms *Geisteswissenschaften* and *Kulturwissenschaften* as interchangeable designations." J. M. Krois, *Cassirer*, p. 125.

7. Cf. P. W. Rosemann, *"Omne agens agit sibi simile." A "Repetition" of Scholastic Metaphysics*, doctoral dissertation, Louvain-la-Neuve, Université catholique de Louvain, Institut supérieur de philosophie, 1995, p. 46 ff.

8. J. Lacan, *Écrits* (Le champ freudien) (Paris, Éditions du Seuil, 1966), p. 9.

Chapter Seven

1. In a letter to Paul Schilpp Cassirer writes: "With regard to content it [*An Essay on Man*] would be new, as it would give here for the first time a thorough (*eingehend*) presentation of my theory of aesthetics. Already in the first sketch (*Entwurf*) of the *Philosophy of Symbolic Forms* a particular volume on art was considered but the disfavor of the times postponed its working out again and again." (cited in *SMC*, p. 25)

2. Quote by D. Verene, in the introduction to *Symbols, Myth and Culture: Essays and Lectures of E. Cassirer, 1939–1945*, p. 25.

3. Cf. D. Verene, ibid., p. 21.

4. Indra Kagis McEwen, *Socrates' Ancestor: An Essay on Architectural Beginnings*. (Cambridge: MIT Press, 1993), p. 43 f.

5. Strictly speaking, these three dimensions are found in every symbol. However, they are only because every symbol has as its support an aesthetic image. When, for example, one listens to a language that one does not understand, all that is heard is the aesthetic gestalt that language employs. The principle difficult of speaking a foreign language lies not in learning its grammar or vocabulary, but rather in reproducing its rhythm or melody. This is to say, in entering into its the aesthetic form of the language.

Conclusion

1. ECN, I, p. 3.

2. In the *Logic of the Cultural Sciences*, Cassirer writes approvingly apropos of Herder that "in the definitive form which his philosophy of history and culture attained in the *Ideen*, the goal of totality no longer lies behind us but before us. With this the entire emphasis of his doctrine shifts. For now the differentiation of the spiritual powers is no longer regarded simply as a secession from the original unity and as a kind of original sin of knowledge, but has attained a positive meaning and value" (*Logic*, p. 11).

3. Cf. " 'Spirit' and 'Life,' " p. 858/33: "Today anew the great antithesis of 'nature' and 'spirit,' the polarity of 'life' and 'knowledge,' looms at the very center of philosophical speculation."

4. Cassirer's attitude toward Hegel is difficult to define. On the one hand, there are numerous critical remarks, such as the ones cited, on the shortcomings of the Hegelian metaphysics of spirit and the injustices it does to life. On the other hand, not only does the *Philosophy of Symbolic Forms* seem to be modeled after the Hegelian project of a phenomenology of spirit, but, more specifically and paradoxically, Cassirer has positive references to the very dialectics of life and spirit in Hegel which he criticizes in other places (cf. " 'Spirit' and 'Life,' " p. 875/53): "Especially as concerns Hegel, it would be a complete misunderstanding of his system to bring against it the reproach that by reason of its panlogistic tendency it denies the rights of life—that it has sacrificed the vital sphere to that of logic. Even a mere glance at the historical development of the Hegelian doctrine is sufficient to invalidate this objection: for it is precisely in the writings of Hegel's earlier period that . . . a new, systematically most fruitful concept of life is coined." Was Cassirer rereading the Hegel of the *Phenomenology of Spirit* in the light of the young Hegel, the logocentrism of spirit in the light of a philosophy of life? The question must remain open at least until the publication of volume 18 of *Ernst Cassirer: Nachgelassene Manuskripte und Texte.*

5. Cf. " 'Spirit' and 'Life,' " p. 876/54: "The spirit *is* only, insofar as it turns against itself in this manner; its own unity (*Einheit*) is thinkable only in such contrariety (*Zwiespältigkeit*)."

6. Cf. K. Hedwig, *Sphaera Lucis: Studien zur Intelligibilität des Seienden im Kontext der mittelalterlichen Lichtspekulation*, Beiträge zur Geschichte der Philosophie und Theologie des Mittelalters, N.F. 18 (Münster: Aschendorff, 1980).

7. Cf. *ECN*, I, p. xi: "Zugleich erfährt Cassirers Darstellung seiner eigenen Philosophie hier eine Vertiefung: mit der Lehre von den *Basisphänomenen* versucht er, der 'Philosophie der symbolischen Formen' den Rahmen und den

Mittelpunkt zu geben, den sie bis dahin—selbst im systematischen dritten Band—nur ansatzweise erhalten hatte."

8. I. Kajon, "Das Problem der Einheit des Bewußtseins im Denken Ernst Cassirers," in H.-J. Braun, H. Holzhey, and E.W. Orth (eds.), *Über Ernst Cassirers Philosophie der symbolischen Formen*, Suhrkamp Taschenbuch Wissenschaft, 706 (Frankfurt am Main: Suhrkamp, 1988), p. 265.

9. M. Heidegger, "Das Ende der Philosophie und die Aufgabe des Denkens," in *Zur Sache des Denkens* (Tübingen: Niemeyer, 1976^2), p. 72.

10. Cf. *PSF*, III, p. 199/232; trans. amended: "For no content (*Inhalt*) of consciousness is in itself merely 'present' (*'präsent'*), or in itself merely 'representative' (*'repräsentativ'*); rather, every actual experience indissolubly embraces both factors (*Momente*). Everything present (*Gegenwärtige*) functions (*fungiert*) in the sense of representing (*Vergegenwärtigung*), just as all representation (*Vergegenwärtigung*) demands a link with something present (*Gegenwärtiges*) in consciousness."

11. For an explanation of the relationship between "texture" and "text," cf. above, chapter 5, p. 135.

12. E. W. Orth, "Geschichte und Literatur als Orientierungsdimensionen in der Philosophie Ernst Cassirers," in E. Rudolph and B.-O. Küppers (eds.), *Kulturkritik nach Ernst Cassirer*, Cassirer-Forschungen, 1 (Hamburg: Meiner, 1995), p. 109.

13. M. Heidegger, "Zeit und Sein," in *Zur Sache des Denkens* p. 2.

Bibliography

In compiling this bibliography, I have selected the material that, on the one hand, has proven to be helpful and, on the other hand, I consider to be central to Cassirer studies. I cite the German editions of Cassirer only when I have used them in the present study—this could be either because the text is not available in English or because it is essential in the context of my argument, so that I have had constant recourse to the original. For a complete and up-to-date bibliography of Cassirer's works and the literature on Cassirer, see the web site of the International Ernst Cassirer Society: www.cassirer.org.

Primary Literature

Books

Cassirer, Ernst. *An Essay on Man: An Introduction to a Philosophy of Human Culture* (New Haven: Yale University Press, 1944).

———. *Determinsim and Indeterminsim in Modern Physics: Historical and Systematic Studies of the Problem of Causality*. Trans. by O. T. Benfey. New Haven: Yale University Press, 1956.

———. *The Individual and the Cosmos in Renaissance Philosophy*. Trans. by Bario Domandi. New York: Harper & Row, 1964.

———. *Kant's Life and Thought*. Trans. by James Haden. New Haven: Yale University Press, 1981.

———. *Language and Myth.* Trans. by Susanne K. Langer. New York: Dover Publication, 1953. (*Sprache und Mythos: Ein Beitrag zum Problem der Gotternamen* [Studien der Bibliothek Warburg, 6]). Leipzig/Berlin: B. G. Teubner, 1925. Reprinted in *Wesen und Wirkung des Symbolbegriffs* [see below], pp. 71-158.)

———. *The Logic of the Cultural Sciences: Five Studies.* Trans. S. G. Lofts. New Haven: Yale University Press, 2000. (*Zur Logik der Kulturwissenschaften: Fünf Studien.* In Göteborgs Högskolas Arsskrift 48. Heft 1 [1942], pp. 1–139.)

———. *The Myth of the State.* New Haven: Yale University Press, 1946.

———. *The Philosophy of the Enlightenment.* Trans. by Frits C. A. Koelln and James P. Pettegrove. Princeton: Princeton University Press, 1951.

———. *Philosophy of Symbolic Forms,* vol. I: *Language.* Trans. by Ralph Manheim. New Haven: Yale University Press, 1953–57. (*Philosophie der symbolischen Formen,* Teil 1: *Die Sprache.* Darmstadt: Wissenschaftliche Buchgemeinschaft, 1988.)

———. *Philosophy of Symbolic Forms,* vol. II: *Mythical Thought.* Trans. by Ralph Manheim. New Haven: Yale University Press, 1955. (*Philosophie der symbolischen Formen.* Teil 2: *Das mythische Denken.* Darmstadt: Wissenschaftliche Buchgemeinschaft, 1987.)

———. *Philosophy of Symbolic Forms,* vol. III: *The Phenomenology of Knowledge.* Trans. by Ralph Manheim. New Haven: Yale University Press, 1957. (*Philosophie der symbolischen Formen,* Teil 3: *Phanomenologie der Erkenntnis.* Darmstadt: Wissenschaftliche Buchgemeinschaft, 1990.)

———. *Philosophy of Symbolic Forms,* vol. 4: *The Metaphysics of Symbolic Forms* (including the text of Cassirer's manuscript on *Basis Phenomena*). Edited by J. M. Krois and D. P. Verene, trans. by J. M. Krois. New Haven: Yale University Press, 1996. (*Nachgelassene Manuskripte und Texte,* vol. I: *Metaphysik der symbolischen Formen.* Edited by J. M. Krois and O. Schwemmer. Hamburg: Felix Meiner, 1995.)

———. *The Platonic Renaissance in England.* Trans. by J. P. Pettegrove. Austin: University of Texas, 1953.

———. *The Problem of Knowledge: Philosophy, Science and History since Hegel*. Trans. by William H. Woglom and Charles W. Hendel. New Haven: Yale University Press, 1950.

———. *The Question of Jean-Jacques Rousseau*. Trans. by Peter Gay. New York: Columbia University Press, 1954.

———. *Rousseau-Kant-Goethe: Two Essays*. Preface by E. Cassirer. Trans. by James Gutmann, Paul Oskar Kristeller, and John Herman Randall Jr. Princeton: Princeton University Press, 1945. Reprinted in New York: Harper & Row, 1963.

———. *Substance and Function and Einstein's Theory of Relativity*. Trans. by William Curtis Swabey and Marie Collins Swabey. Chicago: Open Court Publishing, 1923.

Collections

———. *Freiheit und Form: Studien zur deutschen Geistesgeschichte*. Darmstadt: Wissenschaftliche Buchgesellschaft, 1981.

———. Geist und Leben: Schriften zu den Lebensordnungen von Natur und Kunst, Geschichte und Sprache (Reclam-Bibliothek, 1963). Edited by Ernst W. Orth. Leipzig: Reclam Verlag, 1993.

———. *Symbol, Technik, Sprache: Aufsätze aus den Jahren 1927–1933* (Philosophische Bibliothek, 372). Edited by Ernst W. Orth and John M. Krois. Hamburg: Felix Meiner Verlag, 1985.

———. *Symbols, Myth and Culture: Essays and Lectures of Ernst Cassirer 1935–1945*. Edited by Donald Phillip Verene. New Haven: Yale University Press, 1979.

———. *Wesen und Wirkung des Symbolbegriffs*. Darmstadt: Wissenschaftliche Buchgesellschaft, 1994.

Articles

———. "Albert Schweitzer as Critic of Nineteenth-Century Ethics." In A. A. Roback (ed.), *The Albert Schweitzer Jubilee Book*. Cambridge: Science and Art, 1946, pp. 241–57.

———. "The Concept of Group and the Theory of Perception." *Philosophy and Phenomenological Research* 5.1 (1944): 1–35.

———. "Das Symbolproblem und seine Stellung im System der Philosophie." *Zeitschrift für Ästhetik und allgemeine Kunstwissenschaft* 21 (1927): pp. 295–312.

———. "Davoser Disputation zwischen Ernst Cassirer und Martin Heidegger." In Martin Heidegger, *Kant und das Problem der Metaphysik*. Frankfurt am Main: Vittorio Klostermann, 1973.

———. "Der Begriff der symbolischen Form im Aufbau der Geisteswissenschaften." In *Vorträge der Bibliothek Warburg*, 1921–1922. Leipzig: B. G. Teubner, 1923, pp. 11–39.

———. "A Discussion between Ernst Cassirer and Martin Heidegger." Trans. by Francis Slade. In Nino Langiulli (ed.), *The Existentialist Tradition* (Anchor Books). Garden City, N.Y.: Doubleday, 1971, pp. 192–203.

———. "Eidos und Eidolon: Das Problem des Schönen und der Kunst in Platons Dialogen." In *Vorträge der Bibliothek Warburg*, 1922–1923. Nr. 2. 1924, pp. 1–27.

———. "Enlightenment." *Encyclopaedia of the Social Sciences*, vol. 5, 1931, pp. 547–52.

———. "Ficino's Place in Intellectual History." Review of Paul O. Kristeller, *The Philosophy of Marsilio Ficino*. New York: Columbia University Press, 1943. *Journal of the History of Ideas* 6 (1945): 483–501.

———. "Force and Freedom: Remarks on the English Edition of Jacob Buckhardt's Reflection on History." *The American Scholar* 13 (1944): 407–17.

———. "Form und Technik." In Leo Kestenberg (ed.), *Kunst und Technik*. Berlin Wegweiser Verlag, 1930, pp. 15–61. Reprinted in *Symbol, Technik, Sprache: Aufsätze aus den Jahren 1927–1933*, 1985, pp. 39–90.

———. "From a Philosopher." In E. Lasker, *Chess for Fun and Chess for Blood*. New York: David MacKay, 1942, pp. 15–18.

———. "Galileo: A New Science and a New Spirit." *American Scholar* 12 (1942): 5–19.

———. "Galileo's Platonsim." In M. F. Ashley Montagu (ed.), *Studies and Essays in the History of Science*. New York: H. Schumann, 1946, pp. 276–97.

———. "Giovanni Pico della Mirandola." *Journal of the History of Ideas* 3 (1942): 123–44 and pp. 319–46.

———. "Herman Cohen, 1842–1918." *Social Research* 10 (1943): 219–32.

———. "Inhalt und Umfang des Begriffs: Bemerkungen zu Konrad Marc-Wogau: Inhalt und Umfang des Bergiffs." *Theoria* 2 (1936): 207–32.

———. "The Influence of Language upon the Development of Scientific Thought." *The Journal of Philosophy* 39 (1942): 309–27.

———. "Judaism and the Modern Political Myths." *Contemporary Jewish Record* 7 (1944): 115–26.

———. "Kant and the Problem of Metaphysics: Remarks on Martin Heidegger's Interpretation of Kant." In Molte S. Gram (ed. and trans.), *Kant: Disputed Questions*. Chicago: Quadrangle Books, 1967, pp. 131–57.

———. "Kant und das Problem der Metaphysik: Bemerkungen zu Martin Heideggers Kantinterpretation." *Kant-Studien* 36/1 (1931): 1–26.

———. "Kant." *Encyclopedia of the Social Sciences*, vol. 8, 1932, pp. 538–42.

———. "Le langage et la construction du monde des objets." Trans. by P. Guillaume. *Journal de psychologie normale et pathologique* 1–4 (January 15–April 15, 1933): 18–44.

———. "Leibniz." *Encyclopedia of the Social Sciences*, vol. 9, 1933, pp. 400–402.

———. " 'Life' and 'Spirit' in Contemporary Philosophy." Trans. by R. W. Bretall and P. A. Schilpp. In Paul Arthur Schilpp (ed.), *The Philosophy of Ernst Cassirer* (Library of Living Philosophers, 6). LaSalle, Illinois: Open Court Publishing Company, 1958, pp. 855–80. (" 'Geist' und 'Leben' in der Philosophie der Gegenwart." *Die Neue Rundschau* 41, pp. 244–64. Reprinted in *Geist und Leben Schiften*, 1993, pp. 32–60.)

———. "The Myth of the State." *Fortune* 39 (1944): 164–67, 198, 201–4, 206.

———. "Neo-Kantianism." In *Encyclopaedia Britannica,* 14th ed. London and New York, 1929, vol. 16, pp. 214–15.

———. "Newton and Leibniz." *The Philosophical Review* 52 (1943): 366–91.

———. "The Place of Vesalius in the Culture of the Renaissance." *Yale Journal of Biology and Medicine* 16 (1942): 109–19.

———. "The Problem of the Symbol and Its Place in the System of Philosophy." Trans. by J. M. Krois. *Man and World* 11 (1978): 411–28.

———. "Rationalism." In *Encyclopaedia Britannica,* 14th ed. London and New York, 1929, vol. 18, pp. 991–93.

———. "Reflections on the Concept of Group and the Theory of Perception." In Donald Phillip Verene (ed.), *Symbols, Myth and Culture: Essays and Lectures of Ernst Cassirer 1935–1945.* New Haven: Yale University Press, 1979, pp. 271–92.

———. "Schiller and Shaftesbury." *The Publications of the English Goethe Society* 11 (1935): 37–59.

———. "Science and Ethics: Equal Partnership." *Saturday Review.* March 2, 1957, p. 50.

———. "Some Remarks on the Originality of the Renaissance." *Journal of the History of Ideas* 4 (1943): 49–56.

———. "Structuralism in Modern Linguistics." *Word: Journal of the Linguistic Circle of New York* 1 (1945): 99–120.

———. "Substance." In *Encyclopaedia Britannica,* 14th ed. London and New York, 1929, vol. 21, pp. 500–502.

———. "Transcendalism." In *Encyclopaedia Britannica,* 14th ed. London and New York, 1929, vol. 22, pp. 405–6.

———. "Truth." In *Encyclopaedia Britannica,* 14th ed. London and New York, 1929, vol. 22, pp. 522–24.

———. "Was ist "Subjektivismus"? *Theoria* (Göteborg) 5 (1939): 111–40.

———. "Zur Logik des Symbolbegriffs." *Theoria* (Göteborg) 4 (1938): 145–75. Reprinted in *Wesen und Wirkung des Symbolbegriffs*, 1994, 201–30.

———. "Zur Theorie des Begriffs." *Kant-Studien* 33 (1928): 129–36.

Secondary Literature
Works on Cassirer

Books

Baeten, E. M. *The Magic Mirror. Myth's Abiding Power* (Philosophy of the Social Sciences). Albany: State University of New York Press, 1996.

Cassirer, T. *Mein Leben mit Ernst Cassirer*. Hildesheim: Gerstenberg Verlag, 1981.

Feron, O. *Finitude et sensibilité dans la philosophie d'Ernst Cassirer*. Paris: Éditions Kimé, 1997.

Ferrari, M. *Il giovane Cassirer e la scuola di Marburgo*. Milan: Angeli, 1988.

Ferretti, S. *Cassirer, Panofsky, Warburg*. New Haven: Yale University Press, 1989.

Gaubert, J. *La science politique d'Ernst Cassirer: Pour une refondation symbolique de la raison pratique contre le mythe politique contemporain* (Philosophie-épistémologie). Paris: Éditions Kimé, 1996.

Göller, Th. *Ernst Cassirers kritische Sprachphilosophie*. Würzburg: Könighausen & Neumann, 1986.

Graeser, A. *Ernst Cassirer* (Denker). Munich: Beck, 1994.

Hamburg, C. H. *Symbol and Reality: Studies in the Philosophy of Ernst Cassirer*. The Hague: Martinus Nijhoff, 1956.

Itzkoff, S. *Ernst Cassirer: Philosopher of Culture* (Twayne's World Leader Series, 61). Boston: Twayne Publishers, 1977.

———. *Ernst Cassirer: Scientific Knowledge and the Concept of Man*. Notre Dame: University of Notre Dame Press, 1971.

Knoppe, Th. *Die theoretische Philosophie Ernst Cassirers—Zu den Grundlagen transzendentaler Wissenschafts- und Kulturtheorie*. Hamburg: Meiner, 1992.

Krois, J. M. *Cassirer, Symbolic Forms and History*. New Haven: Yale University Press, 1987.

Lipton, D. R. *Ernst Cassirer: The Dilemma of a Liberal Intellectual in Germany, 1914–1933*. Toronto: University of Toronto Press, 1978.

Lofts, G. S. *La vie de l'esprit: Essai sur l'unité systématique de la philosophie des formes symboliques et de la culture* (Accent). Louvain-Paris: Éditions Peeters, 1997.

Schwemmer, O. *Ernst Cassirer: Ein Philosoph der europäischen Moderne*. Berlin: Akademie-Verlag. 1997.

Paetzold, H. *Die Realität der symbolischen Formen-Die Kulturphilosophie Ernst Cassirers im Kontext*. Darmstadt: Wissenschaftliche Buchgesellschaft, 1994.

———. *Ernst Cassirer: Von Marburg nach New York: Eine philosophische Biographie*. Darmstadt: Wissenscaftliche Buchgesellschaft, 1995.

Collections

Braun, H.-J., Holzhey, H. and Orth, E. W. (eds.). *Über Ernst Cassirers Philosophie der symbolischen Formen* (Suhrkamp Taschenbuch Wissenschaft). Frankfurt am Main: Suhrkamp, 1988.

Figal, G. and Rudolph, E. (eds.). "Ernst Cassirer." Special number of the *Internationale Zeitschrift für Philosophie* 2 (1992).

Frede, Dorothea and Schmücker (eds.). *Ernst Cassirers Werk und Wirkung: Kultur und Philosophie*. Darmstadt: Wissenschaftliche Buchgesellschaft, 1997.

Janz, Nathalie (ed.). *Ernst Cassirer 1945–1995: Science et culture, Revue de l'Université de Lausanne* 1–2 (1997), pp. 63–72.

Rudolph, E. and Küppers, B.-O. (eds.). *Kulturkritik nach Ernst Cassirer* (Cassirer-Forschungen, 1). Hamburg: Felix Meiner, 1995.

Rudolph, E. and Stamatescu, I. O. (eds.). *Von der Philosophie zur Wissenschaft: Cassirers Dialog mit der Naturwissenschaft*. (Cassirer-Forschungen, 3). Hamburg: Felix Meiner, 1997.

Schilpp, P. A. (ed.). *The Philosophy of Ernst Cassirer* (Library of Living Philosophers, 6). LaSalle, Ill.: Open Court, 1958.

Seidengart, J. (ed.). *Ernst Cassirer: De Marbourg à New-York: L'itinéraire philosophique: Acts du colloque de Nanterre* (Passages). Paris: Les Éditionis du Cerf, 1990.

Symbolische Formen, mögliche Welten—Ernst Cassirer. Special number of *Dialektik: Enzyklopädische Zeitschrift für Philosophie und Wissenschaften* 1 (1995).

Articles

Agassi, J. "A Hegelian View of Complementarity." *British Journal for Philosophy of Science* 9 (1958): 57–63.

Alexander, E., "Heidegger's Kant Interpretation: Hermeneutical Violence." *Philosophy Today* 25 (1981): 286–306.

Arnett, W. E., "Ernst Cassirer and the Epistemological Values of Religion." *Journal of Religion* 35 (1955): 160–67.

Awerkamp, D. "Cassirer's Philosophy of the Symbol." *American Catholic Philosophical Association* 27 (1964): 178–228.

Bernet, R. "Perception et herméneutique (Husserl, Cassirer et Heidegger)." In R. Bernet, *La vie du sujet: Études sur Husserl et la phénoménologie* (Épiméthée). Paris: Presses universitaires de France, 1994, pp. 139–62.

Bidney, D. "The Philosophical Anthrolopogy of Ernst Cassirer and Its Significance in Relation to the History of Anthropological Thought." In Paul A. Schipp (ed.), *The Philosophy of Ernst Cassirer* (see above), pp. 465–545.

Blystone, J. "Is Cusanus the Father of Structuralism?" *Philosophy Today* 16 (1972): 296–303.

Brameld, T. "Philosophical Anthropology: The Educational Significance of Ernst Cassirer." *Harvard Educational Review* 26 (1956): 207–32.

Cahoone, L. E. "Cassirer's Interpretation of Galileo." *Journal of the British Society of Phenomenology* 16 (1985): 268–78.

———. "The Interpretation of Galiean Science: Cassirer Contrasted with Husserl and Heidegger." *Studies in History and Philosophy of Science* 17 (1986): 1–21.

Capeillères, F. "Cassirer Penseur Politique: The Myth of the State contre Der Mythus des 20. Jahrhunderts." *Cahiers de Philosophie politique et juridique* (Presse Univesitaire de Caen), 24 (1994): 175–204.

———. "Cassirer and Political Philosophy." In E. Rudolph and Bernad-Olaf Küppers (eds.), *Kulturkritik nach Ernst Cassirer* (see above), pp. 129–42.

———. "Concept, jugement et 'forme sérielle': À propos de la philosophie des formes symboliques comme 'logique des relations.' " *Revue de métaphysique et de morale* 3 (1996): 337–60.

———. "Le sujet de l'action: Le sujet de la connaissance." *Cahiers de philosophie politique et juridique* 28 (1995): 39–59.

———. "Postface." In Ernst Cassirer, *Écrits sur l'art* (Passages). Trans. by Christian Berner, Fabien Capeillères, Jean Carro, and Joël Gaubert. Paris: Les Éditions du Cerf, 1995, pp. 193–253.

———. "Présentatiton." In Ernst Cassirer, *L'idée de l'histoire: Les inédits de Yale et autres écrits d'exil*. Paris: Les Éditions du Cerf, 1988, pp. vii–xxxv.

———. "Sur le néo-kantisme de E. Cassirer." *Revue de métaphysique et de morale* 96 (1992): 517–46.

———. "Unité système et finitude chez Ernst Cassirer: une philosophie du 'globus intellectualis.' *Rivista di storia della filosofia* 4 (1995): 853–69.

Colson, D. and Goodman, D. "Cassirer, and the World." *Kinesis: Graduate Journal in Philosophy* 1 (1981): 1–15.

Dosch, H. G. "The Concept of Sign and Symbol in the Work of Hermann Helmholtz and Heinrich Hertz." In Nathalie Janz (ed.), *Ernst Cassirer 1945–1995: Science et culture*, 1–2 (1997), pp. 47–62.

Durpe, L. *Metaphysics and Culture* (The Aquinas Lecture, 1994). Milwaukee: Marquette University Press, 1994.

Eco, U. "On Symbols." *Semiotic Inquiry* 2 (1982): 15–44.

Erickson, S. A. "Cassirer's Dialectic: A Critical Discussion." *Idealistic Studies* 4 (1974): 251–66.

Ferrari, M. "Cassirer et l'empirisme logique: La discussion entre Cassirer et Schlick." In Nathalie Janz (ed.), *Ernst Cassirer 1945–1995: Science et culture*, 1–2 (1997), pp. 31–46.

———. "Cassirer und der Raum: Sechs Variationen über ein Thema." *Internationale Zeitschrift für Philosophie* 2 (1992): 167–88.

———. "Das Problem der Geisteswissenschaften in den Schriften Cassirers für die Bibliothek Warburg (1921–1923): Ein Beitrag zur Entstehungsgeschichte der Philosophie der symbolischen Formen." In H. J. Braun, H. Holhey, and E. W. Orth (eds.), *Über Ernst Cassirers Philosophie des symbolischen Formen* (see above), pp. 114–33.

———. "Ernst Cassirer und Peirre Duhem." In E. Rudolph and Bernad-Olaf Küppers (eds.), *Kulturkritik nach Ernst Cassirer* (see above), pp. 177–96.

———. "La genèse de Das Erkenntnisproblem." In Jean Seidengart (ed.), *Ernst Cassirer: De Marbourg à New-York* (see above), 1990, pp. 97–114.

———. "La philosophie de l'espace chez Ernst Cassirer," *Revue de métaphysique et de morale* 96 (1992), pp. 455–77.

———. "Préface." In Ernst Cassirer, *Le problème de la connaissance dans la philosophie et la science des temps modernes* (Passages). Trans. by Jean Carro, Joël Gaubert, Pierre Osmo, and Isabelle Thomoas-Fogiel. Paris: Les Éditions du Cerf, 1995.

———. "Teoria del concetto e pensiero mitico in Ernst Cassirer." *Edizioni Universitarie di Lettere Economia Diritto, Annali del Dipartimento di Filosofia dell'Università di Firencze Nuova serie* (1996), pp. 13–26.

———. "Über die Ursprünge des logischen Empirismus, den Neukantianismus und Ernst Cassirer aus der Sicht der neueren Forschung." E. Rudolph and I. O. Stamatescu (eds.), *Von der Philosophie zur Wissenschaft* (see above), pp. 93–132.

———. "Ursprünge und Motive der Sprachphilosophie Ernst Cassirer." *Dialektik. Enzyklopädische Zeitschrift für Philosophie und Wissenschaften* 1 (1995): 109–19.

Fetz, R. L. "Ernst Cassirer und der strukturgenetische Ansatz." In H. J. Braun, H. Holhey, and E. W. Orth (eds.), *Ernst Cassirers Philosophie des symbolischen Formen* (see above), pp. 156–90.

———. "Genetische Semiologie? Symboltheorie im Ausgang von Ernst Cassirer und Jean Piaget." *Freiburger Zeitschrift für Philosophie und Theologie* 28 (1981): 434–70.

———. "Nachahmung, Spiel und Kunst: Fragen einer genetischen Ästhetik." *Freiburger Zeitschrift für Philosophie .und Theologie* 29 (1982): 489–508.

Foucault, M. "Une histoire restée muette." *La Quinzaine littéraire* 8 (1966): 3–4.

Göller, Th. "Ernst Cassirer über Geschichte und Geschichtswissenschaft." *Zeitschrift für Philosophische Forschung* 45 (1991): 224–48.

———. "Zur Frage nach der Auszeichnuung der Sprache in Cassirers Philosophie der symbolischen Formen." In H. J. Braun, H. Holhey, and E. W. Orth (eds.), *Über Ernst Cassirers Philosophie des symbolischen Formen* (see above), pp. 137–55.

Goodman, N. "Words, Works, Worlds." *Erkenntnis* 9 (1975): 53–73.

Harbermas, J. "Hie befreiende Kraft der symbolischen Formgebung Ernst Cassirers humanistisches Erbe und die Bibliothek Warburg." In D. Frede and R. Schmücker (eds.), *Ernst Cassirers Werk und Wirkung* (see above), pp. 79–104.

Heidegger, M. Review: "Mythic Thought [Heidegger's review of volume 2 of the Philosophy of Symbolic Forms]." Trans. by James G. Hart and John G. Maraldo. In *The Piety of Thinking: Essays by Martin Heidegger*. Bloomington: Indiana University Press, 1976. ("Das mythische Denken von Enrst Cassirer," *Deutsche Literaturzeitung* 21 (1928): 1000–1012.)

Janz, N. "Le Symbole cassiréien entre voiles et dévoilement." In Nathalie Janz (ed.), *Ernst Cassirer 1945–1995: Science et culture*, 1–2 (1997), pp. 143–62.

Knoppe, Th. "Idee und Urphänomen: Zur Goethe-Rezeption Ernst Cassirers." In E. Rudolph and Bernad-Olaf Küppers (eds.), *Kulturkritik nach Ernst Cassirer* (see above), pp. 325–52.

Krois, J. M. "Cassirer: Aufklärung und Geschichte." In D. Frede and R. Schmücker (eds.), *Ernst Cassirers Werk und Wirkung: Kultur und Philosophie*. Darmstadt: Wissenschaftliche Buchgesellschaft, 1997, pp. 122–43.

———. "Cassirer's Unpublished Critique of Heidegger." *Philosophy and Rhetoric* 16 (1983): 147–59.

———. "Der Begriff des Mythos bei Ernst Cassirer." In H. Poser, *Philosophie und Mythos-Ein Kolloquium.* Berlin: Walter de Gruyter, 1979, pp. 199–217.

———. "Ernst Cassirer 1874–1945." In *Die Wissenschaftler: Ernst Cassirer, Bruno Snell, Siegfried Landshut* (Hamburgische Lebenbilder, 8). Hamburg: Verlag Verrein für Hamburgische Geschichte, 1994, pp. 9–40.

———. "Ernst Cassirers Semiotik der symbolischen Formen." *Zeitschrift für Semiotik* 6 (1984): 433–44.

———. "Ernst Cassirers Theorie der Technik und ihre Bedeutung für die Sozialphilosophie." *Phänomenologische Forschungen* 15 (1983): 68–93.

———. "Ernst Cassirer's Theory of Technology and Its Import for Social Philosophy." *Research in Philosophy & Technology* 5 (1982): 209–22.

———. "On Editing Cassirer's Unpublished Papers: Technical and Philosophical Perspectives." In Nathalie Janz (ed.), *Ernst Cassirer 1945–1995: Science et culture,* 1–2 (1997), pp. 163–84.

———. "Problematik, Eigenart und Aktualität der Cassirerschen Philosophie der symbolischen Formen." In H. J. Braun, H. Holhey, and E. W. Orth (eds.), *Über Ernst Cassirers Philosophie des symbolischen Formen* (see above), pp. 15–44.

———. "Semiotische Transformation der Philosphie: Verkörperung und Pluralismus bei Cassirer und Peirce." *Dialektik* 1 (1995): 61–72.

———. "Urworte: Cassirer als Goethe-Interpret," in E. Rudolph and Bernad-Olaf Küppers (eds.), *Kulturkritik nach Ernst Cassirer* (see above), pp. 297–324.

Kuderowicz, Z. "Dilthey and Cassirer, Dilemmas of the Philosophy of Culture." *Reports on Philosophy* 5 (1981): 43–60.

Lofts, G. S. "Husserl, Heidegger, Cassirer: Trois philosophes de crise." *Revue philosophique de Louvain,* 90 (1992): 570–84.

———. "La Lecture de l''histoire.' " In Steve G. Lofts and Philipp W. Rosemann (eds.), *Éditer, traduire, interpréter: Essais de méthodologie philosophique* (Philosophes médiévaux). Louvain-la-Neuve: Éditions de l'Institut supérieur de philosophie; Louvain/Paris: Peeters, 1996, pp. 156–73.

———. "L'ordre symboliquue de Jacques Lacan à la lumière du symbolique d'Ernst Cassirer." In Steve G. Lofts and Paul Moyaert (eds.), *La pensée de Jacques Lacan: Questions historiques—Problèmes théoriques* (Bibliothèque Philosophique de Louvain, 39). Louvain-la-Neuve: Éditions de l'Institut supérieur de philosophie; Louvain-Paris: Éditions Peeters, 1994, pp. 83–105.

———. "Une nouvelle approache de la philosophie d'Ernst Cassirer." *Revue philosophique de Louvain* 90 (1992): 523–38.

Lynch, D. A. "Ernst Cassirer and Martin Heidegger: The Davos Debate." *Kant-Studien* 81 (1990): 360–70.

Makkreel, R. A. "Cassirer zwischen Kant and Dilthey." In D. Frede and R. Schmücker (eds.), *Ernst Cassirers Werk und Wirkung* (see above), pp. 145–62.

———. "Vico and Some Kantian Reflections on Historical Judgment." *Man and World* (1980): 99–120.

———. "Wilhem Dilthey and the Neo-Kantians: The Distinction between the Geisteswissenschaften and the Kulturwissenscahften." *Journal of the History of Philosophy* 7 (1969): 423–40.

Marc-Wogau, K. "Der Symbolbegriff in der Philosophie Ernst Cassirers." *Theoria* 2 (1936): 279–332.

———. "Was ist 'Subjektivismus'? Bemerkungen zum gleichnamigen Vortrag E. Cassirer." *Theoria* 6 (1940): 66–74.

Marion, J.-L. "L'interprétation criticiste de Descartes et Leibniz (Critique d'une critique)." In Jean Seidengart (ed.), *Ernst Cassirer: De Marbourg à New-York* (see above), pp. 29–42.

Merrell, F. "Metaphor and Metonymy: A Key to Narrative Structure." *Language and Style* 11.3 (1978): 146–63.

Orth E. W. "Cassirers Philosophie der Lebensordnungen." In E. Cassirer, *Geist und Leben*. Leipzig: Reclam, 1993, pp. 9–30.

———. "Der Begriff der Kulturphilosophie bei Enrst Cassirer." In H. Brackert and F. Wefelmeyer (eds.), *Kultur Bestimmungen im 20: Jahrhundert*. Frankfurt: Suhrkamp, 1990, pp. 156–91.

———. "Die Anthropologische Wende im Neukantianismus: Enrst Cassirer und Richard Hönigswald." *Il cannochiale* 1–2 (1991): 261–87.

———. "Einheit und Vielheit in der Sicht Edmund Husserls und Ernst Cassirers." In Chr. Jamme and O. Pöggeler (eds.), *Phänomenologie und Widerstreit: Zum 50: Geburtstag Edmund Husserls*, 1989, pp. 332–51.

———. "Ernst Cassirers Philosophie der symbolischen Formen und ihre Bedeutung für unsere Gegenwart." *Deutsche Zeitschrift für Philosophie* 1–2 (1992): 119–36.

———. "Geschichte und Literatur als Orientierungsdimensionen in der Philosophie Ernst Cassirers." In E. Rudolph and Bernad-Olaf Küppers (eds.), *Kulturkritik nach Ernst Cassirer* (see above), pp. 105–27.

———. "Interkulturalität und Inter-Intentionalität." *Zeitschrift für philosophische Forschung* 47 (1993): 333–51.

———. "Ist der Neukantianer Ernst Cassirer ein Nominalist? Verlegenheiten der Substanzkritik." *Internationale Zeitschrift für Philosophie* 2 (1992): 261–72.

———. "Operative Begriffe in Ernst Cassirers Philosophie der symbolischen Formen." In H. J. Braun, H. Holhey, and E. W. Orth (eds.), *Über Ernst Cassirers Philosophie des symbolischen Formen* (see above), pp. 45–74.

———. "Phänomenologie in Ernst Cassirers Philosophie der symbolischen Formen." *Dialektik: Enzyklopädische Zeitschrift für Philosophie und Wissenschaften* 1 (1995): 47–60.

———. "Philosophische Anthropologie als Erst Philosophie: Ein Vergleich zwischen Ernst Cassirer und Helmut Plessner." *Dilthey-Jahrbuch für Philosophie und Geschichte der Geiteswissenschaften*, 7, (1990–91): 250–74.

———. "Zugänge zu Ernst Cassirer. Eine Einleitung," in H. J. Braun, H. Holhey, and E. W. Orth (eds.), *Über Ernst Cassirers Philosophie des symbolischen Formen* (see above), pp. 7–11.

———. "Zum Begriff der Technik bei Ernst Cassirer und Martin Heidegger." *Phänomenologische Forschungen* 20 (1987): 91–122.

———. "Zum Zeitegriff Ernst Cassriers." *Phänomenologische Forschungen* 13 (1982): 65–89.

———. "Georg Simmel als Kulturphiosoph zwischen Lebensphilosophie und Neukantianismus." *Jagiellonian University Reports on Philosophy* 14 (1991): 105–20.

Paetzold, H. "Die symbolische Ordnung der Kultur. Ernst Cassirer Beitrag zu einer Theorie der Kulturentwicklung." In D. Frede and R. Schmücker (eds.), *Ernst Cassirers Werk und Wirkung* (see above), pp. 163–84.

———. "Ernst Cassirer und die Idee einer transformierten Transzendentalphilosophie," in Wolfgan Kuhlmann and Dietrich Böhler (eds.), *Kommunikation und Reflexion: Zur Diskussion der Transzendentalpragmatik. Antworten auf Karl-Otto Apel.* Frankfurt am Main: Suhrkamp, 1982.

———. "Ernst Cassirer, 'The Myth of the State' und die 'Dialektik der Aufklärung' von Max Horkheimer und Theodor W. Adorno." U. L. Figge, *Semiotik: Interdisziplinäre und historische Aspekte.* Bochum, 1989, pp. 301–49.

———. "Ernst Cassirers 'Philosophie der symbolischen Formen' und die neuere Entwicklung der Semiotik." In A. Lange-Seidl (ed.), *Zeichenkonstitution: Akten des 2: Semiotischen Kolloquiums Regensburg, 1978.* Berlin: Walter de Gruyter, 1981.

———. "Mythos als symbolische Form. Zu Ernst Cassirers philosophischer Interpretation des Mythos." *Neue Zeitschrift für Systematische Theologie und Religionsphilosophie* 25 (1983): 224–43.

———. "Mythos and Moderne in der Kulturphilosophie Ernst Cassirers." In E. Rudolph and Bernad-Olaf Küppers (eds.), *Kulturkritik nach Ernst Cassirer* (see above), pp. 159–76.

———. "Sprache als symbolische Form: Zur Sprachphilosophie Ernst Cassirers." *Philosophisches Jahrbuch* 88 (1981): 301–15.

Rajan, S. "Cassirer and Wittgenstein." *International Philosophical Quarterly* 7 (1967): 591–610.

Ricœur, P. "Can Fictional Narrative be True?" *The Phenomenology of Man and of the Human Condition: Analecta Husserliana* 14 (1977): 3–19.

Rudolph, E. "Ernst Cassirers Rezeption des Renaissancehumanismus." In D. Frede and R. Schmücker (eds.), *Ernst Cassirers Werk und Wirkung: Kultur und Philosophie.* Darmstadt: Wissenschaftliche Buchgesellschaft, 1997, pp. 105–21.

———. "La Réception cassirérienne de l'humanisme de la Renaissance." In Nathalie Janz (ed.), *Ernst Cassirer 1945–1995: Science et culture,* 1–2 (1997), pp. 99–114.

———. "Les mythes politiques comm phénomènes du culture selon Ernst Cassirer." *Cahiers de Philosophie politique et juridique* 26 (1994), pp. 159–74.

———. "Politische Mythen als Kulturphänomene nach Ernst Cassirer." In E. Rudolph and Bernad-Olaf Küppers (eds.), *Kulturkritik nach Ernst Cassirer* (Cassirer-Forschungen, 1). Hamburg: Felix Meiner, 1995, pp. 143–58.

———. "Raum, Zeit und Bewegung: Cassirer und Reichenbach über die philosophischen Anfänge des physikalischen Relativismus." E. Rudolph and I. O. Stamatescu (eds.), *Von der Philosophie zur Wissenschaft* (see above), pp. 45–62.

———. "Von der Substanz zur Funktion: Leibnizrezeption als Kantkritik bei Ernst Cassirer," *Dialektik Enzyklopädische Zeitschrift für Philosophie und Wissenschaften* 1 (1995): 85–96.

———. "La résurgence de l'aristotélisme de la Renaissance dans la philosophie politique de Cassirer." *Revue de métaphysique et de morale* 96 (1992): 479–90.

Schwemmer, O. "Die Vielfalt der Symbolischen Welten und die Einheit der Vernunft: Zu Ernst Cassirers Philosophie der Symbolischen Formen. Ein Kommentar in Thesen." *Dialektik* 1 (1995): 37–46.

Seidengart, J. "L'héroïsme philosophique de Giodano Bruno à l'apogée de la Renaissance d'après Cassirer." In Nathalie Janz (ed.), *Ernst Cassirer 1945–1995: Science et culture,* 1–2 (1997), pp. 115–42.

———. "Néokantisme et relativité in La Mesure dans les sciences physiques," *Revue philosophiques de la France et de l'étranger* 174 (1984): 201–18.

———. "Symbolische Konfiguraiton und Realität in der modernen Physik." In E. Rudolph and Bernad-Olaf Küppers (eds.), *Kulturkritik nach Ernst Cassirer* (see above), pp. 197–218.

———. "Théorie de la connaisance et épistémologie de la physique selon Cassirer." In Jean Seidengart (ed.), *Ernst Cassirer: De Marbourg à New-York* (see above), pp. 159–76.

———. "Une interprétation néokantienne de la théorie des quanta est-elle possible? Réflexions sur l'épistémologie d'Ernst Cassirer et sur son interprétation de la théorie des quanta dans Determinismus und Indeterminismus in der modernen Physik." *Revue de synthèse* 106 (1985): 395–418.

Silverstone, R. "Ernst Cassirer and Claude Lévi-Strauss: Two Approaches to the Study of Myth." *Archives de sciences sociales des religions* 21 (1976): 25–36.

Troeltsch, E. "Humanismus und Nationalismus in unserem Bildungswesen." In H. Baron (ed.), *Deutscher Geist und Westeuropa*. Aalen: Scientia Verlag, 1966, pp. 231–35.

Verene, D. P. "Cassirer's Concept of Symbolic Form and Human Creativity." *Idealistic Studies* 8 (1978): 14–32.

———. "Cassirer's Philosophy of Culture." *International Philosophical Quarterly* 22 (1982): 133–44.

———. "Cassirer's View of Symbol and Myth." *Monist* 50 (1966): 553–64.

———. "Kant, Hegel, and Cassirer: The Origins of the Philosophy of Symbolic Forms." *Journal of the History of Ideas* 30 (1969): 33–46.

———. "Cassirers Kulturphilosophie, Übertragen aus dem Englischen von Ulrich Lorenz." *Allgemeine Zeitschrift für Philosophie* 9 (1984): 1–18.

———. "Ernst Cassirer: A Bibliography." *Bulletin of Bibliography and Magazine Notes* 24 (1964): 103–6, 125–28.

———. "Introduction: Cassirer's Thought 1935–45." In E. Cassirer, *Symbol, Myth and Culture: Essays and Lectures of Ernst Cassirer, 1939–1945*, pp. 1–45.

Other Literature

Bass, Bernard. *Le désire pur: Parcours philosophiques dans les parages de J. Lacan*. Louvain: Éditions Peeters, 1992.

Bernet, Rudolf. *La vie du sujet: Études sur Husserl et la phénoménologie* (Épiméthée). Paris: Presses universitaires de France, 1994.

Buckley, R. Philip. *Husserl, Heidegger and the Crisis of Philosophical Responsibility* (Phaenomenologica, 125). Dordrecht: Kluwer Academic Publishers, 1992.

Lacan, Jacques. *Écrits* (Le champ freudien). Paris: Éditions du Seuil, 1966.

———. *Le Séminaire de Jacques Lacan,* Livre VII: *L'éthique de la psychanalyse* (Le champ freudien). Paris: Éditions du Seuil, 1986.

———. *Le Séminaire de Jacques Lacan,* Livre XI: *Les quatre concepts fondamentaux de la psychanalyse* (Le champ freudien). Paris: Éditions du Seuil, 1973.

Makkreel, Rudolf. *Imagination and Interpretation in Kant: The Hermeneutical Importance of the Critique of Judgement.* Chicago: University of Chicago Press, 1990.

Puthenpurackal, Johnson, J. *Heidegger through Authentic Totality to Total Authenticity: A Unitary Approach to His Thought in Its Two Phases* (Louvain Philosophical Studies, 2). Leuven: Leuven University Press, 1987.

Index